THE EDGE OF EACH ROUGH REGION

Church and Community in the Great Glen

Adrian Varwell

"Walk about Zion, go round her, count her towers,
consider well her ramparts, view her citadels,
that you may tell of them to the next generation
For this God is our God for ever and ever;
he will be our guide even to the end"
[Psalm 48:12 – 14]

abertarff.wordpress.com

Cover:

The image of the Great Glen is reproduced with permission from Gary Brindle at scotaviaimages (www.scotaviaimages.co.uk). The Celtic knot design was created by Marjory Tait at Highland Celtic Art (www.highlandcelticart.co.uk) and represents the three parishes of Abertarff, Glengarry and Glenmoriston as parts of three larger parishes, whilst having a common interlinked unity at the heart of the Great Glen.

Maps:

The maps for this book were prepared by Angela Henderson (www.angelahenderson.co.uk). They are reproduced under a Creative Commons Attribution 4.0 International (CC-BY) Licence with the permission of the National Library of Scotland.

Biblical References:

The Biblical references throughout serve to emphasise that the Word of God is relevant to, and informs, every area of life: all are from the New International Version unless otherwise stated.

CONTENTS

LIST OF ILLUSTRATIVE MAPS

PREFACE

"Look to the rock from which you were cut
and to the quarry from which you were hewn"
[Isaiah 51:1]

Having been called to be the Minister of Fort Augustus and Glengarry in 2001 I soon found that it was difficult to discover much about the history of the two parishes and their engagement with the local community. Most historical sources dealt with the larger neighbours from which the two parishes had been created, and these accounts carried only scant reference to the communities to which I sought to minister. In the limited time available amongst my ministerial duties I found that both of my parishes did in fact have a rich Christian heritage and that the Fort Augustus district had once formed a significant parish, Abertarff, in its own right. It also became clear that over the centuries the church in Glenmoriston had been closely associated with its southern neighbours. The area in the centre of the Great Glen, which had a natural coherence, had been embraced within larger parishes and largely lost to the pursuit of church history. Therefore, that which had once been central had found itself at "the edge of each rough region" and I believed that it was important to reclaim something of its heritage.

After retirement I became a member of Urquhart and Glenmoriston Parish Church and then spent four years serving as a locum in Fort William and Kilmonivaig: thus over two decades I have been closely involved with most of the parishes within the Great Glen. Furthermore, writing within sight of the old Manse of Kilmore in Drumnadrochit, in a house that stands upon the old glebe of Urquhart looking up to Creag Neamh, the Hill of Heaven, I have a profound sense of the Christian heritage of the Great Glen and of the faithful men and women who served their Lord and bore witness to His grace and love. I am pleased to relate something of this enduring heritage.

Adrian Varwell

ACKNOWLEDGEMENTS

The following have given valuable assistance in preparing this book: Fort Augustus Heritage Group; Fort William Archive Centre; Glengarry Heritage Centre; Glenurquhart Library; Inverness Library; Rev Ian Allan; Rev Richard Baxter; Graham Biggs for access to Cill Chuimein Heritage papers; Rev Bart Buell; George F Campbell; Lynne Davidson; Libby Grey; Angela Henderson for preparing the maps; Colin McAllister; Donald G MacDonald; Duncan MacDonald; Peter MacDonald; Jane Patten; Rev Dr Bruce Ritchie; Alasdair Roberts; Rev Dr John Ross; Hamish Turner, and Simon Varwell for technical assistance. Especial thanks are due to my wife Margaret, who has been so encouraging throughout the preparation of this book.

ABBREVIATIONS

APM: Abertarff Presbytery Minutes [CH2/7/1-9]

FASTI: "Fasti Ecclesiae Scoticanae" (Record of the Ministry of the Church of Scotland)

IFC: Inverness Field Club

IPM: Inverness Presbytery Minutes – within "Records of the Presbyteries of Inverness and Dingwall, 1643-88", SHS Publications, Vol 24, 1896

KKS: Kilmonivaig Kirk Session [CH2/433/1,2]

NLS: National Library of Scotland

NSA: New Statistical Account of Scotland

ODNB: Oxford Dictionary of National Biography

OSA: The "Old" Statistical Account of Scotland

SHS: Scottish History Society

SRO: Scottish Record Office

SRS: Scottish Records Society

TGSI: Transactions of the Gaelic Society of Inverness

TSA: Third Statistical Account

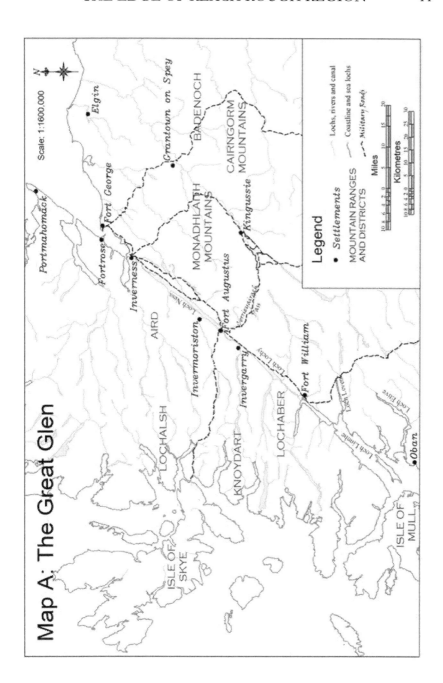

Map A: The Great Glen

FOREWORD

"The boundary lines have fallen for me in pleasant places;
surely I have a delightful inheritance"
[Psalm 16:6]

Remote or Central?

"... we are in a remote place here"
[Luke 9:12]

The Great Glen crosses Scotland from north-east to south-west, and across the centuries it has provided a route for travellers, traders, armies and saints. To the east the Monadhliath Mountains cut off access to Strathspey and routes to the lowlands, whilst to the west various sinuous glens pass beneath high peaks to give access to the Sound of Sleat. The central area of the Great Glen, at the south end of Loch Ness, often called Glen Albyn, has across the centuries found itself to be at "the edge of each rough region" surrounding it: the ancient lands of Moray to the north-east, the district of Aird to the north, and the sea-facing areas of Lochalsh and Lochaber to the west and south. These lands belonged to a number of Clans whose territories marched together in Glen Albyn, the Frasers, the Grants, the Macdonells and the Camerons.

The central area of the Great Glen is also bisected by another unmarked but significant boundary which further defines the marginality of Glen Albyn. The watershed between rivers flowing east to the North Sea and those flowing west to the Atlantic, sometimes known as the Great Ridge of Scotland, "Drumalban", passes through Laggan Achadrom, "the field of the ridge", at the south end of Loch Oich. This is the highest point of the Great Glen valley floor, once suggested to mark the very centre of Scotland.[1] Indeed, the area is overlooked by Creag nan Gobhar from where, it is said, one may see from the Moray Firth to the Atlantic.[2] Glen Albyn, therefore, is at the intersection of many boundaries, north and south, east and west, serving to emphasise that the district is indeed at "the edge of each rough region."

Ancient routes took advantage of the lochs and rivers along the Great Glen, and with high passes to the east and tributary glens to the west, a natural cross-roads was created at the south end of Loch Ness. This would suggest that the broad strath south from the modern Fort Augustus had the capacity for economic development; it could have hosted a significant population and supported a thriving Parish Church. In fact, Fort Augustus and the adjacent Glen Garry and Glen Moriston, have been at the extremities of other parishes for centuries: only in comparatively recent times have they had any independent identity. For this reason much of the early history of the churches in this area has been subsumed within those larger parishes. This study sets out to explore the story of these three modern parishes, and to outline the role of the Christian Church in the communities of this central area of the Great Glen.

"… the most centrical point"

*"I took you from the ends of the earth,
from its farthest corners I called you.
I said to you: You are my servant;
I have chosen you and have not rejected you"
[Isaiah 41:9]*

A modern road map of the Highlands portrays the A82 running south-west to north-east along the Great Glen between Fort William and Inverness. At Invergarry the A87 strikes west to Kyle of Lochalsh, joined on its course by a road from Invermoriston. Apart from a junction with a minor road which threads up the east side of Loch Ness, Fort Augustus would appear to be no more than a halfway roadside village. Yet, to look at older maps charting the ancient drove roads and the military roads of the Eighteenth Century, the broad glen between Loch Lochy and Loch Ness is seen to be a crossroads of routes north and south, east and west. Across the centuries ancient peoples, cattle traders and raiders, armies and fugitives, intrepid travellers and Christian saints have passed through this area, etching a cross on the landscape focussed on the village now known as Fort Augustus.

In the early Eighteenth Century General Wade's roads followed some of the old drove roads, and with its new military status Fort Augustus was at the intersection of a cruciform network of tolerable roads. The Fort and its garrison could have become a major centre, for in 1725 Edmund Burt, the Chief Surveyor to General Wade, wrote that the intention was "that it should be the principal garrison of the Highlands, and the residence of the governor, who was likewise to command the other two in that line …", namely Fort William and Fort George. He went on: "Fort Augustus … is … reckoned to be the most centrical point of the habitable part of the Highlands." However, for a variety of reasons such an advantage did not create an urban centre. Burt related that "there was a civil project on foot, which was, to build a town after the English manner, and procure for it all the privileges and immunities of a royal borough in Scotland."[3] The writer of the first Statistical Account for Boleskine and Abertarff saw Fort Augustus as "the centre of communication betwixt the Western Isles and the South", and noted its potential for the location of a market.[4] However, whilst large towns were created in Strathspey at Grantown and Kingussie, Fort Augustus and its surrounding glens, though central, were peripheral to the seats of power, and the area never fulfilled its natural potential.

The Turnpike Roads of the Nineteenth Century were built for heavier wheeled traffic, and the steep hills and repeated hairpin bends of General Wade's roads were no longer serviceable, so the routes east and west of Fort Augustus fell out of use. The south-west to north-east axis was strengthened with the construction of the Caledonian Canal, completed in 1822, and with the upgrading of the A82 in the 1930s. Apart from the re-routing of the A87 between Glengarry and Glenmoriston in the 1950s no new roads have been built, and the ancient drove-roads are left to the hill-walkers. Fort Augustus is today less central than it once was, but is still a sentinel for the district around about.

Since the early days of the Christian faith, the followers of Jesus have been called to be salt and light in their communities; they were encouraged to create church fellowships and to serve the local populace.[5] Within the Great Glen, Christians have witnessed to their faith for sixteen centuries. Their church fellowships have taken different forms and have borne different names, and yet their witness has remained steadfast. We may identify certain strands of

Christianity, each one having left its heritage in the area: Celtic, Roman, Episcopal, Presbyterian. These, though, are simply labels which, whilst charting the threads of church polity, do little to represent the on-going work of ordinary Christians seeking to live faithfully for their Master. In that sense any and every community, no matter its size, is the central focus for the Christians living there, for that is their mission field. Only at the end of time will the unfolding of this eternal calling be revealed, and any attempt to record the history of any one church and its people can only tell a part.

Within the Great Glen the story of the church in Glenmoriston has been partially covered by William MacKay's history of Urquhart and Glenmoriston[6] and the Free Church "West the Glen" has been well documented by Ian Allan.[7] Furthermore, the history of the Roman Catholic Church in the area is recorded in various places.[8] Alan Lawson's work on the history of Stratherrick has highlighted the story of the church in the Parish of Boleskine which, of course, embraced Abertarff up to 1883.[9]

It is not the purpose here to rewrite earlier works, but rather and especially to focus upon the Church of Scotland in Fort Augustus and Glengarry, and upon Glenmoriston which was and is still closely connected with its southern neighbours in various ways. These are detailed histories, the fruit of several years of research, but they are not shared for the sake of history alone because these church communities did and still do interact with other Christian traditions, and these links will be recognised and celebrated as appropriate. Across the ages, through their faithfulness to their Lord, local Christians have sought to fulfil the Great Commission in this heart of the Highlands. Therefore a final chapter applies lessons from the past to the challenges of the present century. The God of the past is the God of the future and, learning from its history, God's people in the Great Glen and in similar rural areas are encouraged to embrace the possibilities that lie ahead.

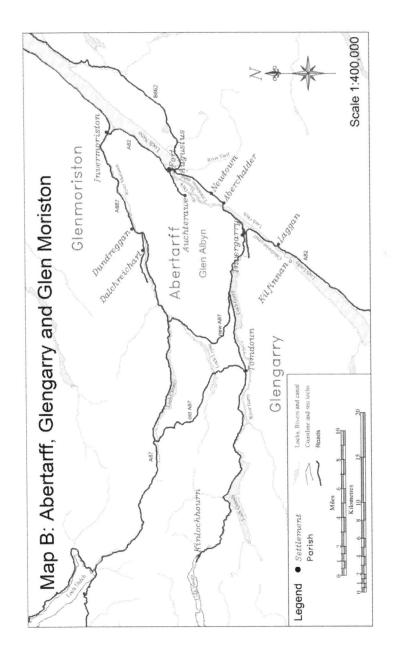

Map B: Abertarff, Glengarry and Glen Moriston

Chapter 1:

THE LIGHT SHINES IN THE DARKNESS

"The light shines in the darkness,
and the darkness has not overcome it"
[John 1:5]

"In the beginning ... the Word" [1]

"How beautiful on the mountains are the feet of those who
bring good news, who proclaim peace,
who bring good tidings, who proclaim salvation ..."
[Isaiah 52:7]

It cannot be known when the Good News of Jesus Christ first reached the Great Glen, but surely it predated the visits of members of Ninian's community. There is evidence of Christians living in the British Isles from the early Third Century: Tertullian wrote about 210AD of "regions of the Britons inaccessible to the Romans but subject to Christ."[2] Travellers, traders and roaming Roman soldiers could well have shared their faith even in the remotest parts of the Highlands.[3]

Whilst the seeds of Christianity were sown during the Roman period "it is significant that the first great mission to Scotland of which we know was that of Ninian to the Picts."[4] At the end of the Third Century this son of a British chief built his church at Whithorn, from where he and his disciples travelled across central and north-east Scotland. Place-name evidence suggests that Ninian or his disciples may have been in the Great Glen[5]: Temple, also known as St Ninian's, on the north shore of Glenurquhart Bay, was perhaps a northern outpost of the Whithorn mission. However, the extent to which Ninian or his followers penetrated the north of Scotland has been a matter for debate: the historian J D Mackie casts doubts upon "the extent and penetration of Ninian's efforts."[6] Nevertheless, in these early years there may have been many faithful Christians sharing their faith as they travelled and traded: "much more missionary work was done by ordinary Christians in the course of their daily business and intercourse than is often realised."[7] Not surprisingly the Great Glen has been called "The Valley of the Saints."

More certainty prevails over the missionary endeavours of Columba and his followers. Although much about Columba's life is unknown, and histories are somewhat idealised, it is clear that he travelled from Ireland to Scotland in the year 563.[8] There is a long-standing tradition that Columba landed and settled on Iona because from there he could no longer behold his native Ireland, but it has been suggested that this is an over-simplification. Finlay argues that Columba must have had a plan of campaign lasting two years or so to build contacts with the Scots, the Picts and their rulers prior to the establishment of a base in Iona.[9] Bradley notes that Iona was not granted to Columba until 574[10], implying that during this time the Irish saint must have had a more-or-less settled base on the mainland from where he established good relationships with Conaill, King of the Scots in Dalraida, and King Brude of the Picts, whose stronghold was near Inverness. It would have been at this time that the conversion of Emchat recorded by Adamnan in his "Life of Columba" took place, perhaps at what later became Urquhart Castle.[11] Finlay suggests that Columba's incursion into Brude's heartland could not have been "made without some prior agreement with the Pictish king" and that some political purpose was more likely to have gained him an audience. It is clear that the foundations of diplomacy and statesmanship preceded the establishment of Columba's mission to the Picts.[12] Such patient preparations meant that "for all of [Brude's] reign, and for years afterwards, Iona monks had unrestricted and unmolested freedom within Pictland."[13] Indeed, whether it was as early as 565 or as late as 580 that Columba finally met King Brude, the saint had been present in his territory for some years.

Given this picture of a gradual and patient beginning to Columba's mission, some theories have been advanced to suggest the location of Columba's early base. George Campbell has speculated that Columba created a religious house at the south end of Loch Ness, and that the "Insula Hinba" referred to by Columba's historian, Adomnan, equated to the peninsula between the Oich and the Tarff. He points to Meall a'Cholumain, south of Fort Augustus, to suggest that this was the hill from which Columba could no longer behold the western seas which led back to Ireland, persuading him that he could now settle his missionary activities in the fertile glen below.[14]   Bradley, along with other scholars, champions Jura as the location of Hinba[15] although a mainland base would have better served Columba's early objectives. More recently Ritchie has stated that "Wherever Hinba was, it was important to Columba, and it may have been his temporary home before he ever saw Iona."[16] Campbell concludes that "prior to the expansion of his community on the island of Iona in Columba's lifetime, Hinba must have been the senior house."[17] This theory has a bearing on the subsequent history of churches in Abertarff or Kilchuimen, the earlier names for Fort Augustus, which will be examined later.

Subsequent to Columba's arrival in the Great Glen, his followers and others may have established cells or preaching stations across the area. Ritchie states that "other monks and other missions, not under [Columba's] authority, were evangelising the land ..."[18] Campbell suggests sites at Auchterawe and Mourvalgan/Murligan close to "Insula Hinba"[19]; whilst Mackay points to Clachan Cholumchille and St Columba's Well at Invermoriston to emphasise the Columban influence.[20] Within Glengarry place names suggest connections with Finnan, Donnan, and an unknown saint who is commemorated at Creag an t'Sagairt, the Priest's Rock. These cells were places of private devotion, bases for prayer, teaching and outreach into the local community. They were the bases for missionaries who "were not only men of education and expert scribes, but also experienced husbandmen, who cultivated the crofts which were attached to their cells, and so maintained themselves and showed the people how to make the earth yield its substance."[21] These were hardy men, "bringing their gifts of knowledge to benefit the people. Gradually their doctrines of mercy and forgiveness supplanted the more barbarous teachings of the former spiritual leaders, the Druids."[22] Their message was radical. In place of multiple and competing gods, they preached of a Trinity, one God in three complementary and co-operating Persons, a sovereign God who created and sustained all the elements of creation.[23]

The "tent-making" ministries of the Celtic Christians followed the example of the Apostle Paul who worked to support himself[24] and was a most appropriate form of mission in its time. It was, however, slow and patient work, building relationships and sowing the seeds of faith by example and friendship. Finlay advances place-name evidence and the testimony of Pictish sculptured stones to conclude that the progress of the Christian faith was slow and geographically patchy, concluding that "the rulers of the Picts were pagans until long after Columba's day."[25] However, the sign of the cross began to appear on Pictish monuments and the foundations of faith were laid.

By the 690s the Picts were a maturing nation. "The spiritual leaders – the bishops and abbots of Christianity – were drawing closer to their secular counterparts – the kings – and were playing major roles in secular affairs."[26] Bishop Curetan, abbot of the monastery at Rosemarkie, which was a major religious centre in the Pictish region, maintained royal and international connections, and his name is preserved in place names within Glen Urquhart.[27] By 700 Christianity was the main religion of the Picts, with a structure of churches and monasteries served by missionaries from Iona and other early foundations.[28] It may be confidently concluded that

"Columba and his Irish monks, alongside native Pictish Christians, took Christian faith deep into Scottish culture and religious belief."[29]

The Men from the North

"I have stirred up one from the north"
[Isaiah 41:25]

The Ninth Century saw the arrival of the Vikings in northern Scotland. The Pictish Christian monastery at Portmahomack was overrun about 800, and the Pictish realm was subdued in the 860's.[30] As they raided and then settled the east and west coasts, control of the Great Glen gave the Vikings a portage route to bind their territory.[31] Their presence in the Great Glen is marked by various place-names: Creag an Iarlain, the Jarl's Rock, stands over Fort Augustus, and names in Glen Urquhart commemorate Monie, a Viking prince supposedly buried at Corriemony. His sister reputedly lived on in the district, and is believed to be buried at Abriachan.[32]

There is some evidence that there were Christian converts amongst the Viking settlers. Writing from a Scandinavian perspective it has been suggested that Vikings "had become familiar with Christianity from friends and relatives who had emigrated to Christian countries ... where the immigrants quickly accepted the local faith.[33]   The presence of the significant monastery at Portmahomack demonstrates the extent of evangelism amongst the Picts prior to the Viking settlement.   George Campbell makes a closer connection between the early Columban site at Abertarff and Scandinavia.   He suggests that Erik Segersall, King of Sweden, married a Danish Queen, came to Scotland to visit the Danish colony in Moray and "acquired the south end of Loch Ness and an entire adjoining strath" before his death in 995.[34] Stratherrick may perpetuate his name. Local tradition tells of a Scandinavian, King Eric, who died in a battle in Glenmoriston, was buried at Achnanconeran, and whose name may be preserved in Coir' Iarairidh.[35]   Erik's son, Olof Skotkonung, significantly "the Scot-king", was the first Christian king of Sweden (995–c1018), and Campbell proposes that he embraced his Christian faith whilst living at Abertarff, perhaps because something of Columba's monastic foundation remained on the shores of Loch Ness.   Furthermore it may be significant that Olof appointed a Christian bishop in Sweden in defiance of his pagan overlord.[36]

Priories and Parishes

"The Lord's message rang out from you"
[1 Thessaloniand 1:8]

Whilst Viking influence penetrated the north and west of Scotland, the majority of the land-mass was consolidated by Malcolm II (1005–1034) at the beginning of the new Millenium. The members of this Celtic monarchy "were generally in alliance with the Church but they had not the support of an organized hierarchy."[37] Because the Celtic church did not have an over-arching hierarchy, and in the absence of a diocesan structure, civil government was exercised through a feudal system that was gradually imposed across Scotland up to the end of the Twelfth Century. Norman families from the south were granted land to replace Pictish leaders. "The Great Glen was particularly important as a strategic objective, since it offered a direct link between the power centres of Moray and Argyll and was therefore fortified in the reign of William the Lion (1165–1214) by a line of castles running from Inverness through Urquhart and Inverlochy to Dunstaffnage."[38]

The loose association of state and church was strengthened under Malcolm III (1057–1093), also known as Malcolm Canmore, and David I (1124–1153). Symbols of military might served to emphasise the new sense of unity. The old order was swept away by David I and his successors, and land was redistributed to loyal supporters who were expected to build strongholds to assert the peace. Urquhart Castle and a motte and bailey at Abertarff were built at this time.[39]

The thirteenth century saw the allocation of lands to the king's supporters and to the church. For instance, it is recorded in the Register of the Diocese of Moray in 1233 that Sir Alan Durward "for the sake of peace, has given to the church of Urquhart half the lands claimed, in pure, free, and perpetual charity."[40] The lands of Glengarry were granted by King Robert the Bruce to Thomas Ranulph in 1307.[41] At the same time the site of the church at Abertarff was gifted to Beauly Priory by Sir John Bissett of Lovat.[42]

At the outset of the thirteenth century the church was becoming as organised and structured as civil society. The Kings of the Scots had in part consolidated their control of the north and west Highlands through the Church in the Twelfth Century. King David I (1124–1153) defeated Oengus of Moray in 1130, all part of a power-struggle for pre-eminence. Thereafter David planted monastic communities at Urquhart (near Elgin, 1136) and Kinloss (1150) and created the Diocese of Moray, although a detailed parochial system took time to develop. For instance, Kilmore Kirk in Glenurquhart was annexed in 1208 to support a Prebend at Spynie Cathedral, the antecedent to Elgin Cathedral, so this church almost certainly predated 1200. Perhaps the church at Abertarff had a similar narrative.

The relative stability created by the Canmore dynasty saw the founding of three monastic houses of the French Valliscaulian order in 1230, Ardchattan, Pluscarden and Beauly. If, as has been suggested, Beauly Priory had a daughter-house at Abertarff, there may be evidence that the Order chose earlier Christian sites.[43] For instance, the priory at Ardchattan "seems to have been deliberately located near to a much earlier Christian site"[44], and continuity may have been the policy at Abertarff. Beauly Priory provides a guide to the church history of the mediaeval period with its noble patron, extensions and rebuilding, and a prosperous hinterland. At the time of the Reformation the then Prior became a Lay Prior, and by 1571 there was still a Prior and four monks in the house. However by 1633 the church was in a state of decay and thereafter some of the ancillary buildings were demolished to build Cromwell's fort at Inverness.[45] This story of change and decline may offer a close parallel to that of the church at the south end of Loch Ness.

By 1509 there was evidence of landowners being expected to make improvements. In Urquhart there was a requirement to "till or reclaim wild land in meadows and pastures, make enclosures, improve the public highway and supervise and care for the common benefits, such as stone and wooden bridges, fold-gates and stiles." The Royal Forest of Cluanie, at the head of Glenmoriston, provided rich hunting grounds amongst the hills where the summer shielings were located[46]. The enclosures protected cereal crops worked on a run-rig system: outside were the moorland grazings for cattle and beyond that were the Highland sheilings for summer grazing. Cattle were the mainstay of Highland farming, and the Act of Union on 1707 opened up English markets. Cattle-droving to the lowland trysts generated a growing income during the Seventeenth Century.[47] Within the Great Glen there were small-scale activities such as the felling of timber which was floated down-river from Glen Garry and Glenmoriston and on to Inverness for domestic use and ship-building. Charcoal-fired iron manufacture took place at Invergarry during the Eighteenth Century and perhaps earlier.[48]

Cattle raised on the uplands offered rich pickings in less settled times. In the Fifteenth Century "the large herds reared on the pasture lands of Urquhart and Glenmoriston were an irresistible temptation to the cattle-lifting hordes of Lochaber and the West …"[49] Such lawlessness persisted across the Highlands, for as late as 1672 Inverness Presbytery recorded that a proposed visitation at

Daviot and Dunlichity was cancelled since the heritors and elders had "to abyd in the glens to shelter and keep their bestiall and goods from the Lochaber and Glencoa robbers."[50]

Social upheavals testified to the spiritual failure of the church. Early in the Sixteenth Century the dioceses, which should have given structure and oversight "were administered not from the rural heartland of the Highlands ... but from the relative safety of cathedral cities situated, for the most part, on the edge of the Highlands". Dunkeld, Elgin, and even Fortrose were distant from the Great Glen. More locally "the parish structure, though long complete, remained much weaker and less developed than the cohesive and compact system operating in the south."[51] Furthermore, the process described as The Reformation, which commenced in 1560, created a century of ecclesiastical turmoil which saw periods of episcopal and presbyterian government alternating and intermingling. There was a lack of continuity, and in the Highlands especially, distant from the centre of diocesan or presbyterian authority, it may be concluded that the church in the region "had developed in somewhat erratic fashion in the decades after 1560. Weaknesses in the structure, therefore, could often lead to shortcomings in the parishes." James Kirk concludes that the bishops "had largely failed to supply the initiative and direction needed to succeed in the missionary enterprise upon which the kirk had embarked."[52] Any administrative failure of the Church was, however, accompanied by the loss of financial foundations. In the third quarter of the Sixteenth Century ecclesiastical order had disintegrated due to "the appropriation by secular property-owners of the extensive estates which various abbeys and bishoprics had earlier accumulated."[53]

A Partial Reformation

"… put in order what was left unfinished"
[Titus 1:5]

The process of religious change known as The Reformation was actually a long period of transition. Its origins are well recorded elsewhere[54], and the events that shaped its progress took place far from the Great Glen. It saw a movement from the Roman Catholicism, which had transformed the Celtic Church, to the Presbyterian hegemony which dominated Scotland in the Eighteenth Century. In the course of a century the Church in Scotland experienced inter-twined periods of episcopacy and presbyterian governance which sometimes confuses the historical narrative, especially when the church was governed by presbyteries under a bishop. Some of the clergy adapted their allegiances according to the times, whilst others were forced into exile or diplomatic silence. Indeed, the ecclesiastical changes were largely restricted to the towns in the first instance because clergymen who adhered to the Reformation principles were few and far between. Thus, the upheavals of the Reformation did not bring about an immediate transformation of the church and its mission. In 1567 the "Province of Murray" had but eight ministers adhering to Reformation principles, whilst the Bishop of the time was one of those who adhered most strongly to the old Church. The Province served the area between the Rivers Ness and Spey, although it is interesting to note one of their ministers, "Maister Robert Pont", was appointed as "Commissioner to plant kirks" across the Province.[55]

The organisation of parishes was such that they covered vast areas. In 1567 the ministers in the "Province of Murray" were assisted by "exhorters and readers"; there were eighteen exhorters and nineteen more readers located across the Laigh of Moray and south to Badenoch. Exhorters were often lay preachers, whilst readers had the task of reading the scriptures for the benefit of the illiterate at church services. One exhorter is named for "Urquhart and Glenmorisoun", and another who served as exhorter and reader in "Durris (Dores), Bolleskene, Abirtarff."[56] The latter, James Duff, was described thirteen years later as the vicar of Dunlichity, Daviot, Boleskine, Dores, Dalrossie and Moy, a territory stretching from Strathdearn to Glen Albyn. More local ministry would have been supplied by "Readers": in 1567 James Farquharson is listed as exhorter for Urquhart and Glenmoriston. By 1574 the Reader at Glenmoriston was granted a stipend along with the income from the "Kirklands" "to be payit out of the chancellarie of Murray [by] the takkismen or parochinaris of Glenmoreistown, or [by] the chancellare, as the reidare sall choose."[57]

Following the outset of the Reformation "the immediate emphasis was on repairing kirks and securing reformed service for the existing parish system. The Reformation, of course, was nowhere effected overnight."[58] Geography and poor roads meant that it was difficult to serve Highland parishes, but within a short time there was a thinly-spread distribution of ministers. A reorganisation of the kirk's finances, begun by the crown in 1573, saw one minister in charge of three or four adjacent parishes with a resident reader in each. This "had the merit of providing every parish with the prospect of, at least, the service of a reader, supervised and supplemented by a neighbouring minister, until such time as additional finance and recruitment to the ministry were secured."[59]

With the appointment of the first protestant Archbishop of Glasgow in 1603 the Reformation asserted its ascendency: "the doctrines of the Reformation began to create a spirit of unrest among the Scottish people. The work of the Reformers was greatly facilitated by the unworthy lives of some of the clergy."[60]　In fact there were only a "few priests left in the country who had not conformed to the new religion. Not more than about half a dozen priests remained, and in 1605 it was reported that there was only one. From 1603 to 1653 the few remaining Catholics in Scotland were left without even a rudimentary organised Church."[61]　The Reformation saw different patterns of church organisation. The early protestant bishops had been less than assiduous in their advocacy of reformation principles, but the General Assembly of 1576 saw "diocesan episcopacy effectively eclipsed" and the old dioceses were subdivided into presbyteries. After 1603 King James decided that "bishops were essential for his success in church and state;" with the result that within a short time-span the majority of Highland parishes had a settled ministry and "firm foundations were laid for the presence of the reformed kirk in parishes throughout the Highlands.[62]　King James' reforms and episcopalian church government, however, were to be reversed and reversed again before the end of the century.

In 1633 King Charles I and Archbishop Laud visited Scotland and condemned the Presbyterian system of church governance, insisting that a new Liturgy and Book of Canons should be used throughout the land. This created much ferment, with the result that in 1638 the National Covenant pledged its signatories to maintain the freedom of the Church. This attracted widespread support, and in November of that year the first "free" General Assembly met since 1596. In spite of orders from the king "they deposed the prelates, abolished the Articles that enslaved the Church, and re-established Presbyterianism."[63] The following decade saw unrest erupting into armed conflict in both England and Scotland, caused by a complex mixture of political and religious factors: the King was executed in 1649 against the will of the Scottish Parliament, and this ushered in the ascendency of Oliver Cromwell. With the Restoration of the Monarchy in 1661 Charles II re-imposed episcopacy, leading to ferocious opposition from the Covenanters. It was only in 1690, following the accession of William III, that Presbyterianism was restored in Scotland.

Despite the upheavals of the Reformation in urban Scotland life in the Highlands saw little change. The area was "hardly touched by the political and religious tensions which affected the Lowlands so acutely in the fifteenth and early sixteenth centuries." The reforming zeal which was fuelled by the teachings of John Calvin made little initial impact. There was at first "no general or systematic attempt ... to convert the Highlanders and Islanders to Calvinism. There was a lack of Gaelic-speaking priests to minister to them and so they drifted into a state of semi-paganism, though retaining many Catholic traditions. The [Catholic] faith just faded out; it was never suppressed." Nonetheless, missionaries still made forays into the Great Glen area: they were active in Glenelg and Lochaber in the 1630s, and worked from a base at Invergarry Castle from 1655 to 1679. Later in the century three of them were at work in Glengarry and Knoydart.[64]

Beyond the towns organisation of the Reformed church was slow. Well-formed, community-focussed parishes took time to emerge. There was a shortage of protestant clergy, especially in the rural areas. For instance, it is recorded that in 1607 Andrew Macphail was appointed minister of Boleskine, Moy, Daviot and Dunlichity, a territory that included Abertarff at this time. In 1614 Boleskine was amalgamated with Abertarff and Dores for three years, and thereafter Boleskine and Abertarff forged a common identity. Not surprisingly "remote Highland parishes had at best a very intermittent service from their ministers. How could it be otherwise when many miles of wild hill country separated them from the parish church and ministers had to make their way among them on rough tracks, either on foot or on horseback?"[65]

The provision of manses was not always straightforward because this depended not on the congregations but upon the landowners and heritors. Some landowners had no such responsibilities, but they and others designated as heritors were liable for the payment of public burdens such as the minister's and schoolmaster's stipends, the upkeep of churches, manses and glebes, the poor rates and the maintenance of roads and bridges. Not surprisingly, some landowners and heritors were reluctant to support Presbyterian ministers if they had Episcopalian or Catholic leanings. A minister could supplement his stipend by farming the glebe, but during the years of ecclesiastical turmoil some landowners absorbed the glebes into their own lands, thereby denying a minister that additional source of income. As late as 1779 Anne Grant writes of settling in Laggan in Badenoch upon her marriage to Rev James Grant where: "they found themselves housed in a small cottage at the farm of Gaskbeg. There was no church, no manse, and no glebe. They were to receive an extra £20 a year to compensate for the lack of a manse."[66] The absence of a manse was by no means unusual: Kilmonivaig's minister was accommodated in a local landowner's house, and the same occurred in Urquhart.[67]

Records from the Synod of Argyll show that from 1639 onwards "the eldership began to assume a new political importance as the covenanting crisis deepened" and that efforts were being made to secure Gaelic-speaking ministers, schools and bursaries. Within Lochaber, however, "Cameron of Locheil and other heritors petitioned in 1642 for the appointment of a new minister for the kirks of Kilmonivaig and Kilmallie, since, as they claimed, not only were 'many souls ignorant of the Word of God throw the want of the preaching thereof', but the parishioners were 'forced to repair to other kirks long distant ... to baptize infants and get lawfull mareages'."[68]

Any progress in bringing Christian ministry to the area, whether by Catholic priests or Protestant ministers, must have been frustrated by the on-going political and economic uncertainties that affected the Great Glen during the Seventeenth Century. The Marquis of Montrose camped with his army just south of Loch Ness in January 1645 during his campaign against Clan Campbell, but used his brief sojourn to prepare the "Killiwheimen Band." Its purpose was to "unite the Loyalty of the Highlands against the Power of Argyle", and it expressed sentiments that would not be out of place today: "each and everie one of us doe faithfullie promeis, mutuallie to assist one another heirin, as we shall be desired, or the occasione requyr: All of which befor God and his angels we most solomnlie … vow and promeis firmly till adhere to, and never to swerve from, as we would be reputed famous men, and Christians, and expect the blessing of Almighty God in this lyf, or his eternal happiness hereafter." Two Earls and over fifty clan heads subscribed their names to this declaration of loyalty to the King and to each other.[69]

Such a declaration, however, did not bring a peaceful resolution of religious and clan strife, nor did it guarantee lasting prosperity. In April Montrose and his troops passed through Glengarry where the castle was burnt down. In 1689 John Graham, Viscount Dundee, who maintained allegiance to King James VII once William of Orange had come to the throne, led an army which comprised many local clans through the Great Glen and the parallel Glen Buck and Glen Loy.[70] At the same time there were harvest failures and famines recorded in the latter part of the century. "In the 1690s the Scottish grain harvest failed for four successive years and there was a famine in both Highlands and Lowlands. So severe was it that it is estimated between a quarter and a third of the population either died or left the country …"[71]

"... a melancholy and afflicting picture"

"... you are lukewarm – neither hot nor cold"
[Revelation 3:16]

In 1695 the Vatican had appointed the first Scottish Vicar-Apostolic, Bishop Nicolson. Unwilling to take the Oath of Allegiance to William and Mary he kept a low profile, but managed a visit to the Highlands and Islands in 1700, passing through the Great Glen and Glengarry.[72] It was noted that "Catholic advances in the Highlands between 1700 and 1750 were identified in Lochaber, Glenmoriston ... Abertarff and Fort Augustus. This advance was put down to the activity of priests in these areas."[73]

The signs of revival amidst the Catholic community prompted the concern of some Presbyterians to establish in 1701 the "Society in Scotland for Propagating Christian Knowledge" or SSPCK, with the intention of planting schools based upon Protestant principles. The SSPCK "resolved to open the first school in the parish of Abertarf ... because it was "the centre of a country where Popery does much abound." The school, however, met with such opposition from mainly Papist parents that it had to be closed after a year and a half."[74] The schools introduced new personnel to the Highlands, often young men intending to enter the parish ministry.

They had to be "a person of Piety, Loyalty, Prudence, Gravity, competent (in) knowledge and literature and endued with other Christian qualifications suited to that station."[75] As such they could be able co-workers alongside the resident ministers, "particularly on the Lord's Day, when they pray and read with the inhabitants, and instruct them in the principles of religion."[76]

Opposition to the perceived Catholic resurgence combined with growing concern about the social conditions of the Highland population. The dawn of the Eighteenth Century saw the creation in Edinburgh of the Society for the Reformation of Manners, founded for the purpose of "labouring in the dark and dreary regions of their own country where a high northern latitude, a surly climate, a stubborn sterile soil, civil oppression, and a gloomy religious superstition combined to present a melancholy and afflicting picture of accumulated human misery."[77] Abertarff was chosen as being most in need, but the project did not advance.

Dramatic change, however, came from another direction and the rest of the Eighteenth Century was to bring significant developments to the Great Glen. The Rising of 1715 had little immediate impact upon the area, although the Laird of Glengarry raised five hundred men for the cause.[78] Estates of Jacobite sympathisers, Glengarry included, were appropriated and managed

by the Commissioners of the Forfeited Estates: they were charged
with realising these assets, many of which were sold to the York
Buildings Company which took an interest in the forests of the
Highlands and their potential for fuelling iron smelting in Glengarry
and elsewhere. However, it was the Battle of Glenshiel in 1719 that
strengthened the Government's nervousness about Highland
sympathies, and this led to the creation of a network of barracks,
including that at Kilchuimen. This was followed by the building of
a military road from end to end of the Great Glen.

Designed and supervised by General Wade, these roads were just
a part of his strategy to control the Highlands. By 1729 a new fort
was under construction to replace the Kilchuimen barracks; it was
completed in 1742. In 1731 the new road west to Glenelg was
finished. The road east over the Corrieyairach Pass to Laggan was
completed shortly afterwards. Such road building enabled the rapid
movement of troops who harried Catholics, sought out priests and
no doubt contributed to revived Jacobite unrest.[79] The creation of
a crossroads at the south end of Loch Ness gave rise to a busy
community with a range of local trades and services.

Whilst military developments proceeded there were other moves
to consolidate the influence of Protestantism. Following a new
Oath of Allegiance passed by Parliament in 1723 George I granted

£1000 to promote Protestantism in the Highlands and Islands, and in the following year the Royal Bounty Committee was set up to support itinerant preachers, catechists and teachers. Later on the Commissioners of the Forfeited Estates gave further assistance. The Church of Scotland General Assembly of 1722 was told there were four thousand Catholics in the Hebrides and the western mainland, with numerous enclaves "in Glengarry, Glenmoriston, Glenurquhart and Strathglass" although the Catholic historian Peter Anson feels this number may have been exaggerated.[80]

In an attempt to improve the Christian presence in the region, the new Synod of Glenelg was established in 1724 "designed to bring fresh vigour and effectiveness to the work of the established church in the Western Highlands and Islands."[81] The Synod was a church court interposed between the General Assembly and the more local presbyteries. At the same time the Presbytery of Abertarff was created, comprising the parishes of Kilmallie, Kilmonivaig, Abertarff, Boleskine, Urquhart, Glenmoriston, and Laggan in Upper Strathspey, the latter included because of the direct route over the Corrieyairach Pass. This ecclesiastical innovation placed Abertarff at the geographical centre of a vast rural region which stretched in the north from the upper reaches of Glenurquhart to Loch Leven in the south, and from Strathdearn and

Dalwhinnie in the east to the west coast between Acharacle and Loch Hourn.[82] Presbytery meetings were usually convened at Abertarff, the most central, and possibly the largest settlement within its bounds. It is significant that the Presbytery took its name from the ancient church of Abertarff despite the fact that it did not regain its status as a parish until 1883. The Presbytery of Abertarff, which was superseded by Lochaber Presbytery in 1923 following a realignment of parishes, was the only administrative area ever to be centred upon Glen Albyn.

In 1725 the General Assembly was presented with a report from the Synod of Glenelg listing the vacant churches, large parishes, lack of schools, and the poor state of church buildings, manses and glebes.[83] A typical church building at this time was little more than a shed or barn, "no more than forty by sixteen feet, and without seats or bells."[84] The itinerant missionaries did not always have such shelter: three of them reported that "not having the convenience of preaching houses ... we are obliged to preach in the open air, exposed to the heat in summer, and in winter to the inclemency of the weather; generally in wet clothes, and sometimes without the benefit of necessary refreshments, which render these missions extremely troublesome, dangerous and prejudicial to health."[85] Many have suggested that "until near the close of the eighteenth century the impression made by the Church was trivial. Change, when it came, was due to men of intensely evangelical faith."[86] More significant change was, however, about to come about across the Highlands due to events focussed upon Fort Augustus.

The Military Years

> "... *flashing swords and glittering spears!*
> *Many casualties, piles of dead, bodies without*
> *number, people stumbling over the corpses ..."*
> *[Nahum 3:3]*

The final Jacobite Rising was triggered by the arrival of Prince Charles Edward in Moidart in August 1745. His Standard was raised at Glenfinnan on 19 August and amongst the twelve hundred clansmen present were Glengarry MacDonalds and Glenmoriston Grants. The progress of the Rising is well documented elsewhere, and within the Great Glen there was much activity, with Jacobites commandeering Kilchuimen Barracks and then pounding the new and lower Fort with cannon fire. The culmination of the campaign was at Culloden on 16 April 1746. What immediately followed brought great suffering to the Highland glens, and was to cause a set-back to the Christian communities, both Catholic and Protestant. Indeed, "In the twelve months that followed Culloden a whole ancient civilization and way of life were dismantled. Like most others, it had its faults and its shortcomings, but was certainly no worse than what, under different auspices, was now to replace it."[87] The events at Fort Augustus and amongst the surrounding glens precipitated that new era.

The Duke of Cumberland moved his headquarters and victorious troops to Fort Augustus on 16 May 1746. During the reprisals that followed over a period of two months some eight battalions of Redcoats scoured the surrounding glens for Jacobites and their sympathisers. There was an element of revenge in what followed: "every day a company or two of infantry would draw rations and ammunition and sally forth into the hills from Fort Augustus to burn and murder and plunder and rape. The discovery of the bodies of nine Redcoats in a well behind the barracks had put the troops in a conveniently revengeful frame of mind. With savage enthusiasm they burned down every house they came to, large or small, carried off the contents, raped the women, old or young, and cut down or shot any clansmen they came on, without, for the most part, stopping to ascertain their loyalties or allegiance."[88] From this and other campaigns about three and a half thousand men, women and children were imprisoned, and nine hundred transported.

The Catholics, Jacobite sympathisers or not, suffered heavily:

"orders were issued that all Papist chapels or places where Mass was being celebrated must be demolished, and all priests arrested."[89] In England anti-Catholic sentiment was widespread and continued for some years. It has been suggested "that the failure of the 'Forty-Five' held back the progress of the Catholic Mission in Scotland for more than a quarter-of-a-century. It also led to wholesale destruction of many of the castles and country houses which has sheltered mission priests for nearly two hundred years"[90], among them Invergarry Castle. Catholic sources agreed with the Church of Scotland estimate that one in ten of the Highland population adhered to the Catholic Church, these being supported by just four secular priests and two Jesuits ministering to their widely-scattered flocks. However, by 1764 Bishop Hugh Macdonald, in his Report on the Highland Vicariate, was able to note some fourteen hundred Catholics under the charge of their priest. "Glengarry was the most important mission in the Highland Vicariate"[91], but it was further noted the same priest ministered to over a thousand Catholics in Brae Lochaber and the Braes of Badenoch! The Bishop also records that in Fort Augustus "there are many Protestants, but the rest of the region is all Catholic."[92]

Anson reflects that "the cause of Protestantism had gained little from the brutal efforts made by the Duke of Cumberland and his red-coats".[93] A Church of Scotland General Assembly report in 1765 charted a growing Catholic community in the Highlands, mentioning "the assiduity of the Roman priests", and specifying that in Glenmoriston and other parts of Inverness-shire Protestantism "was decaying and Popery increasing."[94]

Following Cumberland's departure to London, Government troops continued their patrols for some years, well after the escape of "Bonnie" Prince Charles to France in September 1746. The military task was to hunt down his sympathisers and to enforce the Disarming Acts and the ban on Highland dress. Records exist of one of the smaller patrol areas based at Laggan Achadrom from whence the Redcoats ventured as far as Strathglass and Glen Roy. It is recorded that the senior officer "advertised his orders on the church doors in his district ..."[95] This emphasises the importance of churches as community hubs but there is, alas, no helpful record of the location of those church doors!

Within Protestant circles the work of the SSPCK, with support from the Royal Bounty Committee, enabled teachers, schools and catechists to gradually build up the Church of Scotland in the Highlands. This led in turn to talk of planting new churches in areas distant from the historic parish churches. For instance, in 1760 the Royal Bounty Committee, formed to administer the incomes of the

Forfeited Estates following the '45, recommended that the Glengarry area be disjoined from Kilmonivaig and joined to Fort Augustus, something not achieved until 1987.

Despite the diligence of both Christian communities following Culloden, there was another significant change across the Highlands prompted by the re-organisation of estates and so-called agricultural improvement.   It is thought that around 50,000 Highlanders emigrated between 1763 and 1775.   Many crofts in Glengarry, Glenmoriston and Glenurquhart were abandoned as families moved to Canada or to the lowlands of Scotland. In Glengarry, along with Knoydart, there had been a population of 5000 and the clearances there removed many settlements from the landscape. In 1792 one hundred and fifty emigrants left Glengarry for Canada, giving their native glen's name to Glengarry County in Ontario. Migration of Highlanders, both Catholic and Protestant, to Canada reached a peak in 1817, by which time 35,000 Gaelic-speakers had made their home in Nova Scotia.[96] In Fort Augustus in 1775 Anne Grant tells of "another ship load of emigrants, marching off to their Chaldea."[97]

In 1818 the General Assembly received a Petition from the Presbytery of Abertarff in the name of its Moderator, William Fraser of Boleskine, asking the Assembly to approach the Lords of the Treasury requesting greater support for churches in the Highlands.

The Petition, which was circulated widely, stated that due to geography and "paucity of the Clergy it is absolutely impossible that the people whose spiritual interests are confided to the Presbytery can have Divine Ordinances, or Religious edification dispensed to them as often, or as regularly as they would require, should their few Pastors possess all the zeal of the Apostles, united with Herculean strength." Within its own bounds Presbytery recommended the creation of five new parishes, including Glenmoriston, Abertarff and Glengarry.[98] Whilst the Royal Bounty Committee's missionaries did serve Glenmoriston, Glengarry and Fort Augustus and elsewhere, it would be 1864 before Glengarry became a parish in its own right. Fort Augustus achieved this in 1883, followed by Glenmoriston in 1891.

The Disruption

"… the churches were strengthened in the faith"
[Acts 16:5]

The causes of the Disruption of 1843 are many and various. The Clearances, agricultural "improvement", social injustices and reaction to the power of the lairds were just some of the grounds fuelling the desire for change, as well as a growing evangelical thrust within the Highland churches. The role and influence of some ministers upon their congregations and communities was transformational, and there was a quickening of spiritual concern generated by catechists and elders. The influence and example of schoolmasters working for the SSPCK was also significant. Matters came to a head at the 1843 General Assembly of the Church of Scotland when over four hundred ministers left to create the 'Church of Scotland Free'.

In many parts of the Highlands, the Disruption emptied the Church of Scotland congregations, as was the case in Urquhart. In Kilmallie, two-thirds of the congregation left with their minister.[99] William Lauder, the missionary-minister at Glengarry, took on the task of establishing the Free Church in the area. He was the only local leader to adhere to the new denomination, although he had only limited success in Glengarry. He did, however, make headway in Glenmoriston and Fort Augustus. By June 1843 four elders were elected and ordained at Fort Augustus, three of them residing in Glenmoriston. These elders, however, were the only men who had adhered to the Free Church in the district. Thus, in that area at least, the Disruption was not the seismic event that denuded the Establish Church in Urquhart of all but a few of its adherents. As will be related, Mr Lauder had secured a site for a new church at Fort

Augustus within weeks, although it was 1857 before a new building was opened in Glenmoriston. Progress in Glengarry was much more difficult because the landowner refused a site for a new church. Eventually, in 1860, a church was built at Gairlochy, west of Spean Bridge, with the congregation also meeting at Laggan.[100]

The Disruption created new challenges for the Church of Scotland Presbytery of Abertarff. It was minuted that "Our people are assailed by no fewer than six Free Church Ministers and five Popish priests stationed within the bounds, and also by other itinerating emissaries of the Free Church and that of Rome."[101] The Presbytery, which lost four ministers to the Free Church, acted as fast as it could to fill its vacancies, appointing William Sutherland as missionary for Glengarry, Fort Augustus and Glenmoriston as early as July 1843. The rifts between the two denominations ran deep, with families and communities divided, and the national leaders of the two churches making claims and counter-claims about which claimed the spiritual and moral high ground. The Church of Scotland minister at Kilmallie, commenting upon the 1851 Census which showed that the Free Church performed less than a half of the marriages as those by the Church of Scotland, said "Yet the Free Church represents itself as comprising almost the whole population of Scotland …"[102] Over the years the Free Church congregations in Fort Augustus and Glenmoriston were to follow a pattern of association which mirrored that of the Established Church. From 1844 to 1878 the two congregations were formally linked, then Glenmoriston became a separate charge, with a new manse built alongside the church in 1882. In 1909 it reunited with Fort Augustus and the two were united with the Glenurquhart congregation in 1983. The new Free Church congregation in Glengarry was united with Kilmonivaig from 1844 to 1858; it was then an independent congregation for a short while before rejoining its southern neighbour of Kilmonivaig. The progress of the Free Church in Fort Augustus, Glemoriston and Glengarry, and the creation of the United Free Church in 1900, is charted in following chapters.

Two Centuries of Development

> *"Praise be to the name of God for ever and ever ...*
> *He changes times and seasons"*
> *[Daniel 2:20,21]*

Ways through the Glens

> *"I am making a way in the wilderness"*
> *[Isaiah 43:19]*

Plans for new churches in the early 1800s coincided with a significant example of government-backed economic development in the Highlands. Thomas Telford was tasked by the Treasury to plan improved communications and to consider the causes of emigration from the Highlands. This led to the building of "Parliamentary" roads, upgrading and expanding the network created in the previous century by General Wade and his successors. Within the Great Glen new roads were built from Invergarry to Kinloch Hourn and Glenshiel, along with much needed bridges at Torgyle and Aberchalder.[103] The vital bridge over the River Oich at Fort Augustus was completed by 1813.

The benefit of a canal from west to east, exploiting the lochs of the Great Glen, had been widely promoted and was closely championed by Telford. Construction of the Caledonian Canal commenced in 1802. One of the largest civil engineering projects involved the diversion of the River Oich where it flowed into Loch Ness, the construction of a flight of five locks alongside Fort Augustus, the cutting of five miles of canal from Loch Ness to Loch Oich, and then a summit section beyond Loch Oich to Loch Lochy. The scale of this enterprise cannot be underestimated, and its impact on the district was immense. The flight of locks rising from Loch Ness created a focus around which the modern settlement of Fort

Augustus was to coalesce. There were many temporary villages created to accommodate the navvies, but there is little evidence of any provision for their spiritual welfare apart, perhaps, from the building of Laggan Church in 1820. However, as will be recounted later, the Sabbath was respected, and many of the navvies led informal worship in their huts.

Today the Caledonian Canal carries little commercial traffic: its primary focus is leisure boating and cruising, and the towpaths are incorporated into the long-distance footpath and cycleway, the Great Glen Way. There is a boat-hire business at Laggan Locks and a Canal Heritage Centre at Fort Augustus, and the Canal and its users make a significant contribution to the local economy and services.

Nearly a century after the commencement of works to build the Caledonian Canal the Invergarry and Fort Augustus Railway was under construction, creating a branch line from the West Highland Railway at Spean Bridge. With extensive earthworks and viaducts the railway brought a fresh influx of navvies to the district. Minutes of the Presbytery of Abertarff note that a Lay Missionary had been obtained to minister to the workmen engaged on the project.[104] Once completed, the line fell victim to railway rivalries meaning that any idea of continuing the line to Inverness soon withered, as did

the passenger and freight traffic once road improvements and
motorised transport revolutionised communications after the First
World War. The line finally closed in 1946 leaving a legacy of
viaducts and a tunnel along its length. In recent years Invergarry
Station has been restored by a group of enthusiastic volunteers.

Transformation of the Land

> " … *the land will yield its fruit*"
> *[Leviticus 25:19]*

The years following Culloden saw the deterioration of the traditional
agricultural economy. Crofts were extinguished by landowners
imposing increasing rentals, the sheilings abandoned and new farms
created. In Glenmoriston the coming of the new, extensive sheep
farms were seen to mark the disruption of good relationships
between landlord and people: John Grant, a local bard, claimed that
if the laird were still running the estate:

> "The tenants would be well managed
> No people would be evicted
> And arrogance without dignity
> Would not take advantage of the commons
> Each landed proprietor
> In the north, here, is mistaken
> Turning his back on his people
> For the tarred sheep."

For the bard, emigration was unavoidable and he looked to divine protection:

> "I shall be going and will not be stopped
> And I shall collect my baggage
> And I shall be with the others
> Who will not leave me on the shore
> But, O King! on the throne,
> who art both herdsman and Father
> Keep watch over the flock
> Who have gone to plough the seas."[105]

By 1845 the switch from cattle to sheep was all but complete. Around Fort Augustus sheep farms were created west of the Oich in the 1820s, and at Cullachy in the 1850s, but deterioration of the land and growing competition from Australian wool hastened the development of the sporting estates. By 1900 there were five such estates around Fort Augustus alone.[106]

The Glengarry lands were perhaps the most extensive in the Highlands, but the rental income was less than £300 per annum. The Clan chief needed to improve his fortunes, and he did so first in 1782 by leasing Glenquioch to Thomas Gillespie "provided the five hundred people living there were removed." More Glengarry tenants were evicted from 1785 until 1802, the majority from the Knoydart area, with many taking emigrant passages to Nova Scotia.

Thomas Telford reported that in 1801 alone eleven ships had sailed from Fort William with 3,300 emigrants aboard.[107] Glengarry estate was divided into many sheep-walks, but Duncan Macdonell, the fifteenth Chief, died in 1828 with personal debts of £80,000. The scene was set for further changes that would be exacerbated by serious harvest failure in 1836 and the potato blight which brought destitution to the Highlands in 1846 and 1847. This in turn became another impetus to emigration.[108] During the half-century of agricultural transition the estates in the Great Glen remained intact although by 1848 their ownership had passed to "rich English capitalists".[109] Meanwhile the scale of emigration cannot be denied, nor can the suffering of the populace be ignored; by these dramatic social changes the traditional bond between clan chief and his people was all-but destroyed.

The Nineteenth Century saw the development of the sporting estates as landowners sought to maximise the income from their marginal land. Once Queen Victoria bought Balmoral in 1852 the Highlands became fashionable. New mansions and lodges were built in the glens, and game-keepers and stalkers were housed in some very remote locations as testified by the Baptismal Roll for Glengarry parish. The lodges were let for the season, and were tenanted by wealthy individuals who were not necessarily aware of the local culture. The factor advised one individual who proposed shooting at Balmacaan in Glenurquhart from 12 August "that it would be best if he delayed his arrival until after 18th August when Communion Week would be over."[110] Many tenants and other seasonal visitors, however, did make significant contributions to the local churches, as will be related.

Development of the estates was helped by improved communications. Steamers on the Caledonian Canal, the building of bridges and road improvements brought the guests, and once the railway reached Inverness the Great Glen became much more accessible.

The sporting estates depended upon the efficient administration of the factor, and a large staff. On Balmacaan in the 1870s there was a head-keeper, five under-keepers, four stalkers, as well as dog-men, pony-men, gillies and a skinner, not to mention the casual labour involved in driving game and the rearing of pheasants.[111] An extract from the Glen Quoich Game Book records the "bags" from 1840 to 1862, nearly 18,000 grouse and 700 stags and hinds. A parallel list of "vermin" killed across the Glengarry estate gives a sorry tale of eagles, wild cats and other wild life destroyed over the same period.[112]

The Forestry Commission

"Let all the trees of the forest sing for joy"
[Psalm 96:12]

The end of the First World War saw the creation of the Forestry Commission, the fruit of many years of campaigning and lobbying by Lord Lovat. He saw large-scale afforestation as an essential strategic policy, and as a means of stemming the tide of rural depopulation. As a major landowner in the Great Glen, Lovat saw the potential: part of what later became the Port Clair Forest was one of the first purchases of the Commission after its inauguration in 1919. Inchnacardoch Forest followed a year later, then Port Clair and South Laggan and ten years later the local workforce had risen to eighty: two large nurseries had been established along with an experimental station at Aucherawe. By 1939 the Commission owned eleven forests in the Great Glen, and there were around one hundred and thirty employees in the Fort Augustus area. A further nursery was operating at South Laggan, and with offices and workshops at Fort Augustus the forestry community expanded in the post-war era. It has been suggested that an 8% rise in the local population between 1931 and 1951, against the trend elsewhere in the Highlands, was partly due to the expansion of forestry.[113]

Forestry brought a new dimension to the communities of the Great Glen, with staff housing being built at Jenkins Park in Fort Augustus, North Laggan, Glenmoriston and elsewhere, as well as some unique forestry "crofts" at Auchterawe and South Laggan which enabled forestry workers and their families to grow crops and raise cattle, sheep and hens. There were also bothies and hostels to accommodate other workers. All told the Forestry Commission made a significant contribution to the district.[114]

Many of the employees played a role in the life of the local churches. The Baptismal Registers for Glengarry and Fort Augustus chart the gradual evolution of the Great Glen community, where the infants of the estate workers at the end of the Nineteenth Century are succeeded by those of railway staff, forestry workers and lorry drivers as the Twentieth Century progresses.

Tourism and the Environment

"Go into all the world and preach the gospel to all creation"
[Mark 16:15]

Queen Victoria may have set the trend for tourism within the Great Glen when she travelled through the Caledonian Canal in 1873 aboard the SS Gondolier, although apparently she was not amused that the crowds at Fort Augustus locks were able to watch her eating lunch! A century later the employment offered by the Caledonian Canal, the Forestry Commission and the hydro-power industry has declined – due to the use of contractors, the centralisation of management and technical innovations – whilst the growth of tourist-related employment has created new economic opportunities. Fort Augustus Abbey has been transformed into The Highland Club resort, but this is just one of several tourist developments. The creation of residential leisure parks, the designation of the Great Glen Way and other long-distance routes, camping and caravan sites, and the expansion of hotels, hostels and guest houses, restaurants and recreational facilities all mean that the area is busier than ever – all the year round. There is, of course, every reason for the Christian community to engage with visitors as much as with the local residents.

Such tourist developments both inform and are informed by the growing concern for the environment. In the early 1800s Alasdair Macdonnel of Glengarry protested against the building of the Caledonian Canal on the grounds of damage to the fisheries in Loch Oich and invasion of privacy because boats would be seen passing the windows of his mansion house.[115] There was vociferous opposition to the early hydro-electric schemes, but later developments and windfarms attracted less concern. More recently forestry management has moved away from blanket planting of commercial species towards a regeneration of native trees. The conservation charity Trees for Life purchased the Dundreggan Estate in Glenmoriston in 2008 with an ambitious programme of tree-planting, education and re-wilding: the project brings many volunteers and visitors to the area. For Christians, charged with care for Creation, there is ample scope for involvement with the environmental issues within the Great Glen.

A Centre of Power

"They tunnel through the rock; their eyes see all its treasures.
They dam up the sources of the rivers
and bring hidden things to light"
[Job 28:10,11]

The changes wrought by the canal, the railway and forestry were as nothing compared to the ambitious hydro-electric projects which followed the Second World War. Although the monks at Fort Augustus Abbey had created a small hydro-scheme in 1890, supplying electricity to the Abbey and to some local homes, larger-scale development was presaged by the Foyers Aluminium Works built in 1895.[116] Early in the Twentieth Century Kinlochhourn was identified as a possible site for a second aluminium works, served by the waters of Loch Quoich, but Kinlochleven was then chosen as a better location.

However, the dreams of post-war reconstruction after the Second World War, against a background of Highland depopulation from 1921 onwards, created the North of Scotland Hydro-Electric Board and brought electricity to the Highlands. Glengarry and Glen Moriston were the location for major projects commenced in the 1950s and completed in 1957. The Garry scheme dammed two lochs and created two power stations, whilst the Moriston scheme dammed three lochs and saw three power stations built. Both schemes required large labour forces, and apart from the dams and power stations there were miles of tunnels, aqueducts and roads to be built. The raising of Loch Loyne, part of the Garry scheme, necessitated the diversion of the main road to Skye between Tomdoun and Cluanie to a new route from Invergarry to Bunloyne.[117] The majority of the work forces on both schemes were accommodated in camps and, as will be related, the churches rose to the challenge of ministering to these temporary communities. Upon completion of the schemes electric power lines connected the power stations both with local consumers and with customers further south. In his capacity as a County Councillor, Rev Hugh

Gillies, minister at Fort Augustus, switched on the new supply to his community in 1951. A switching station was built at Aucherawe, and a range of employees were settled locally. Bespoke housing was built at The Riggs in Fort Augustus. Again, some hydro staff were valued members of local churches.

The present century has seen a new round of hydro developments in the Great Glen, many of them small-scale run-of-river schemes, although by far the largest was the Glendoe scheme, north-east of Fort Augustus, commenced in 2005. Again the labour-force was largely recruited from outside the area, and six hundred personnel were accommodated at a camp above the village. The Parish Minister had opportunities to engage with the project, and was invited to conduct acts of worship in the tunnels and at the commissioning of the dam.[118] Some senior staff resided locally and joined with the churches.

Further hydro-schemes are planned south-west of Invergarry and to the north of Invermoriston; these will no doubt provide more opportunities for involvement by the churches. Recent hydro schemes have been accompanied by the development of wind-turbine farms located east and west of the Great Glen, although these have not required large transient labour forces to be housed locally. Today the area around the Great Glen is a significant centre for renewable energy generation. It is interesting to reflect that whilst Fort Augustus never became the town and economic centre once envisaged, and having lost its status as a hub for Wade's road network, its large switching station lies at the heart of the extensive electricity transmission network. In one sense, at least, the village in the middle of the Great Glen has finally become a centre of power!

Renewing the Community

> *"… they … went from village to village,*
> *proclaiming the good news" [Luke 9:6]*

In the first decade of the current century the Church of Scotland Presbytery of Lochaber created a plan to centre its ministries upon the catchment areas of the five secondary schools within its bounds. Whilst school chaplaincy is only a part of a parish minister's role, it was seen that the secondary schools, with their educational role and good community facilities, are a focus for local sentiment and an agent for social cohesion. The Presbytery has grouped linkages of parishes around the secondary schools at Kinlochleven, Strontian, Mallaig and Fort William. The fifth school, Kilchuimen Academy at Fort Augustus, is close to the parish church and manse: good relationships between school and church have been mutually beneficial. The catchment area of the Fort Augustus secondary school embraces Glengarry and Glenmoriston whilst the primary school serves just Fort Augustus and Glenmoriston, although the northern glen falls within the adjoining parish and presbytery. Had the parish boundary readjustments of the 1980s reached a different conclusion the ministry centred at Fort Augustus would have been identical with the school catchment areas.

In 1975 local government reorganisation placed Fort Augustus and Glenmoriston within the area of Inverness District Council, and the two within one Community Council. Glengarry came under Lochaber District Council. Further reorganisation abolished the District Councils and united the Great Glen once again within a one-tier Highland Council. However, Glengarry retains its own Community Council whilst the Fort Augustus and Glenmoriston Community Council has become a vital player in the renewable energy developments, shaping the consequent community benefit funds that have flowed from these projects. Voluntary organisations, charities, householders, students and social enterprises have greatly benefited: in 2018–2019 over three quarters of a million pounds was channelled into the central Great Glen area.[119]   Thanks to such funding the Fort Augustus and Glenmoriston Community Company has developed various social, economic and practical programmes. Glengarry has promoted similar projects with its own community benefit funds. All three communities have recently joined together to create the Three Glens Health and Social Care Group to develop a Community Care programme.

The first Regional Plan created by Highland Regional Council in the 1970s recognised the role of Fort Augustus as a service hub, with Glengarry and Glenmoriston as satellites, and despite the advent of online shopping this pattern persists nearly fifty years on. Over the last fifty years the wisdom of this association has been borne out, and the central area of the Great Glen has strengthened its identity. In some parts of Scotland the national church has sometimes failed to consider the geographical realities of presbytery areas, although the proposed creation of a pan-Highland Presbytery for the Church of Scotland may yet abolish one ecclesiastical boundary with positive effect.

Following this broad account of the Great Glen over sixteen centuries of Christian witness, it is helpful to focus more closely on the three parishes that have shaped the ministry and mission within the central area of the Glen. The configurations of these parishes have varied over that time, being associated with their neighbours and with each other in varied patterns. Church buildings have been established, abandoned, and relocated according to the needs of successive ages, and it is hoped that something of the worshipping communities that resided in the area and used these buildings can be recorded and celebrated.

The Lord alone led his people
without the help of a foreign god
He let them rule the highlands,
and they ate what grew in the fields
They found wild honey among the rocks;
their trees flourished in stony ground;
their cows and goats gave plenty of milk;
they had the best sheep, goats and cattle,
the finest wheat and the choicest wine
[Deuteronomy 32:12 – 14]

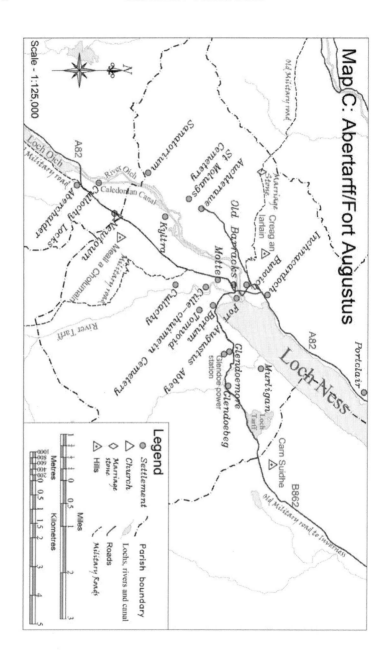

Map C: Abertarff/Fort Augustus

Chapter 2:

ABERTARFF

"On those living in the land of the shadow of death
a light has dawned"
[Matthew 4:16]

"Abertarff" denotes the mouth of the River Tarff where it enters
Loch Ness, and this designation of the district pre-dates that of
Kilchuimen. That more modern name has been taken by many to
indicate that the settlement in Abertarff takes its name from
Cuimen, a colleague of Columba and later the abbot of Iona.
However, several informed writers suggest that it takes its name
from the Comyn or Cummin/Cummings family, who held a vast
area of Moray which stretched in ancient times well into Lochaber
and Glenmoriston. This derivation also occurs in a story recorded
by Dr Archibald Clerk in 1864, where Cumming, fearing for his life
following the murders of his sons, fled Lochaber, died of a broken
heart at Suidhe Chuimein, and was buried at the south end of Loch
Ness, thence called 'Cill a'Chuimein'.[1] In 1689 "A New Map of
Scotland" shows Moray as stretching from the mouth of the Spey
to Ardnamurchan Point, with Abertarff in the middle of the

territory.[2] Suidhe Chuimein, standing above the watershed between Glendoe and Stratherrick, gives a fine vista over much of the Comyn's land, although in earlier years it may well have been a look-out point for the Celtic saints such as Cuimen.

Nonetheless, there is evidence of other early saints in the district, notably Moluag, whose main base was the island of Lismore. At Auchterawe: "is a little cemetery dedicated to Saint Molua, called Kilmalomaig. ... another of the early Irish missionaries (who) ... lived to extreme old age, and died at Rosemarkie ... in 592. In times gone by, there was a church here beside the burying-ground, but now all trace of it has disappeared. This was once the centre of a densely-populated district ..." St Moluag's chapel at Aucherawe may be the shrine of "Quittra", or Kytra, visited by Mary Queen of Scots in September 1562.[3] Campbell suggests that a monk named Fergnae had a hermitage at the "muirbolc mor" which he identifies as Morvalgan or Murlighan Hill east of Abertarff.[4] These are but two of the early Christian sites in the district. Whether best described as cells, shrines or churches, these ancient places of worship were surely small, flimsy, and have left no trace. It is significant that the church close to Urquhart Bay was called Kilmore, "A' Chille Mhor", the Great Cell, because its size contrasted with the smaller buildings more typical of the age.[5]

The Lost Churches

"So I turned my mind to understand,
to investigate and to search out"
[Ecclesiastes 7:25]

There is some evidence for a church at the south end of Loch Ness in the mediaeval period, but its location remains to be confirmed. If Columba had settled a base on the shores of Loch Ness, however temporary, or if Cummein, the abbot of Iona, or his followers had a cell there, no matter how humble, then it would have been small and would not have survived the ravages of time.[6] Campbell proposes a Christian presence continuing from those early days through the Viking period and into the thirteenth century when Abertarff is first mentioned in 1208 by Bricius, the Bishop of Moray. Bricius refers to "Gillibride, Persona de Abirtarff" as a witness to a deed. That there was a "parson" at Abertarff bears testimony to a church of some status that warranted its own priest.[7] King David I (1124–1153) used a new set of landowners and markets to settle the territory and to develop a pastoral economy. In 1225 land was granted at Abertarff to support the Rector of the Parish Church: there is some evidence to suggest that the church was at the mouth of the River Tarff on the shore of Loch Ness.[8] Abertarff Church supported the new Priory at Beauly through its valuable tiend income, a one-tenth tax levied on local agricultural income, especially its salmon, so Abertarff was valuable real-estate. Sheep, cattle, cheese and hides were all important products, due to good low-level land and the summer grazings around the higher sheilings. A new Lordship was granted to Thomas of Thirlestane who built "the Old Castle of Kilwimmin" just to the east of the present Kilchuimen Cemetery.[9] He had the reputation as a thief because it is alleged that he appropriated church lands, leaving the priest with only a "toft and croft" – a house and garden ground. This confirms the significance of the Church of Abertarff, whether or not it was a Columban foundation, and not least because it was a priory church associated with Beauly Priory.[10]   It may be concluded with confidence, therefore, that there was a church of some importance at Abertarff in the thirteenth century.

Thirlestane's castle was burned down in 1228 by rebellious Moraymen[11] and later, in 1240, the Byset (Bisset) family was granted the Lordship at Abertarff, with William Bisset appointed Patron of the Church of Abertarff. All this suggests that the community of Abertarff was thriving in the Thirteenth Century, and that the Church there had an important role within the ecclesiastical structure of the time. However, the local economy went downhill after 1280 when the weather became cooler and wetter, perhaps due to a significant volcanic eruption in South America. This led to cattle disease and sheep scab which decimated the herds and led to the impoverishment of the population.[12]

The ascendency of Robert the Bruce, and the increasing consolidation of the various regions of Scotland, led to Hugh Fraser of Lovat being confirmed in the Barony of Abertarff in 1422[13]. Predations from the west, however, put the Great Glen under pressure: one of the bloodiest incidents followed when the MacDonalds overran Abertarff and Stratherrick causing much destruction. The outcome was the Battle of Kinlochlochy (or the Battle of the Shirts) in 1544. Fought at the head of Loch Lochy close to Laggan Achadrom, only a few combatants survived[14]. The Great Glen was to remain vulnerable to civil disturbance for another two hundred years, and the role of the church somewhat parlous. As predations continued, the economy declined and landowners increased their control of communal resources, so the place of the church in Abertarff, at least, declined. With the early signs of a radical religious reformation in the mid-1550s whatever remained of the original Abertarff Church and its assets were assigned to the sixth Lord Lovat: it would be over three hundred years before the Lovat family would return the ancient site to ecclesiastical use.[15]

In 1614 the churches of Dores, Boleskine and Kilchuimin were amalgamated, although Dores was separated three years later. "Thus came into being the combined parish of Boleskine and Abertarff which was to continue for 270 years, except for the years 1676–1688 when Abertarff was joined with Glenmoriston". There must have been some substance to the church of Kilchuimen because in 1636 "the Synod granted the minister, Andrew Fraser of Boleskine, liberty 'to intromit with [*ie. to appropriate*] the burial silver of Abertarff' to erect 'ane stane house, as some evil disposed persones had already burned his present dwelling hows'".[16] Thus Abertarff's resources were sold to provide a manse at Boleskine.

The precise location of Abertarff church, however, remains difficult to pinpoint. Walter MacFarlane's "Geographical Collections" brings together topographical reports from the Seventeenth and Eighteenth Centuries. One report from around 1719 tells of the ruins of a castle on the shore of Loch Ness "supposed to be built by the Cummings from whom it had its name to this day but now scarce the vestiges of it remain, being demolished for the Barracks use."[17] Another report, possibly from a century earlier states that at the mouth of the River Erigh (Oich) "there is ane ancient Castle and verie pleasant plaine of Corneland about this antient Castle and it stands at the Southwest heid of

Lochnes. There is ane Church toune not half a myll from the mouth of the river which is called Killchuimen in Abirtarff, and there is no church in this toune but it is the Paroch of Abirtarff and where the church should stand, there is a river called Tarff …" Further, with reference to an account of Statherrick, we read of "certaine Churches in Abirtarff and Straharrigaik Kilquhimen in Abirtarff and Boleskie in Straharrigaick …"[18]

There are two conundrums to explore in these reports. Firstly, is the ancient castle referred to at the mouth of the Oich one that predated General Monck's fortification of 1654, or is it Thirlestane's motte burnt down in 1228? The location of the castle may be a guide to the "Church toune" which was within half a mile of the castle, although allowances must be made for the generalisations of a casual observer. The distance from the mouth of the Oich to Kilchuimen Cemetery, which has been suggested as the site of the church, is well over half a mile, whilst the site of the motte is virtually adjacent to the cemetery. However, the reference to the River Tarff "where the church should stand" hints that there had been a place of worship beside the river. This may refer to the ancient "Kirk of Kilchuma" at the shore of Loch Ness as marked on Pont's map of c1583–1596, or it may simply suggest that the writer felt that there should have been a church at the settlement of Kilchuimen.

Secondly, having stated that there was "no church" it is reported that there was a church at "Kilquhimen in Abirtarff". It is impossible to resolve this contradiction unless the information comes from different reports at different times, or it may be that these reports suggest that there was in fact no church building despite the fact that the parish retained its status and integrity. Neither of these riddles may be resolved without further research. If Andrew Fraser sold the Abertarff silver in 1636 it is more than likely that the church beside Loch Ness was in a parlous state, so much so that eighteen years later it was considered to be of no importance whatsoever.

Marked on Timothy Pont's map[19] in the late 1500s as "K. of Kilchuma", the building at the mouth of the Tarff was probably demolished in 1654 to make way for a fortification built by General Monck as part of Cromwell's chain of strongholds from Inverlochy to Inverness. Campbell observes that this was part of a deliberate pacification strategy, with the new strongholds being built from stones plundered from religious houses: stones from Beauly Priory had been used to build the Citadel at Inverness. Although he points out that Abertarff Priory "was already defunct long before the military took an interest in it" (as was the case at Beauly and Fortrose), "these foundations stood as cultural monuments for a native population who now had to be put in their place."[20]

"… the Kirk was fallen"

> *"… all that we treasured lies in ruins"*
> *[Isaiah 64:11]*

Two decades later, on 30 March 1675, the Church of Scotland Presbytery undertook a visitation to the Parish of Boleskine. This took place at a period when the Presbytery was administered by a bishop in Elgin and a governing Synod. The Minutes record that Mr Thomas Houistone was asked "if this visitation was tymouslie intimated" to both his congregations of Boleskin and Kilcummeing. During questions addressed to the elders it was said that the minister celebrated the sacrament of the Lord's Supper at Boleskine three years ago, but at Kilcuming "to there knowledge, never." Later the visitation committee told Mr Houistone that "He was desired to celebrat the sacrament of the Lords supper yearly once, and being enquired qt was the reason that did never celebrat the s'd sacrament in Kilchuming, Answered that he had not an kirk to celebrat it in, except he should celebrat it in the open fields, yt the Kirk was fallen, and though he used the law against the Heritors, yet none of them valued any procedour he used." The visiting party clearly took this revelation seriously, for it is further minuted that "The Bretheren refers this case to the advise of ye Bishope and Synod, what shall such Bretheren do in reference to the celebration of the Lords supper in such places as want a church to celebrat the same comelie and orderlie in."[21]

The plea did not fall upon deaf ears, and at the beginning of the following year the Presbytery minutes bear witness to consultations involving the diocesan hierarchy and local parties. The solution was the creation of a new charge of Abertarff and Glenmoriston under the ministry of Mr Robert Monroe, "The Bretheren taking the condition of the said bounds to their serious condition ..." Mr Monro had yet to have his trials prior to ordination, although he "was now a great while a preacher in this province and elsewhere", and these were to be completed quickly because of "the peoples necessity requiring heast."[22]

Whilst Mr Munro underwent his trials to test his preaching ability, his knowledge of Hebrew and Greek and so on, the necessary legalities were presented to the Bishop, and this "Supplication" from the "heretuors, gentlemen, and Elders of Abertarfe and Glenmoriston" was approved by the Bishop and Chancellor early in the following year. At the same time an Edict was served at both churches, and at the beginning of March Mr Munro was ordained by the Bishop at Elgin and Presbytery arranged for his institution at Kilchuimen on 12 March 1676.[23] The Supplication is an interesting document containing some useful insights into the religious situation in Abertarff and Glenmoriston: along with the minute of 12 March, it is reproduced in Annex 1.

The Presbytery minutes charting the course to Mr Monro's arrival in Abertarff and Glenmoriston highlight some issues that would not be resolved easily. It is interesting that when the Supplication was presented to the Presbytery it is stated that the ministers of Boleskine and Urquhart wished to have Mr Monro "settled as Minister and their helper in the said bounds of Abertarff and Glenmoriston". This suggests that the new charge was not a new independent parish, and that the minister would be working under his senior colleagues: this was to be a source of conflict a decade later, as will be related in Chapter 4. The Supplication which gained the Bishop's approval called upon Mr Monro to serve alternately at Abertarff and Glenmoriston not only because of the presence of Catholic priests working in the district, but because the ministers of Boleskine and Urquhart could not work effectively because of "the distance of these places and the dangerous waters interjected betwixt them and our usual residence in our other congregations."[24]

Two more minutes raise an intriguing problem that is not easily resolved. At the visitation of March 1675 it was reported that the Kirk at Abertarff "was fallen" and clearly unusable, but then on 13 February 1676 the heritors and Elders "were cited at the Church door". A month later, at his institution at Kilchuimen on 12 March, Mr Monro was presented with "the keys of the Churches doors" and Mr Huison (Houston, minister of Boleskine) "declared that he gave the said Mr. Robert reall possession and infeftment in the manse and gleib by delivering to him timber, stone, and earth, as is usuall in such cases."[25] Had the church been repaired, rebuilt or relocated? The glebe still existed, but was it there that Mr Monro had to build himself a manse? Where were the edicts read for his new ministry, and where did the installation take place? The fact that "the Kirk was fallen" in 1675 bears testimony to an earlier church building, but what remained?

Just eighteen months after Mr Monro's installation another Presbytery visitation yields some more clues as to the condition and location of the church at Abertarff. By the time of the visitation on 25 September 1677 it would seem that Robert Monro had entered his charge with some zeal, for whereas there had been no Elders in Abertarff in 1675 the minute two years later records the names of ten Elders and another five for Glenmoriston. When questioned the elders stated "*una voce* that they were wele satisfied" with their minister. However, all was not well in the two parishes. Mr Monro is reported as saying "that for want of an edifice since the kirk fell, that they had no place to put delinquents in for public repentance, yrfore he entreated the Bretheren to tak an serious course w't the heritors for seting up and building a place for Gods worship." The Elders were asked "why they were not buildeing a kirk" and "they answered that they sent some gentlemen to the session of Boleskine in ther Easter Parioch to concur with them jointly in building the said edifice, seeing they are concerned as wele as they, and have not got an satisfactory answer with these commissioners." The Presbytery advised that two men should be sent on the next Lord's Day to the Boleskine Session, the minister to report to the next Presbytery meeting. Alas, there are no surviving minutes to record the outcome of their endeavours.

The church building was not the only problem brought before the meeting. Mr Monro stated that he "regrated that the Bridge was ruinous: the Elders were exhorted to use all diligence for setting up the s'd Bridge, and that because the water is interjacent betuixt the Kirk and ye people that resort for the ordinances, which the people do regrate, bot that they are not able of themselves to set up that bridge without the assistance of the whole parioch afar off as wele as neere at hand." This would refer to the bridge across the River Tarff, because Mr Monro went on to raise another difficulty. "The minister regrated that there was not a ferrie boat on the water of Ovaich [the River Oich] for transporteing of himself and parishioners, to qch the gentlemen present replyed that Malcolme Fraser of Culduthell [on the promontory south of Cherry Island] did oblige himself to uphold a boat there, that the Parishioners would pay the boatman conforme to former condescendence, which the boatman sought not as yet, yrfor the Minr and Elders are desired to keep yr condescendence to Culduthell that he may keepe conditione with them." This was not the end of his troubles. As will be related in Chapter 4 the elders of Glenmoriston expressed their disappointment that the minister was not with them every second Sabbath, and Mr Monro said that he did not have a boat to get him there.[26]

Mr Monro faced a number of challenges: no church in Abertarff, no local landowners prepared to build a new one, no bridge over the Tarff, no boats to take him across the Oich or to Glenmoriston where also there was no suitable place for worship within the parish. As late as the early 1700s it was reported that the Oich "is seldom fordable from October to March, yet no bridge or ferry boat on it."[27] The minute of the 1677 meeting is a little unclear, but it would seem that the visiting committee found the Church Officer responsible for looking after the building and some parish duties was wanting: "it was declared he was deficient in office... rebuked by the Moderator and ordained to waite on his office more diligently under the payne of deposition."[28] Mr Monro later led a controversial life: he was upbraided in 1688 for conducting marriages in irregular circumstances![29]

The account of the visitation of 1677 not only highlights the difficulties facing anyone seeking to minister the gospel in the area, but it also helps to confirm the location of Abertarff Kirk. The kirk was east of the Oich, and the River Tarff stood between the church building and the people and, of course, the rest of Boleskine Parish. Maps of the area give some evidence of a migration of a church building from the Sixteenth to the Eighteenth Centuries. Timothy Pont's map dated 1583–1596 places "K. of Kilchuma" on the peninsula between the two rivers with a symbol representing a church.[30] This must be the church suggested by Campbell as the successor to Columba's possible first base, Abertarff Abbey or Priory, established by the French Order of Valliscaulians around 1230.[31] This same building must be that reported by the minister, Thomas Houston, as being "fallen" in 1675. It is significant that Blaeu's Atlas of Scotland of 1654 shows "Kibyhuimen"(?) and

"Abyrtorf" east of the Tarff, with Borlum to the west[32], but does not mark any church building.

Half a century on, "A plan of the Barrack at Kilwhiman" dated 1718 shows no church on the peninsula, though it does not cover the area east of the Tarff.[33] A few years later a map of c1724 by R. Debize on behalf of General Wade shows houses labelled "Killiwhymen" in the area of the present Kilchuimen Cemetery, but very significantly labels "Borlum" across the river, along with a black rectangle with a cross on its longer side drawn 90 degrees to the horizontal.[34] An extract of this map is reproduced as Map C. Another map of c1727 shows a cross-symbol, perhaps indicating a church at the mouth of the River Tarff on the shores of Loch Ness.[35] Roy's Military Survey of Scotland dated 1747–1755 shows no churches, but "Kilchuimen" is identified of the west side of the Tarff in the vicinity of the present cemetery, and there are houses and cultivated land indicated across the river.[36] It is not until another map, dated only as "18th Century", but certainly in the latter half of the century, that a plain rectangular building marked as a church is to be seen located to the south of the old barracks and this is clearly the church of 1774, on the site of the present place of worship.[37] That though anticipates another chapter in the story of Fort Augustus Church.

Whilst the accuracy of early mapmakers cannot always be relied upon, given that place-names can migrate as old settlements are superseded by new, and remembering that "Kilchuimen" does not necessarily represent the location of a church, one can only tentatively identify the places of worship prior to the Eighteenth Century. Whilst Kilchuimen graveyard appears to be of some antiquity and has been suggested by some to be the site of the original church, it was not enclosed until 1796 and there is little evidence of a building within its walls. This is borne out in the Archaeology Notes on Cille-Chuimein Burial Ground where it is concluded that there is no trace of a church on this site.[38] The New Statistical Account of 1815, referring to the previous Statistical Account, tells of a glebe "on the banks of the Tarff, forming chiefly a level plot of ground without a stone or any impediment to interrupt a plough" which lends credence to the church building portrayed at Borlum in the Debize map of 1724. In the same account it is reported that in the middle of the Eighteenth Century the glebe was taken over by the Commissioners of the Forfeited Estates to create a new glebe for the minister of Boleskine.[39]

The cartographical and archaeological evidence, along with the testimony of Mr Monro, leads to the firm conclusion that the Seventeenth Century church was not at the site of Kilchuimen

Cemetery at all, but may well have been on the other side of the river on the lands of the present Borlum Farm. The residences of the elders listed on the occasion of the 1677 visitation may support this notion: three are stated to be "of Borlume", three from "Ardochie", one from "Little Glendo" and one from "Murvalgan" [Murligan], all east of the Tarff. Of the two others, one is from "Inshnacardich" west of the Oich, and one from "Killchumen" between the two rivers.[40] It is clear that there was a large population east of the Tarff, for Glen Doe supplied one hundred fighting men for the 1745 uprising, and Borlum Hill and Murligan Hill were crofting lands before the age of agricultural improvement.[41]   The Baptismal Register for Fort Augustus confirms the presence of a substantial population at Glendomor, Glendobeg, Murlagan and Tomvoid in the second half of the Eighteenth Century.[42]

One must conclude that in 1724, at least, there was a church at Borlum, although it remains to be determined just where "at Kilchuimen" Robert Monro was ordained to the Parish of Abertarff and Glenmoriston in 1676. The association of these two parishes ended in 1688: perhaps Monro's discipline for marriage irregularities that year was a fortunate pretext. In any case it seems that the lack of endowment and administrative commitment are to blame. Lachlan Shaw, writing in the 1770s, states that "Attempts have been made to unite Glenmoriston and Abertarff in one parish, but have failed for want of a maintenance." He continues that "the civil sanction was not obtained, and therefore Abertarf was again annexed to Boleskine ...": there is no record of a resident minister in Abertarff from 1688 until 1726.[43]

The provision of education was equally tardy. The Scottish Society for the Propogation of Christian Knoweledge (SSPCK), having identified Abertarff as its first priority for a school in 1701, made a renewed attempt ten years later, but then "refused to send a teacher to Abertarff until the heritor had erected a pariochial school and constructed a bridge for the convenience of pupils." However, an SSPCK school was started in "Killichuiman" in 1722 with forty-two pupils.[44] At just its second meeting in 1725 the newly-created Presbytery of Abertarff was asked by the schoolmaster to support his request to the SSPCK for books and writing paper.[45]

The absence of a bridge over the River Oich had for a long time proved to be a barrier to progress in the area. School, church and community were all disadvantaged by the lack of such a vital link. The Jacobite Risings of 1715 and 1745 ensured that Kilchuimen was to become the centre of military activity. Thus a new bridge was an early priority in the improvement of communications within the

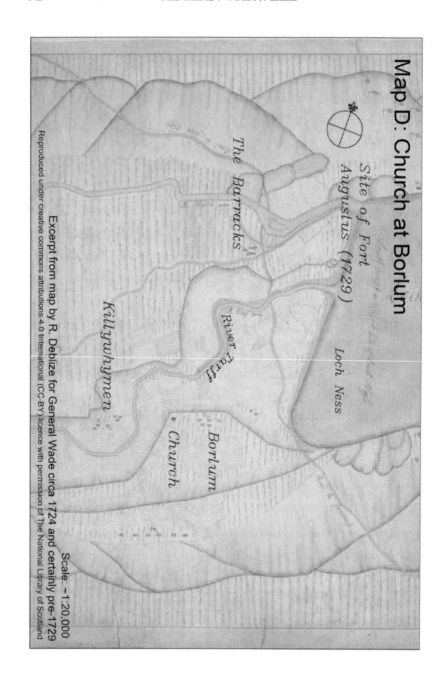

Map D: Church at Borlum

Site of Fort
Augustus (1729)

Loch Ness

The Barracks

Killgwhymen

River Tarff

Borlum

Church

Excerpt from map by R. Deblize for General Wade circa 1724 and certainly pre-1729

Scale: ~1:20,000

Great Glen area. The Jacobites had largely by-passed the Great Glen in 1715, but in August 1745 around two thousand supporters from the local glens assembled at Aberchalder prior to marching over the Corrieyairach Pass.[46] Within nine months the area would ring to a very different beat.

The Jacobite Years

"The shields of the soldiers are red:
the warriors are clad in scarlet"
[Nahum 2:3]

Following the first uprising in 1715 a network of barracks was built across the Highlands. Kilchuimen Barracks were built between 1718 and 1721 on a bluff between the Rivers Oich and Tarff, one wall of which remains at the rear of the Lovat Arms Hotel and is best viewed from the grounds of the present church. The substantial building dominated the area: described at the time as the largest built in the Highlands, it was three storeys high and could accommodate three-hundred and sixty soldiers in thirty-six barrack rooms: it did not, however, include a place of worship. A Galley was built to bring supplies along the length of Loch Ness.[47]

Following the 1715 rising the Lovat estates were taken over by

the Commissioners of the Forfeited Estates, with the consequence
that the lands around Abertarff, including the site of the earliest
place of worship, were handed over to the Crown. This facilitated
the further military development of this strategic area. The barracks
were replaced by a new and well-fortified edifice which was built
closer to Loch Ness over a period of thirteen years commencing in
1729. An early Board of Ordnance plan of 1729 for the new bastion
proposed a "Chappel" above the gatehouse[48] although a later plan
of 1742 has no reference to a place of worship within the Fort. It is
interesting to note that even at the much larger Fort George, built
between 1748 and 1769 for a complement of two thousand, a chapel
was very much an afterthought.[49] Spiritual welfare for the soldiers
was clearly not a priority.

There was a fitful association between the military and the
community throughout this period. It is noted that Fort William
and Fort Augustus "were dependent to some extent upon the
Bounty Fund for the provision of preachers. The general policy was
to make use of the local ministers ... But it was chronically difficult
to fill the pulpits of some of these Highland charges, and the Bounty
Committee had, on occasion, to appoint a minister to the Fort who
would also serve the neighbourhood."[50] The first such appointment
appears to have been George Anderson, formerly a chaplain to the

Scots troops in Holland. He was appointed by the Royal Bounty Committee in November 1728 and ordained as "Missioner at Maryburgh [*i.e. Fort William*] and Kilchuiman", a post he quit in 1729: the Committee recorded in 1730 that he had "failed to return"! Clearly Mr Anderson was a loose cannon, for he was re-appointed as Chaplain at Maryburgh between 1733 and 1737, then in 1741 he became Master of George Watson's Hospital in Edinburgh. It is recorded that "a combative tendency ... is apparent throughout the Scottish phase of his career" since he was a campaigner against stage plays through various tracts published between 1732 and 1756.[51]

Before he departed in 1729 it was George Anderson who was asked by Presbytery to speak to the Commanding Officer about the "gross immoralities and Sabbath breaking committed by soldiers and others about Kilchuimen." Three years later Thomas Fraser, the minister of Boleskine and Abertarff, brought a more explicit concern to the Presbytery: from its creation the Presbytery held its meetings in the village so no doubt the assembled brethren could see the evidence around them. "Master Thomas Fraser reported that to his great grief since the Barracks were built at Fort Augustus, there are many prophanations of the Lord's Day in many aspects, not only within the District of the Barracks but in the adjacent villages; as also that a great number of ... women resort thither from all corners and that his hands are much weakened by reason he cannot get Discipline put duly in execution against persons who lurk … in the flatts about said Barracks and villages, and therefore craved the presbytery's advice on this case." The Presbytery advised Master Fraser "that he and one or two of the most considerable gentlemen who are Elders in his parish may wait upon his Excellency General Wade, and deal with him to lay his orders upon the Commanding Officer in the Barracks to concur with the Kirk Session of Bleskine and Abertarph in obliging all within the District of the said Barrack to abstain from such abuses in becoming, and also punishing all those who have hitherto or may hereafter be guilty of the same or the like Immoralities … and [for] Delinquents without the bounds of the said Barracks they did advise the said Master Fraser to make application to the Civil Magistrate to have them punished according to law …" There was a meeting with General Wade[52], but worse was to come fourteen years later. Such was the growing military presence that in 1741 the Presbytery began to record its meetings at "Fort Augustus" rather than the traditional "Abertarff". The village had now become an army garrison!

There would appear to have been no minister based in Abertarff from 1729 until 1739 when Patrick Grant was appointed. He was appointed by the Bounty Committee to Fort Augustus in August, but a year later was moved to Fort William. He returned north for just short of twelve months in 1741 before another move to Kilmonivaig. He became the minister of Logie Easter in 1744[53]. The next minister, William Grant, arrived at Fort Augustus in the summer of 1743 to be ordained as the Missionary Minister at Abertarff and possibly Glenmoriston too. He remained for seven years when he took the charge at Kilmonivaig where he ministered until 1775. During the early 1740s Jacobite sentiment was growing and consolidating: in March 1746 their forces took control of the barracks and achieved a direct hit upon the Fort, destroying the powder magazine.[54] Having captured the Fort the Jacobites wrecked the bastions and, it is alleged, put several Redcoats to the sword.

Without any contemporary accounts it is difficult to know how William Grant ministered to both the army and the locals during the months leading up to the '45 and the period of harsh retribution that followed Culloden. However, his sympathetic petition regarding sixty-eight Glenmoriston men may indicate a pastoral concern for local residents caught up in the "rebellion".[55] It is more than likely that publicly, at least, he held the line for the Government and its forces in suppressing the rebellion for "the bulk of the ministers of the Church of Scotland gave all the help they could as recruiting agents and as 'intelligencers', from the moment Prince Charlie's ships were sighted until he was taken away again by ship."[56] Perhaps it was with a hint of frustration that the Caledonian Mercury reported in August 1745 that they had seen letters "from the Moderator and Ministers of the Presbytery of Abertarff, met last Friday at Fort Augustus ... and they contain not one Syllable of Intelligence, except the good News of the Prospect of a plentiful Crop."[57]

William Grant's colleague at the schoolhouse, Alexander Dallas, was told in 1746 by his employers (the SSPCK) "that in respect of present circumstances of the country about Fort Augustus" he should move to a new post at Rannoch. However in September the Lt Governor at the Fort, William Caulfield, petitioned the Society asking for Dallas to be left in post: this was agreed. Had the teacher been too outspoken for one side or the other, or was it his health that caused a change of mind? Either way, he had built up good relations with the military for it had been reported that he had been a great favourite of the Duke of Cumberland and that his employers noted that "he spent much of his time about the barracks."[58] Alexander Dallas died in 1750 but clearly he had built up a valued educational facility in the district because it is recorded that the school had over one-hundred pupils in 1748.[59]

These must have been turbulent and testing years, and from a distant viewpoint it is unnecessary to pass judgement. However it may be concluded "that the clergy, torn by conflicting loyalties, were faithful in their service on either side in the strife".[60] Just two Great Glen ministers were identified with the Jacobite cause: John Cameron of Fort William who was to assist the fugitive prince to escape from Scotland, and John Grant of Glenurquhart who, although not at Culloden, was arrested as a sympathiser and tried on the charge of "explaining the Pretender's Manifesto from the Pulpit". He was discharged and allowed to return home.[61]

"… this diamond in the midst of hell"[62]

"… soldiers as numerous as the sand on the seashore …"
[1 Sam 13:5]

It would be an understatement to say that the district of Abertarff and the citadel of Fort Augustus played a significant role during the '45 and thereafter. The Duke of Cumberland saw the strategic advantage of Fort Augustus, "being the most centrical place for sending out Detachments, and receiving Accounts of their success" at the intersection of Wade's roads.[63] For six weeks from 16 May 1746 the Duke of Cumberland oversaw a period of violent retribution: "in that time the whole of Lochaber and most of

Badenoch rotted from the poison they brought."[64]   Given that the Fort had been quite damaged by the Jacobites in March 1746 a vast encampment was created between the Oich and the Tarff.   There followed "days of burning and murder and plunder", as livestock was rounded up and gathered at Fort Augustus to be sold to the Lowlands.   In time the homeless, orphaned and widowed of the district gathered around the camp to beg for food.   By mid-June it was reported that "The Countries of Glengarry and Glenmorison belonging to the MacDonalds and Grants, are mostly burnt, and their Cattle taken into the Army."   The report continues: "There were found dead last Week two Women and four Children dead in the Hills, who perished through Want, their Hutts being burnt."[65]

Life for the government soldiers was also harsh: again in mid-June two soldiers were sentenced by Court-martial to receive 900 lashes for letting the Chief of Glengarry's son escape; others received harsher punishments for looting.[66]   As was the tradition, many of the soldiers were accompanied by wives and other women. "Such women were soon as restless as the men at Fort Augustus, and the Duke satisfied them all by organizing horse-races" and the sight of women riding astride the ponies and bare-backed created something of a scandal.[67]   The military imperatives were not neglected, however, and so by the end of June fine houses and humble huts were in ruins, and prisoners including Simon, Lord Lovat, and five-hundred "rebels"had been taken and shipped south.[68]   At the same time all soldiers were on constant patrol looking out for the rebel Prince Charlie.

An unidentified minister wrote a letter to The Caledonian Mercury published on 30 June: "As most of this parish is burnt to ashes and all the cattle belonging to the Rebels carried off by His Majesty's forces, there is no such thing as money or a pennyworth to be got in this desolate place. I beg therefore you'll advise me what steps I shall take to recover my stipends. My family is now much increased, by the wives and infants of those in the rebellion in my parish crowding for a mouthful of bread to keep them from starving; which no good Christian can refuse, notwithstanding the villainy of their husbands and fathers to deprive us of our religion, liberty and bread."[69] The anguish of this conflicted minister must have been shared by William Grant who was "in the midst of hell" in Fort Augustus.

By contrast to its earlier comments about indiscipline around the Barracks, the Presbytery was silent about these most recent events in Fort Augustus: indeed it made no comment on the uprising, nor upon the Battle of Culloden. However, they did meet at Fort Augustus in June 1746, a meeting postponed from the previous

October, and recorded the following minute: "The Moderator represented that as the Presbytery had been prevented from meeting according to their last Adjournment by the late wicked and unnatural Rebellion which had raged till the sixteenth day of April last when his Royal Highness the Duke of Comberland had entirely defeat the Rebels at Culloden; and altho the designs of the Rebellious and disaffected were by this defeat totally baffled, yet the [?] in the cornes by the marchings and counter-marchings of the troops who were pursuing the Rebels that were partly keeping in Bothies and partly lurking in the hills, he had not thought it safe to call the Brethren ... sooner."[70]

Cumberland finally left Fort Augustus on 18 July 1746 for the lionizing crowds of Edinburgh and London.[71] Despite the continuing patrols, however, Prince Charlie's supporters still managed to get food and brandy from Fort Augustus to supply the Prince and his supporters holed up in a remote cave in Glenmoriston during the days before his escape to France in September.[72]

Fort Augustus, its garrison and its desolate population, was left to recover and rebuild. In 1747 work commenced on a major reconstruction of the damaged Fort, and it became the military headquarters for the campaign of pacification. The Disarming Acts and the subsequent banning of tartan in August 1747 gave additional work for the ongoing patrols radiating from Fort Augustus, bringing more deaths and imprisonment. The soldiers' lives were, though, "poor and unrewarding."[73] In theory, at least, soldiers and officers were required to attend Divine service; this was re-emphasised by the Duke of Cumberland in 1747[74], and when John Grant was appointed "Itinerant Minister and Catechist at the Garrison of Fort Augustus" in 1752 it was instructed "when there is a Chaplain in said Garrison, that Mr Grant officiate at Glenmorison."[75] It was only when proscription was lifted in 1782 that the Fort's importance was downgraded, with veterans maintaining a military presence. As will be recorded, the parish church built in the 1770s was to include a gallery set apart for the Fort's residents. It was not until 1818 that the last of the veterans were removed, along with the defensive cannons.

The number of missionary ministers serving in Abertarff, and the intervals between them, was not conducive to any sustained ministry, nor to accurate record keeping. William Fraser, the minister of Boleskine and Abertarff, writing in the New Statistical Account of 1835 comments that Abertarff had separate registers of baptisms and marriages kept since 1737 and 1753 respectively, but "on the appointment of another missionary, to whose charge they

were given, they were totally neglected for a period of ten years."
He claimed that the records were lost when someone dropped them
when crossing a rapid stream![76]　However, whilst many vital
documents from the past have been lost in similar accidents, what
appears to have been a transcription of the lost records was found
and handed over to the minister in 1881: this is now within the
Boleskine archive.[77] This Register contains an incomplete record of
baptisms and marriages between 1737 and 1815 but it illustrates the
extent of the military presence in Fort Augustus. For instance, in
1767 there were sixteen baptisms, ten of them the children of
soldiers. The Register also charts the growth of a community
around the Fort, with many varied occupations listed such as bakers,
shoemakers, weavers, merchants, masons, wrights, millers and
vintners.

Such growth was in part encouraged by the policy of the local
military leadership to allow the creation of homes, gardens, barns
and businesses on government land surrounding the Fort. This was
to the mutual benefit of both the military and civilian population.
Alas, no titles were issued and there were as a consequence various
legal wrangles in the years that followed, something that was to
affect the Church of Scotland as well. The development of a village
around the Fort gave a spur to Alexander Fraser of Culduthel to

form a village west of the bridge over the River Oich on his land around 1780. Called Bunoich or Balfrishel, this new settlement helped to create a thriving community at the south end of Loch Ness.[78]

The pattern of short-term ministries continued after 1750.[79] One of these appointments, that of 27 year old Ludovic Grant who served briefly in 1755, had a salary of £30, and he preached in English and 'Erse'. He is described as an itinerant preacher and catechist at the Garrison of Fort Augustus and as officiating at Glenmoriston.[80] In every case it must be assumed that these missionary-ministers were appointed with the expectation that residents at the Fort would be treated as parishioners. This is underlined by a Minute of the Bounty Committee in June 1759 which reads: "the Committee finding that both the stations at Fort William and Fort Augustus are presently vacant, Agreed that ... Mr Alexander Fraser be employed as Itinerant Preacher at the Garrison in Fort William ... and that he preach by turns in the Church of Kilmallie during the vacancy in that Parish and the Presbytery are hereby authorised ... to look out for a proper person to be employed as Missionary at Fort Augustus."[81] This reference is somewhat curious since Alexander Falconer was ordained as a Missionary to Fort Augustus in June 1758 and remained until 1763, whilst Colin M'Farquhar was ordained as minister at an unknown date in 1759. This lack of clarity serves to emphasise the fluidity of the ministry at this time. Indeed, in 1754 the Presbytery of Abertarff was censured by the Synod of Glenelg for "their unaccountable neglect of the Sacrament of the Lord's Supper" mentioning the parish of Boleskine by name.[82] Perhaps being mindful of the lack of continuity in ministry the Royal Bounty Committee recommended in 1760 that Abertarff should be joined with Glengarry, although this was never implemented.

Schoolmasters, too, scarcely bettered the record of the Church ministers. Between 1750 and 1795 there were nine of them all appointed by the SSPCK. One of them, Alexander Munro, acted as Session Clerk for Abertarff, but was dismissed in 1758 for neglecting his duties, and he took the minutes with him! Twenty years later the schoolhouse was in disrepair, and in 1795 the school closed because the heritors refused to provide a parish school and the Synod condemned the Presbytery for not forcing the heritors to fulfil their lawful duties![83] Ministers and schoolmasters came and went, and the support of heritors could not be guaranteed, but perhaps the local church members gave some stability: Dugald Mactavish, a merchant in Fort Augustus was described as the principal Elder in 1760. He was something of a businessman since he built and sold properties on both sides of the River Oich.[84]

Perhaps due to the continuing military presence at Fort Augustus, the minister of Boleskine and Abertarff was moved to complain to Presbytery in 1758 that the glebe at Abertarff had been encroached.[85] Alexander Trapaud, the Deputy Governor of Fort Augustus from 1752 to 1796, had obtained a lease of parts of Easter and Wester Borlum, presumably from the Forfeited Estates Commission, and in 1769 he applied to have his lease extended and the land enclosed.[86] This denied the church its income, and perhaps explains some of the subsequent problems of financing church building in Fort Augustus. Just when the church at Borlum was abandoned is not clear, but the November Presbytery minutes of 1774 record that "there is a new church at Fort Augustus built by subscription."[87] Perhaps it was his Hugenot heritage or a sense of guilt that moved Trapaud to subscribe £50 to the new church in 1777.[88] In any case, his gravestone at Kilchuimen Cemetery commemorates "a brave Officer and Pious Christian and Faithful Friend."

"… a very snug, comfortable church"

"On the first day of the week
we came together to break bread."
[Acts 20:7]

The impetus towards the building of the new church came in 1773 when the Minister of Boleskine, Patrick Grant, told the Presbytery that he had obtained permission from the Court of Session to move his church, manse, and office houses from Boleskine to Drumtemple, "being more Centrical and Convenient for the Parishioners and Minister", which was certainly true. The Court of Session "ordered and Directed that the equivalent of the Glebe at Boleskine and the Glebe in Clachan of Abertarph be given of the farm of Drumtemple … quantity and quality considered."[89] This is perhaps the hardest evidence of a glebe at Abertarff, and helps to fix the location of the glebe and a church amongst a community on the lands of Borlum.

Mr Grant's detailed plans for a new church, manse and glebe required the financial support of the heritors, but the sole heritor south of Carn Suidhe was clearly not prepared to contribute towards the Minister's proposals. At the November 1773 meeting, Presbytery records that the Factor for Mr Hall, heritor of the Lands of Abertarph "craves, that as he apprehends the Parish of Abertarph should accommodate itself in a Place of Worship, that an opportunity should be given him to instruct his Right and Title thereto: and that it is well known the Church proposed to be built at Drumtemple (lying at the Distance of ten or eleven English miles from the place of worship here) cannot possibly accommodate the Parish of Abertarph – that the Presbytery would delay passing decreet for the Church proposed to be built at said place untill such time as his Constituents mind shall be known: which request the Presbytery find reasonable and allow him until the first Tuesday in April next for that purpose."[90] Mr Hall had laid down the gauntlet and Presbytery acquiesced. Then in April the Factor again appeared at Presbytery, asking them to "delay taking any further steps with regard to the Church to be built at Drumtemple ... because a great part of Abertarph he apprehends is to have a new Master who when in capacity to act will no doubt co-operate with Mr Hall in his Proposal of having a Church built at Fort Augustus to accommodate the whole of Abertarff", something with which the Presbytery once more agreed.[91] The reference to "a new Master" may refer to Simon Fraser, Lord Lovat. In 1774 he successfully petitioned the king for the return of his family estates: they cost him £20,000, but came without the Government lands around the Fort.[92]

Mr Hall and his Factor must have moved fast, for just seven months later the Presbytery records that "there is a new Church built in Fort Augustus by Subscription." The Minister of Boleskine complained that neither Mr Hall nor his Factor "has … not done any one thing" towards the church and church yard dyke at Drumtemple, and he pressed his Brethren to proceed with this work.[93] By the following April it was clear that Mr Hall, having ensured a new church for Fort Augustus, wanted no part in the new church at Boleskine.[94] The fact that the Fort Augustus Church was built so speedily implies the co-operation of the military authorities and, perhaps, the good offices of Rev James Grant, who had been appointed as Missionary to Fort Augustus in 1769. The church was built on Crown Land, freely granted, to the south of the old Kilchuimen Barracks, and it may be guessed that stone and other materials from there was utilised. Quite who subscribed to the cost is not clear, although there are some hints in the following minute, but the military were clearly supportive for in June 1776 the Presbytery met at the church along with Governor Trapaud, Mr McVicar, Barrackmaster and others to allocate the seats. The Minute gives some insight into the layout of the church and to the nature of the congregation: it was "agreed to by all present that Governour Trapaud and the better sort of people in this village and in Abertarph who contributed, should posses all from the left hand of the pulpit until the west gabel south side and seat it regularly: and that Glengarry, Glenmoristone and the subscribers in Stratherrick should possess and seat regularly all from the right hand of the pulpit to East Gabel, and the minister of Boleskine makes choice and fixes his seat to be next the Gabel. It is also agreed unanimously that the whole north side be laid out in regular forms [benches], fixed and never removed at any time or interfere with Communion Tables."[95] From this description it may be seen that the church, lying west to east, had the pulpit on the long south wall with the congregation gathered around. A gallery was to be added at a later date.

Governor Trapaud sustained his concern for the new church by demanding more of the missionary ministers' time. These men were typically spending every third Sunday in Glenmoriston and were often covering Glengarry too. In 1784 he wrote to the Royal Bounty Committee asking in which of these three areas "the missionary can officiate with the greatest advantage for accomplishing the ends of the Mission" and asking how many attended his services in Glengarry.[96] The Presbytery was somewhat affronted that they had not been consulted first, but it did highlight both the growing importance of the Fort Augustus church, and the need for better ministry in Glengarry as will be related in the next chapter. There were repeated occasions when the Presbytery vented its frustrations with the Royal Bounty Committee for not filling vacancies at Fort Augustus in a speedy manner, noting the unfailing efforts of Catholic priests at work in the district.[97] The new church, later to be described as snug and comfortable, had opened a new chapter for Fort Augustus, and it is possible to learn much more about the association of the garrison and the parish through the eyes of a remarkable witness and her "Letters from the Mountains".

Letters from the Mountains

"May the mountains bring prosperity to the people,
the hills the fruit of righteousness"
[Psalm 72:3]

In 1809 the letters of Anne Grant were published. She had written these from 1773 onwards, when she accompanied her father to a new posting at Fort Augustus. Anne's father, Capt. Duncan MacVicar, had been appointed Barrack-Master (a senior Officer) at the Fort, and her letters give an insight into the landscape and community surrounding the Fort just twenty-seven years after the devastations of the Duke of Cumberland and his troops. Furthermore she gives some useful information about the new kirk.

In 1775 she writes "we have got a new church, built by subscription, mind, that it would do your heart good to see, and your soul good to hear sermon in."[98]   Earlier, in May 1773 she writes that "The clergyman of the place was the only stranger, of whom I was previously told that he was handsomer than any body: he appeared more modest than most handsome men …"[99]   The clergyman, the Rev James Grant, had been appointed as Royal Bounty Missionary to Fort Augustus in 1769, and was later described as "A man of cultivated tastes and amiable in manner, and greatly revered and loved". He was translated to Laggan in Badenoch in 1775, when Anne Grant wrote: "Mr G. left us last week to be settled in Badenoch. Our parting was – almost affecting …"[100]   It is not surprising therefore that Anne and James were married in 1779!

Mr Grant had no doubt created a close working relationship between the church and the military, for the New Statistical Account, published in 1835, gives more details about Fort Augustus Church: it accommodated three hundred persons, there were no seat-rents, but "the galleries are understood to be Government property", presumably to accommodate the residents of the Fort who, in 1755 comprised eighteen families and seventy invalids. More evidence of the galleries is to be seen in a map of Fort Augustus properties drawn up prior to the construction of the

Caledonian Canal[101] which depicts the church with two
hemispherical appendages on each of the long walls suggesting stairs
to the galleries on the north side and to the pulpit on the south. It
is described as "a very snug, comfortable church, originally built and
kept in repair by voluntary subscription, to which the Government
a few years ago liberally contributed."[102] This contribution may refer
to the donation of £50 paid by the Commissioners of the Annexed
Estates in 1777 towards "building a new Kirk at Fort Augustus" out
of the arrears of the Lovat Estate.[103] In later years James Grant
revived his association with the military when he served as Chaplain
to the Perthshire Volunteers (90th Foot).

Apart from information about the church and its incumbent, the
young Anne MacVicar's letters tell much about the setting of the
Fort and its surroundings, and she gives details of a cruise on Loch
Ness. She has a poignant description of the circumstances of the
death of a young soldier and his burial at Kilchuimen Cemetery in
1773. Her Christian commitment shines through when, in 1778 she
tells that she had not gone with others on a visit to Fort George,
"but I could not, being the week of our sacrament." Then a month
later she recounts her visits to bereaved daughters living half a mile
from the village following the death of their father whom she
describes as "the principal bulwark of religion in this place"; she

does so "since our present pastor does not reside", referring to James Grant's successor. Here she gives a rare insight into the qualities of an unknown pillar of the church who is described as "a man of primitive simplicity of manners, and undeviating rectitude of principle [who] discharged the duties of his useful though humble station with peculiar diligence and fidelity." Anne MacVicar hints that she had little support for her Christian service, saying that "scarce one of our circle had the humanity to go near them" and "I have been teased, and plagued beyond sufferance with people of a very different description. To bear our share of the sorrows of our friends is a duty we are born to ... but to be worn out with the follies and absurdities of those who are incapable of friendship is truly hard."[104]

These comments, whilst shining a light upon the church in Fort Augustus, convey some insights into the poor state of the local populace. Anne MacVicar described the settlement of Laggan Achadrom with its "forty distinct buildings" as being inhabited by cattle thieves, the King's Inn in Fort Augustus as providing "the worst inn's worst room", and the locals as taking "a great deal too much pleasure in turning each other into ridicule", adding "one is greatly amused; but I don't know that we ought to indulge such amusement." Then in 1775 she writes: "Lament with me, for we have had another ship load of emigrants, marching off to their Chaldea."[105] The spiritual, social and economic fortunes of the area were indeed at a low ebb. The Commissioners for the Forfeited Estates attempted some development: the short-lived Linen Manufactory at Invermoriston trained spinners and weavers in the wider district, and limestone was quarried at Abertarff and transported to improve the new farms being laid out around the Beauly Firth.

Life at the Fort was somewhat insulated from the woes of the village. "Towards the end of the 18th century, Governor Trapaud had created a little paradise of flower gardens ... No doubt he was able to do this because of the labour available from a garrison who had plenty of time on their hands. Indeed, the gardening tradition was maintained there by Captain Spalding until at least 1847, and possibly until the garrison was finally removed."[106]

Anne's handsome Mr Grant was replaced by John M'Kilican in 1776 who in 1778, we have learned, did not reside locally: then in 1785, with his imminent departure in mind, concern was raised in Presbytery that an urgent replacement was required since "priests might avail themselves of perverting Protestants, particularly by baptising infants when no minister was at hand."[107] Three years later John Macdonell was appointed missionary minister to serve the huge territory of Boleskine, Urquhart and Kilmonivaig. The time he was able to spend in any one community of this vast district can only be guessed! Thereafter, and up to 1843, there were seven appointments to Fort Augustus of varying lengths of time, from one to twelve years. Although there is no record of James Stewart's ministry the others were Highlanders and all progressed to parish appointments elsewhere in the north. Amongst these seven was John M'Intyre (1824–1828), a son of the Minister of Kilmallie who had acted as Tutor to Aeneas Macdonell, son of Col. Alexander Macdonell of Glengarry. As will be recounted in the next chapter, John MacIntyre no doubt played a part in the ecumenical outlook of the Chief's family. Macdonell, as patron of the parish of Kilmonivaig, presented him to that parish in 1828 and, interestingly, MacIntyre's son ministered in the same parish between 1901 and 1924.

Whilst there was a new church in Fort Augustus there was no distinct provision for the comforts of the missionary ministers. The Royal Bounty Committee insisted that the heritors should provide "a house (consisting of at least two apartments and a kitchen), a garden, a cow-house, a cow's grass in summer, and ground sufficient to furnish provender for her during the winter; and that peats for fuel shall be cut and driven to his house, free of expence." They added that missions would be withdrawn where such accommodation was refused.[108]   These demanding terms were required at a time when heritors were increasingly ignoring their responsibilities towards the parish churches and manses. Presbytery responded that "from their knowledge of the temper that prevails among Heritors in general, and from the silence of some, and the tenor of the answers made by others ... they are firmly of the opinion that the accommodations required will not be granted." All this, they stated, will be "most ruinous to the Interests of Religion within their Bounds." They further noted that there may be a favourable response from the heritors at Glenmoriston and Fort Augustus.[109]

The ultimatum from the Royal Bounty Committee drew an interesting response from the congregation in Fort Augustus, and which revealed the lodging place of the minister. Seven local farmers wrote to the Presbytery saying "we feel it a duty incumbent on ourselves to prevent, if possible, the withdrawing of the Mission; and therefore, we hereby bind and oblige ourselves to furnish the required accommodations, during the currency of our Leases, on condition that it shall be continued, and that the labours of the Missioner shall be confined to Abertarff. Should this, however, not meet with the concurrence of Presbytery and Committee, we expect that, if the Missioner be made to officiate every third Sunday in Glenmoriston, the Proprietor of that Country or his Tenants will contribute one third of the expences. We also beg leave to suggest that, while the Missioner continues to enjoy Lodgings within the Garrison, an equivalent in money for the accommodations required by the Committee shall be made to him." The letter continued with a pledge to raise the finance within three months, and to continue payment twice yearly. The Presbytery expressed its gratitude and "their sense of obligation to the Farmers of Abertarff, and to Glenmoriston and his Curators", and then requested the Royal Bounty Committee to continue the Mission "under the present arrangement."[110]

The fact that any Missionary had found lodgings within the Fort was, perhaps, a mixed blessing. Earlier in 1808 it had been alleged the Rev William Macrae had fathered a child to another resident of the Garrison, something that both he and the woman concerned vigorously denied. After an enquiry, and the evidence of many witnesses, the perpetrator of the allegations was ordered to "stand in the face of the Congregation in the Church here, and publickly to confess her guilt."[111]

Housing in the Great Glen would have been at a premium anyway following the commencement of the building of the

Caledonian Canal in 1804. The engineer Joseph Mitchell, who have spent some childhood years in Bunoich wrote that it was "a curiously sequestered village. It had arisen round the fortress and barracks ... At that time the fortress was in military occupation. There was a governor, with from eighty to a hundred old soldiers (invalids they were called), who kept regular military guard. The governor, in full uniform, with cocked hat and epaulettes, inspired great awe amongst the simple inhabitants of the village. I recall witnessing with much interest ... the parade of the soldiers in the square of the fort. The Inn, or King's House, as it was called, was built by the Government, and kept by a Sergeant Harrower and his active wife. The sergeant was an old veteran, who encouraged by example the consumption of mountain dew. There was a post-office in the village, a blacksmith and various tradespeople."[112] Robert Southey's record of his visit in 1819 bears testimony to the village as a "poor place" and he gives graphic descriptions of the "stupendous" civil engineering work on the canal. By contrast he reports that within the Fort's walls there was a haven of peace, calling it "very pretty – a quiet collegiate sort of place, just fit for a University, if one were to be established ..."[113] Did Southey foresee the Abbey and its school that would occupy the Fort sixty years later?

The building of the Caledonian Canal involved around three thousand men for a period of twenty years, and Fort Augustus was one of the principal construction sites. In 1819 there were two-hundred and fifty men working at Fort Augustus, two-hundred at Loch Oich and over two-hundred at Laggan. The effect on Fort Augustus was significant: "The village benefited from the spending power of the workers and began to share trade with the world outside. For the first time the timber of the Great Glen could be exported and in 1820 one and a half million birch staves were sent out for making herring barrels. Incoming coals became cheaper and were burned in some Fort Augustus fireplaces for the first time."[114] Joseph Mitchell was for a while supervising works at Kyllachy Locks, five miles to the south, and he recalls that "Although there was no church in the neighbourhood, the Sunday was reverently kept. One of the men read portions of Scripture in the forenoon, and in the evening chapters of the Old and New Testament. Psalms were sung, and some of the men gave very earnest, extemporary prayers."[115] This bears testimony to the faithfulness of ordinary Christians in the absence of support from the wider church. The Boleskine archive records seven baptisms and two marriages between 1806 and 1814 involving canal workers.[116]

The canal was not the panacea for all the woes of the district. Poverty and lack of opportunity still drove many to consider emigration. A petition to the Commissioners for the Caledonian Canal in 1808 called for construction of the central section to be speeded up to provide employment for those who might otherwise contemplate emigration. The Colonial Department received petitions pleading for financial assistance to emigrate, including one in the 1820s from Fort Augustus on behalf of over three hundred people who "are desirous of going to Canada, but are utterly unable to pay for their passage."[117] Parts of the canal required to be rebuilt during the 1840s, thus providing more local employment.[118]

By the 1830s the community around Fort Augustus had regained a sense of equanimity after a century of turmoil. The population of "Cill Chuiman" including the garrison numbered two hundred and sixteen, and the settlement of Balfrishel, west of the Oich, had one hundred and fifty-nine persons. The area, however, remained a part of Boleskine parish although the missionary minister was able to convene the local elders to allocate the Poor Fund and to adjudicate on disciplinary matters and collect fines and fees. From 1824 the Boleskine Kirk Session occasionally met in Fort Augustus: indeed, in that year they noted that "as there are no other funds to meet cases peculiar to the Church here, such as the Repair of it,

Communion Tent, Cloth and Cups and Bell; and therefore they resolved that the half of the Fines shall in future be set apart to furnish by degrees these things, and that a Bell shall be the first article to be provided ..."[119] The bell was duly obtained and hung, but there is no record of the other items ever being provided.

The minister wrote in the New Statistical Account that the association between the two parishes "has been injudicious, - there being a hill seven miles long intervening between the inhabited districts of the two parishes, and the greater part of the intervening space being, from its height, frequently impassible in winter."[120] Yet the "snug, comfortable" church built in the mid-1770s and mentioned by the young Anne Grant offered a place of worship that was clearly superior to that at Boleskine. Just why it needed to be replaced less than a century later will be explained in due course. By then a second Presbyterian church had been established within the village with the creation of the Free Church in 1843.

Ministers, Missionaries and Schoolmasters

"The act of faith is what distinguished our ancestors, set them above the crowd"
[Hebrews 11:2 (The Message)]

As mentioned earlier, the Disruption of 1843 was a significant event within the Church of Scotland although its impact in the Great Glen was less pronounced than elsewhere. Following the General Assembly of that year a majority of the Church of Scotland congregations in Urquhart and Glenmoriston adhered to the Free Church, but the effect was less marked in Fort Augustus and Glengarry. However, amongst the clergy it was only William Lauder, the ordained missionary at Glengarry, who left the established church. Lauder established a congregation in Fort Augustus which initially met in "a large malt-barn"[121], and he secured a site for a new church just weeks after the Disruption: a foundation stone was laid in March 1844. By the end of that year, and no doubt to the disappointment of the newly-formed congregation, Mr Lauder had been called to Argyll. A new minister was called very quickly.

The creation of the Free Church in Fort Augustus is all the more remarkable given the social and economic condition of the area. The mid-1840s saw famine and destitution across the north of Scotland, and the Great Glen was not immune. Amongst lengthy reports headed "The Highland Poor," the local press carried one from Captain Spalding, the barrack-master at Fort Augustus. His report is harrowing and is worth stating at length:

"The money collected at the chapel of the mission is distributed among the poor; and on extraordinary occasions the inhabitants endeavour to raise money further by subscription ...   There are a great many old persons about Fort-Augustus entirely dependent on the charity of their neighbours – a great number

of those unable to do anything, particularly women and some old men; and there are a great many destitute children, orphans, and widows with children. The last collection, of which he took charge, amounted to about £20, which he distributed among fifty-one families – from two hundred to three hundred individuals. A great many more families required assistance. The houses of the poor people are, generally speaking, very bad; indeed, half of them do not keep out the rain. He has been obliged himself to have thatch put on their houses, and to give them blankets ... and to give them coals ...Their bedding is as bad as anything can be – many of them without bedsteads, lying on straw chaff on the ground, and, what is worse, without blankets, many lying on heather. They suffer dreadful privations from want of food, chiefly from December till June. This great destitution has been owing, in some cases, to the efficient members of families having gone to America and Australia, leaving their aged and infirm relatives in this country – in others, to the natural privations occasioned by the death of parents who have left destitute children. None of the proprietors of land reside in the country. When he made up the last subscription, Abertarff gave him £3; Lord Lovat, £3; Glenmoriston, £3: he subscribed £3, and made up the rest by small subscription."[122]

The Church of Scotland Kirk Session in Fort Augustus was faced with increased demands upon the Poor Fund and appealed to the Heritors to make generous donations.[123] The Presbytery of Abertarff, which rarely recorded events beyond its immediate concerns, did appoint "a day of humiliation and prayer ... on account of the failure of the potato crop and threatened destitution" in 1846.[124]

A dozen years later the welfare of Fort Augustus was little improved. The complement at the Fort was down to a token of "six men and a serjeant" in 1855[125] yet the village was still subject to the stultifying management of government authorities. In 1857 the local press carried a report from the Daily Mail relating that "the dilapidated state of this beautifully-situated, and, at one time, neat and thriving village, has at length been brought under the notice of the Government, in a petition which was substantially backed and corroborated by a certificate from the Presbytery of Abertarff, who hold their meetings at Fort-Augustus. The Presbytery and the public have no other place to look to for the necessary refreshment and accommodation between Invergarry and Invermorison ... excepting the inn at Fort Augustus, which, together with the whole village and the surrounding lands, are the property of the Government."[126] The article went on to state that there were moves afoot to re-instate a market in the village in a bid to improve local trade.[127]

Despite such privations, the early 1800s saw one valuable development in Fort Augustus, namely the creation of a Church of Scotland school. This replaced the earlier SSPCK charity school which was possibly removed to make way for the construction of the Caledonian Canal. In 1811 a committee of local persons, including William Macrae the parish minister, gathered to take action to establish the Church school. Their meeting, "having taken into consideration the neglected state of the youth of the District of Abertarff for several years arising from the want of a proper school at Fort Augustus, and of suitable encouragement to a teacher of respectability, and considering there is no fund appropriated for the support of an Institution so important to the welfare of the community; have resolved to open a Subscription for the purpose of building a commodious Schoolhouse and accommodation for a teacher." Ten months later the building located close to the church was opened, and its first teacher appointed. In 1828 it came under the oversight of the General Assembly.[128] The school offered a wide range of subjects, and by 1834 ten teachers had served with good effect. The Minutes tell of a curriculum that embraced Latin, mathematics, arithmetic and English reading, writing and recitation: at least one student received tuition in Greek. The schoolmasters were generally seen as a lieutenant to the minister. They had to subscribe to the Established Church and often acted as catechist, elder or Session-Clerk.[129] However, in 1819, Hugh Junor was upbraided for allowing the schoolroom to be used by an itinerant preacher "unconnected with the established church." This may well have been a lay evangelist financed by the Haldane brothers who promoted Baptist churches across Scotland: such independent denominations never gained a foothold within the Great Glen.[130]

An insight into the spiritual heritage of Fort Augustus is illustrated by two schoolmasters and a scholar. John Forbes, brought up in Strathglass, was appointed as schoolmaster in 1838; he published "A Double Grammar of English and Gaelic" in 1843, and became a Tutor in Gaelic at the Church of Scotland's Normal College in Edinburgh in 1848. He was subsequently Assistant Minister at St Stephen's Edinburgh and later became the minister of

Sleat in Skye. He was described as "among the best Gaelic scholars of his time."[131] Duncan MacGregor, the son of another schoolmaster, was born in 1854. Although his family moved away when he was quite young, he served as a missionary in eastern Scotland before ordination to Inverallochy in 1881. He too was a noted Gaelic scholar and wrote extensively on Columba and the Celtic Church. His translations of two hymns attributed to Columba are in the Church of Scotland's 2005 Church Hymnary. Then the Rev Hugh Fraser, born at Aberchalder in 1835, received his early education at Fort Augustus. He later became the minister at Berriedale and then at Fearn.[132]

Whilst the Free Church congregation made steady progress after the Disruption in 1843, the semi-detached status of the Church of Scotland congregation up to 1883 had placed it at a serious disadvantage: Fort Augustus was served by a succession of short-term missionary-ministers who all moved on to appointments elsewhere. Often such men had completed their divinity training, but they were not ordained when first appointed, thus restricting their usefulness to their senior parish minister. Across Scotland such appointments serving parts of larger parishes did not help the spiritual welfare of the people. This was recognised as early as 1838 when a Church of Scotland journal commented: "By all means let our preachers be set to work in those large parishes which cannot be immediately broken in pieces. But let it be fully understood that this is only a temporary expedient, – a transition state; and that we can never look upon our object as at all attained, until the preacher's labours have paved the way for something more, – until the preaching station become a church, the district a parish, and the missionary an ordained minister, the head of an effective kirk-session, a presbyter and bishop of the flock of Christ."[133] Such an aspiration must have encouraged the move towards securing parish status for Fort Augustus and its neighbours.

Presbytery was regularly imploring the Royal Bounty Committee to fill vacancies swiftly, and so it began to highlight the problems of over-large parishes. When Donald Chisholm became the minister of Boleskine and Abertarff in 1840 the Presbytery "considering the union of extensive Parishes in the Highlands of Scotland to be a great evil which Presbyteries should use all constitutional means to get removed, Resolve to take into serious consideration the present union of the Parishes of Boleskine and Abertarff.[134] One solution which the Presbytery recommended to the Royal Bounty Committee in 1844 was to amalgamate the Mission Districts of Glengarry, Fort Augustus and Glenmoriston "with a salary of at least one hundred pounds per annum in order to enable such

Missionary to discharge as far as practicable the onerous districts."[135] William Sutherland, who had been appointed to the tripartite charge in 1843 on the usual salary of £60pa, was offered an additional £40 to cover the neighbouring districts during their vacancies "to enable him to keep a horse and bear the other necessary charges incurred."[136] Perhaps the gesture came too late for by the end of the year Sutherland had been appointed to the Parish of Harris.

With vacancies in all three contiguous mission districts the Presbytery again complained that "the people thereof are constantly assailed by the machinations and importunities of Free Church Ministers as well as Popish priests"[137], but there were no appointments to Fort Augustus between September 1844 and 1849; this perhaps led Presbytery to make a rash appointment which brought them, and the name of Fort Augustus, before the General Assembly of 1847. Prompted by the shortage of ministers and missionaries following the Disruption, the Presbytery had been pleased to receive an application from Daniel Monro, who was a student with the United Associate Synod, one of the smaller Presbyterian denominations, and he was recommended for Fort Augustus in September 1845.[138] His licensing was approved by both the Presbytery and the Synod of Glenelg, but the Committee of the Royal Bounty held this to be irregular, since Mr Monro had not gone through the prescribed course of study. The Presbytery expressed their regret at this ruling, mentioning "the unprecedented difficulties in which they are placed." They stated "that if they have not proceeded in that matter according to the letter of the law of the Church, they have acted according to its spirit." Once again they pressed upon the Committee the vastness of the mission districts and the activities of clergy from the other two denominations, to whom they feared "a serious defection unless a missionary be forthwith appointed."[139] The affair rumbled on until 1847 when General Assembly censured both Presbytery and Synod, and prohibited them "from deviating in future from the rules of the Church."[140]

The concerns of the Fort Augustus congregation surfaced again in 1848 when the Presbytery met in the village and took note of "statements made to them this day by several respectable parties connected with the congregation … in consequence of the want of ministrations in the Church … for such long intervals, and that their attachment to the Church is very much shaken in consequence that they are in danger of being misled into separation and secession from the Church of Scotland." The solution was to ask the ministers of Presbytery to take it in turns to supply at Fort Augustus, but later in the year a Petition was presented signed by one hundred persons "praying for the appointment of a Missionary to that Station and setting forth that in the present impossibility of getting a Gaelic-speaking Missionary they shall be content with the services of an English-speaking Missionary." Presbytery resisted such a cultural change, but once again resolved to do their best to find a suitable candidate. Not for the first time they impressed upon the Royal Bounty Committee that Fort Augustus and Glenmoriston, which had been vacant for seven years, "could make a useful unit together" and reminded the Committee that they had sanctioned three separate missions in 1844, again mentioning the enticement of the Free Church.[141]

Such were the concerns of Presbytery that when Edward Rodgers was appointed in 1849 he was urged "to repair to Fort Augustus immediately." He was to remain for three years, and after eighteen years at Tweedmouth he went to Canada where he was described as "the best pulpit orator in the Owen Sound Presbytery" although "he paid little attention to visiting as a pastoral duty and his congregation never warmed to him …"[142] A reverse migration took place in 1858 when James Mackenzie from Nova Scotia was appointed, though he stayed for little more than a year before taking a parish in Ross-shire. Another Nova Scotian, Simon Macgregor, served from 1881 to 1882.

Most interesting among these Nineteenth Century missionary ministers was Donald Macleod, son of the minister at Onich. He was ordained to Fort Augustus in 1862, but within nine months he had taken the charge at Dornoch. Thereafter he moved rapidly to Dumfries, Montrose, Dundee and Jedburgh, before being appointed to London's Crown Court Church in 1881. There he worked to create the Church of Scotland's prestigious congregation in the West End, St Columba's, Pont Street, and he became its first minister in 1884 until his retirement in 1901.

Abertarff Presbytery minutes give some insights into the church at Fort Augustus during the 1850s. Describing the Mission of Fort Augustus as "very important", Presbytery asked the Royal Bounty Committee to fill the current vacancy, stressing "that it is necessary for the success of a Missionary there that he should be an able Gaelic Preacher." They also noted the need for a "well qualified teacher" to be appointed to the Assembly School as soon as possible."[143] A month later there were meetings to vote for candidates for the vacant charge of Boleskine and Abertarff. Those taking part from Fort Augustus were recorded as Angus McGruer of Dalcataig, Capt Ewen Ross and Mr Johnstone "Distiller"; James Lawrence, a weaver, and Donald Fraser, a carpenter, both resided at Bunoich. There were two candidates for the vacancy and Patrick MacGregor, the missionary minister at Glengarry, received the majority vote, his case having been championed by Lord Ward, Laird of Glengarry. However, Presbytery received a petition complaining that he was "deficient in knowledge of the Gaelic language." Eventually a third party, Malcolm McIntyre was appointed.[144]

A memoir by Archibald Clerk, minister of Kilmallie, shines an amusing light on the polity of Abertarff Presbytery and its relationship with the Free Church Presbytery. The Free Church maintained the exact pattern of meetings set by the Church of Scotland. In 1864 Clerk records: "On the last Wednesday of March I attended the usual meeting of Presbytery at Fort Augustus – nothing of much consequence. Mr Ellice of Glenquioch sent us a Salmon and a bottle of Champagne. The former we divided with the Free Church Presbytery."[145] Salmon and champagne may not be the usual fare for a Presbytery meeting today, although at this time the distances travelled by ministers and elders would have required that meals were provided, along with overnight accommodation. It is significant that many meetings within the Great Glen area were held at the King's Inn and the Lovat Arms in Fort Augustus, and at the Invergarry Inn. By 1860 it would appear that Fort Augustus Church was not a fit location for Presbytery or the congregation.

A Valuable Notebook[146]

> *"... those who were engaged in the work laboured,*
> *and the repairing went forward in their hands,*
> *and they restored the house of God to its proper*
> *condition and strengthened it"*
> *[2 Chronicles 24:13 (RSV)]*

The mystery surrounding the fate of the "snug, comfortable" church at Fort Augustus was unlocked by a plain notebook within the Presbytery Archives held at Fort William. Entitled "Congregational Committee 1860–1867" it contains more valuable information than the title would at first suggest. The first minute records a "Meeting of the congregation of Fort Augustus and district of Abertarff" chaired by Capt. Ewen Ross on 3 December 1860, and states that "there are certain very necessary repairs upon the church and schoolhouse required without delay", and that the meeting "resolves to receive estimates for having these executed". The school minutes for the period 1811 to 1835 reveal a long catalogue of repairs to the schoolhouse, as does a Presbytery minute in 1858: the building gave endless trouble, and its condition may explain something of the quality of the church building too![147]

Things moved quickly, for eight days later a meeting held within the schoolhouse received a report listing the repairs needed on the church, which was approved, and the schoolhouse, which was amended, with arrangements made for sealed offers from contractors to be received just seven days later. At the same meeting the Chairman asked for a review of the seat-rents, an important element of congregational income, and it was minuted that there was no "regular or satisfactory system pursued at present". However, it was agreed to make no changes in the meantime "until an opportunity be had of examining such Documents as may exist in possession of the Kirk Session or other responsible parties, referring to a scheme of the Church Seats and the claims of the various parties to their seats by prescription or otherwise." Yet again the subsidiary status of Fort Augustus church was clearly illustrated.

Seven days later a public meeting of the congregation was informed that a tender for the repairs had been accepted from Mr Thomas Fraser, Kinlochuanagan, for £11. One cannot doubt the scale of tender at the time, but it is placed into context when, at a meeting in January 1861 it was decided to install a stove into the church at the cost of 5 guineas. This seems to have stimulated a renewed interest in the fabric and surroundings of the building. At a public meeting in March a record of gratitude was minuted for a gift of £5 towards church repairs from Mr F J Rufford, "and also to Mrs Rufford, who, it was reported … had contributed handsomely towards improving the approach to and the grounds around the Church." The minute continues: "It was proposed that the Church greens should be enclosed, leaving a wicket at both ends – further that Captain Ross, Mr Thos. McKenzie, Mr Robert Grant and Mr John McBean be appointed to a committee to take into consideration the expediency of planting a double row of trees round the green, enclosing them with a wire fence." The church stove was by now installed, and Mrs Murdoch Grant was appointed to light the stove and clean the church for a fee of £1 per annum. By the end of the year the proposals for the church grounds were on hold "the season being rather far advanced", but a different project was in hand, namely the creation of a Sabbath School Library thanks, in part, to "a very liberal contribution in books" from Mr and Mrs Rufford. In January 1862 the Rules and Regulations for that library were approved, and it was noted that the library would be open to both weekday and Sabbath School scholars.

Church fabric issues, however, had not been resolved. In March 1862 it was reported that the new stove was not working well, and the suggestion was made that the vestry chimney should be heightened. By the end of the year the stove was still causing problems and it was agreed to build a chimney stack to carry off the smoke. Then in January 1863 the committee decided "that the present church stove is useless, and never likely to be of service": they agreed to remove it immediately but, with a note of good management, "retain it on hand until such time as it can be to advantage disposed of"! The urgent necessity of upgrading the building is emphasised by a comment in the Presbytery minutes in 1862 that "the Mission of Fort Augustus is a very populous one, and that from the neighbourhood being frequented by many influential families from the South during the summer and autumn it is of much importance."[148]   Meanwhile, the notebook records some interesting financial matters.   In September 1862 the annual accounts note that Mr William McKinnon and Mr Alexander Munro both received £2, the former as Precentor, the latter for ringing the bell and cleaning the church.   More seriously, a congregational meeting in October was told that six months' salary was due to the minister, Mr Donald MacLeod.

This casts an interesting light upon the ministers who served at Fort Augustus.   Although a part of Boleskine Parish, those who served at Fort Augustus were paid for and appointed by the Royal Bounty Committee.   By the middle of the Nineteenth Century it appears that these ministers were Divinity Graduates undertaking something akin to a probationary period, with Ordination following at a later date. This was important, for ordination enabled the missionary ministers to conduct the Sacraments, thus relieving the distant parish minister of additional duties. In Mr MacLeod's case, the October meeting was told that he was due the sum of £30 for the period from June to November, "during which time he has been officiating as Minister of Fort Augustus." Since Mr MacLeod was ordained to Fort Augustus on 26 November, this suggests that he came following his graduation, and was acting as "minister" prior to ordination.

The minute of 14 October records that the £30 due to Mr MacLeod had been guaranteed by Mr McIntyre, the Parish Minister of Boleskine, but it was up to the congregation of Fort Augustus to pay the salary. The minute continues: "A statement forwarded by Mr McIntyre anent this matter being read, it was proposed and unanimously approved that Capt. Ross should wait upon the members of the Congregation and Adherents, and thus afford an opportunity to all inclined to aid in furthering this object. Mrs Rufford being present, signified to the Committee that she and Mr Rufford were to contribute £10 and also willingly continue the said donation yearly to Mr MacLeod – on condition that the rest of the congregation supplement the usual income to the amount of £100." It is not clear from this record if the congregation remained responsible for the support of their ministers once ordained. In any case, Mr MacLeod was ordained at the end of November, and nine months later was translated to Dornoch. As noted earlier, his subsequent ministry took him eventually to the congregation of St Columba's in London's fashionable west-end!

If 1862 saw progress with the church fabric and finances, one further area remained to be settled, the matter of seat-rents first raised in 1860. At a meeting at the end of November a congregational meeting, chaired by Mr McIntyre, was called to investigate "the claims of each parties as think they possess a right to one or more seats in the church at Fort Augustus." The outcome was a list, reproduced in Annex 2, which gives a fascinating insight into the congregation at the end of 1862. Having recorded the claims, it was minuted that "The Committee accordingly appoint that the above seats may be allotted to such parties as may desire to occupy them – giving always a prior claim to the present occupant. They also resolve that each proprietor shall have his own seat at a certain sum which may be found sufficient to repair it, and that those seats belonging to the Kirk Session be let at a sum that may hereafter be fixed upon by the committee."

Very quickly it became apparent that those church seats were in a poor state. In January 1863 the committee agreed to defer consideration of the repairing of the church seats until their next meeting, the go-ahead being given in February, and completion of the repairs being reported to the May meeting. Only then did the Committee set about the task of letting the seats and setting a sum to defray the cost of repairs. The 1863 arrangements are set out in Annex 2, along with details of the seating in the three galleries, something not recorded a year earlier. The north-side gallery appears to be allocated to the residents of the Fort, presumably the gallery that attracted a contribution when the church was built nearly a century earlier. By August 1863 it seemed that the congregation was in good shape: they had an ordained minister in post, many repairs had been undertaken, and the finances were sorted. The meeting on 26 August records that: "The Committee having now freed the church of debts beg leave to resign – as they hereby do – and Mr MacLeod is requested to intimate the same to the congregation on Sabbath – that they may take such steps as may be thought necessary to elect a new Committee." Mr MacLeod, however, "intimated to the committee that he had resigned the mission of Fort Augustus – and that therefore this would be the last meeting he would be privileged to attend." However, within the following six days the congregation was to face an even greater blow.

"… such a dilapidated state"

"The bricks have fallen down, but we will rebuild"
[Isaiah 9:10]

In the closing days of August the church building suffered a serious collapse. A congregational meeting on 1 September 1863 considered the condition of the East Gable of the church. It was "unanimously agreed that, in order to remove any cause of alarm as to the immediate safety of the congregation while worshipping to put four strong posts under the gallery and the roof adjacent to the East gable." The cause of this structural failure is not recorded: it may be that the gallery was added as an afterthought, as previously suggested, but it is instructive to note that in 1836 the Old Kirk at Kilmore in the Parish of Urquhart had been in a parlous state due to the "crazy" state of the galleries, prompting the building of the new parish church.[149] Six days later a new committee "to manage the affairs of the Church and congregation for the period of twelve months from this date" was appointed. It comprised Captain Ewan Ross JP, Messrs John McBean, Robert Grant, William Burton, George Shaw and William Finlay, along with the Parish Minister *ex officio.* "it was agreed that no important repairs could be done on the church walls till Spring, and that in the meantime it should be ascertained what repairs are actually required to be done on the whole church."

Whatever the committee may have done about the repairs is not recorded until a meeting in March 1865. It would seem that the church continued in use because in July 1864 it was agreed by the committee to replace the vestry door and to replace two panes of window glass. During this eighteen-month period the committee appointed William McKinnon as Precentor in Gaelic and English, at £2 and ten shillings per annum, Alexander Fraser as Assistant Precentor at the same honorarium, and Alexander Munro as Church Officer at £2 and twelve shillings per annum. The same Mr Munro was confirmed as grave digger "in order to prevent any ... disputes about the burying ground at Fort Augustus". In September 1864 the Committee expressed "great annoyance that the Sacrament of the Lord's Supper is not administered on the same day as it is done with the Free Church as they hold it annually on the same day."

The state of the building was raised at last in March 1865 when "it was moved and unanimously agreed to, that in consequence of the dilapidated state of School House and church, the Revd Mr McDougall [the minister at Fort Augustus] should write to Mr McIntyre [the parish minister of Boleskine] to ascertain who are the parties to apply for funds to complete the necessary repairs." The reply to that letter underlined the lowly status of the daughter church of the Parish because on 21 March the committee heard that "there was no legal provision made for keeping the said buildings in repairs"; as a consequence they agreed to circulate a Subscription Paper "to all the members and adherents of the Congregation for defraying the expenses connected with any repairs that may be made …" The Presbytery was asked for contributions, and it recommended the cause to its members.[150]

Eight days later another committee meeting was held, the Boleskine minister, along with F J Rufford Esq of Inchnacardoch and others being present. It was revealed that the Subscription Paper was not circulated because Mr Rufford "with certain Members of Committee" had taken a significant action. This subgroup, along with "an experienced Tradesman from Inverness" had inspected the Church and School House and reported and recommended as follows:

"1st With regard to the School House:
That it should be gutted out – the roof to be taken off, the present walls lowered: and then a new roof be put on and the present windows heightened and otherwise altered, and the walls outside and inside be put into the best order and in short the

whole building to be put into perfect repair. Said repairs being estimated to cost £100stg.

2nd With regard to the Church:

That it should be put into the best possible state of repair: specifying at the same time the required alterations to be made on the East Gable: harling the walls, securing the roof and especially the skews with slates & otherwise. And also with regard to the inside of the Church that the seats should be put into proper order – the opening of them widened and painted – the doors & windows & face of Gallery to be also repaired and painted, and in short the whole to be thoroughly repaired. Said repairs on the Church being also estimated to cost £100stg.

"Mr Rufford further reported other repairs on the ground & walls around said buildings which he specified would cost £25stg. The whole of the above repairs being thus estimated to cost £225stg."

These reports give an insight into the poor state of the buildings and the cramped nature of the seating in the church which, apart from the failure of the East Gable, clearly needed much attention. That this was a serious financial challenge for the congregation is underlined by the generosity of Mr Rufford, as the minute of 29

March records: "Mr Rufford then offered to give £100stg towards completing said repairs, on the condition that the Committee within two months from this date guarantee that they will provide the remaining £125stg necessary to carry out the proposed plans."

Francis Rufford, who tenanted Inchnacardoch Lodge and its sporting rights from the Lovat Estate, is described as a "Landowner and Firebrick Manufacturer" in the West Midlands of England, a business that extended to the manufacture of sinks and baths. At the 1861 Census he lived at Prescott House in Stourbridge with ten live-in servants.[151] In 1870 he gifted land for the building of St Mark's Church in Lye, close to his home and brickyards. His wealth was such that he owned a steam-yacht which in 1871 was seen lying in Inchnacardoch Bay.[152] His business acumen was to be invaluable to the church in Fort Augustus.

Mr Rufford's generosity galvanised the committee; the minute continues: "The meeting unanimously agreed to record their deep sense of gratitude for Mr Rufford's exceedingly handsome and munificent offer in this matter as well as his own & his Lady's uniform kindness and generosity in promoting the highest interests of this district: and at the same time resolved to begin without any delay to endeavour to get the said sum of £125stg and with that view appointed the Rev Mr McIntyre, Minister of the Parish, to apply to the Heritors of the Parish and to the Committees of the Church for donations & Captain Ross & Mr McDougall to obtain the subscriptions of the congregation. Mr McBean to apply to the Commissioners of the Woods and Forest[153] and Captain Ross to apply to Mr Ellice of Glengarry & to other persons spoken of, and likewise every member of the Committee to use his utmost endeavour towards making up the required sum. And, in the meantime, they resolved without delay to gut out the School-House in order to give the required height to the walls to satisfy the regulations of the Committee on Education." Two months later, on 22 May, the committee notes "that the amount required to put Mr Rufford's munificent offer was nearly accomplished." At the beginning of June 1865 it was reported that work on the "office-houses connected with the School-House" had been undertaken, and in March 1866 it was further stated that repairs to "School windows and water closet were complete".

There was, however, some difficulty in establishing the ownership of the land on which the church had been built. As mentioned earlier the local military leadership had encouraged settlement around the Fort, but in the absence of legal titles there had been various problems about legitimate claims to ownership. The Presbytery minutes[154] and meetings of the local committee through to the Spring of 1866 tell of letters and enquiries made to the Parish Minister, the Presbytery, the Church of Scotland in Edinburgh and the Commissioners of Woods and Forests, apparently to little effect. This sense of drift was reflected in a meeting on 24 March when it was noted that Mr McDougall, the Fort Augustus minister, had not attended the previous five meetings of the committee, and that he had failed to hand over a Deposit Receipt for £120 and two shillings. It was agreed that Mr McDougall cease to be the Treasurer and that the paper be handed to the Chairman.

New impetus was evident when, on 20 March 1866, the committee "moved and agreed to that Capt Ross continue Chairman until the repairs of Church and School be completed." Captain Ross had clearly recruited an ally in the shape of Alexander Ross, the Inverness architect, who was invited to visit Fort Augustus to prepare a plan to be laid before the Presbytery of Abertarff which was to meet in Fort William just a week later. Mr Ross had recently completed the new church at Glengarry[155], and was rapidly gaining recognition as a church architect across the Highlands. Captain Ross and Mr Robert Grant met with Mr Ross on Monday 26 March, just a day before Presbytery met. The Presbytery was told that the Church Building Committee "had now collected £290stg for repairing Church and Schoolhouse, but that a sum of fully £100 more is required for the completion of the work." They also noted that there was a delay in obtaining the title to the land but that nonetheless the Committee could proceed with their work as soon as they wished. At the same time Presbytery agreed to approach the Home Mission Committee for a grant towards the project.[156]

Whether it was Alexander Ross's advice, or the opinion of Presbytery, the local committee received a serious setback when it met on 2 April. Following the Fort William meeting the Presbytery Clerk stated "that as the church is in such a dilapidated state that it is necessary to pull down the church and put ... additional sittings in the new building." The Committee does not appear to have taken this advice, and perhaps it baulked at the likely price of a new-build, for not only is Mr Ross the architect's name never mentioned again, but on 23 April the minute reads that the meeting "was to consider what repairs are really necessary to be done to Church & School as there are not sufficient funds in hand to enable them to build the Church anew. It was moved and agreed that Capt Ross, Mr Grant and Mr John McBean meet the Presbytery on the 25th of this month to arrange about proceeding with the repairs as early as possible."

At this point the Presbytery of Abertarff took the initiative. The minute book records the Report of the Committee of the Presbytery appointed to consider repairs to Fort Augustus Church and Schoolhouse which met within the church on the 25 April. Progress was reported on two fronts. First, Capt Ross stated that the Building Committee had raised £294, nineteen shillings and tenpence, and Rev Mr McIntyre of Boleskine spoke of an additional £30 which had been obtained from another source. Second, Capt Ross presented a letter from the Commissioners of HM Woods and Forests "to the effect that the site of the present Church and Schoolhouse will as soon as practical be conveyed by them to the Church of Scotland."

Such progress drew the praise of the Presbytery Committee: "The Committee desires to record their obligation to & their admiration of the Church Committee for their energy and success in collecting such a large amount of funds." The underlining emphasised the committee's appreciation of the action. However, the Committee did not adhere to its earlier advice that the church should be pulled down. Instead it recommended that the committee "employ Mr Burrell, Road Inspector, Fort William, to furnish plans & specifications showing the extent of repairs and improvement which can be effected on the present Church and Schoolhouse with the amount of money now in hand & also what can be done with the amount of £425; it being highly probable that an additional sum of £100 will be contributed by the Home Missions Committee to which application for aid has been made both by the Presbytery & by Mr McIntyre, Minister of the Parish."[157] Mr Burrell had built the first Duncansburgh Church in Fort William in 1860 and then that town's Belford Hospital in 1863, and he would go on to build schools in Roy Bridge and Strontian.[158]

With renewed optimism and a new professional partner the congregational committee moved ahead at speed. Meetings in May and June considered and approved plans and specifications. Then invitations for Estimates from contractors were advertised in the local press[159], with a closing date set for 6 July. At the same time, the financial situation was reviewed. On 13 June it was reported that Rev J McDougall still had £120 and two shillings in hand, that Capt Ross and Mr McBean had just over £132, and Rev McIntyre £31, plus a further guaranteed sum of £30. By the end of the month it was minuted that Mr McDougall had sent a letter of resignation as Treasurer and member of the Committee, and a letter was sent to him "requesting him to hand the collection Book and balance of money in his hands to Mr William Finlay who was appointed Treasurer." Mr McDougall left for another parish in September from whence he was eventually suspended for "inefficiency"![160]

The committee also appointed a superintendent:

"After consideration as to the best plan to adopt in order to conduct & superintend the operation connected with the repairs in a sufficient and satisfactory manner, it was unanimously and very cordially resolved that inasmuch as Mr Rufford of Inchnacardoch has taken such a deep interest in this work & given so munificent a contribution to the funds, he should be most respectfully but earnestly requested to as the Committee and Congregation the further great favour of agreeing to act as Treasurer of the sums subscribed, and to see the work carried out agreeably to the specifications & plans …"

Eight days later the minute recorded Mr Rufford's agreement to act as Treasurer and to oversee the work and he rose to the challenge of his new responsibilities. The scene was set for a significant advance.

A New Canopy

"Over all the glory will be a canopy … a shelter and shade from the heat of the day, and a refuge and hiding place from the storm and rain"
[Isaiah 4:5,6]

A committee meeting held on 18 August 1866 records an unexpected development. "Since the last meeting Mr Rufford had liberally come forward and paid the sum of £107.10.00 for the Museum Building of the late Mr G Cumming in order to have the roof placed over the Church. In consequence of this the former plans and specifications were departed from as a <u>new</u> building of the same dimensions <u>inside</u> as the Museum was <u>necessary</u> for the roof." So the plans for repairs were torn up, and the new building called for by Presbytery in April was to come about thanks to the good offices of Mr Rufford, and the demise of the Museum.

The museum had been created by Mr Roualeyn George Gordon-Cumming, the second son of Sir William Gordon-Cumming of Altyre and Gordonstoun who, after Army service in India and South Africa, had become a big-game hunter. His suitably preserved trophies were exhibited at the Great Exhibition of 1851 to great acclaim. Gordon-Cumming secured his reputation further with the publication of his book "The Lion Hunter of South Africa" in 1856. Two years later he moved to Fort Augustus and built a museum beside the Canal to house his trophies. Victorian travellers would visit the museum as the steamers passed through the flight of locks.[161] Sadly, Gordon-Cumming died in 1866, aged 46, and his assets were sold. A copy of an Account prepared for his Trustees and Executors shows that upon his death he had only £16, five shillings and tenpence to his name. Local sales of his assets raised

£154, fifteen shillings and a penny, and a London sale of the Museum contents raised £1611 and eight shillings. It is believed that the exhibits from the museum were purchased by Barnum's Circus. The final item on the Account records "Price for the Building Materials of the Museum for removal as sold to F T Rufford Esq. Fort Augustus ... £107.10.00."[162]

Interestingly, in a letter dated 1906 obtained by Jane Patten, it appears that relatives of the deceased were still contesting the value of Gordon-Cumming's assets forty years later! The letter states: "The principal value was of course the museum building with its beautiful woodwork – the whole of which I was told at the time, had been knocked down unopposed for £10 to the contractor for the new church – in which it now is." The price quoted by the letter-writer is at variance with the Account. It is fascinating to realise that the roof of Fort Augustus Church is older than the building itself, and that the timbers that once sheltered the mighty animals of Creation now provides a canopy for those who worship their Creator!

With the fortuitous provision of a ready-made roof, and the co-operation of Mr Burrell the Architect, work proceeded apace. The same minute of 18 August 1866 states that "Messrs McKay of Inverness, contractors for the Church and Schools agreed to have

the works complete by the 20th November for the sum of £280."
This sum was considerably lower than that quoted earlier in the year,
despite the need to demolish much of the existing church building
and to set new foundations to accord with the shape of the museum
roof. How many of the walls and stones of the old building were
incorporated within the new can only be guessed at. That the
project was definitely viewed as a new-build was underlined at the
next meeting of the committee just six days later when arrangements
were made for the laying of a Foundation Stone on 28 August. One
month later the minute gives a full account of the momentous event:

"the foundation stone of the new Church was laid on the 28th
August by Mrs Rufford & assisted by Capt Ewen Ross in
presence of some of the Presbytery & the Church's working
Committee & a great number of the Congregation & other
denominations. Prayers were offered up by the Rev Malcolm
McIntyre of Boleskine. A number of newspapers viz. Inverness
Courier, Glasgow Herald, Edinburgh [*Evening*] Courant & five
coins with a statement of the different Gentlemen who took an
interest in providing site and money among whom were Mr Ellice
of Glengarry & Mrs Rufford of Inchnacardoch & was placed
under the foundation stone. The Chairman had much pleasure

in producing a true copy of the Deed of Conveyance & the ...
Warrants conveying the land ... by the Church Committee to the
Church of Scotland in perpetuity and for ever. The Deed of
Conveyance & all the expenses attending it amounted to
£6.6.03."

At last, with the Foundation Stone in place and the question of land
ownership finally resolved by the Crown Charter of 6 September
1866, the building of the new church could proceed. It soon
appears, though, that the finances were still a consideration. A
committee meeting in November 1866 recommended that
advertisements be placed in the Inverness Courier to invite further
subscriptions: it actually appeared on 18 October and is reproduced
below.

The committee suggested that the Presbytery Clerk should apply
to the Home Mission of the Church of Scotland to pay the costs of
the Deed of Conveyance "as the funds for Church repairs are so
low". The Home Mission Committee subsequently gave £112 and
ten shillings towards "funds collected by the congregation at Fort-
Augustus for building their handsome new church."[163]   In
November 1866 the Presbytery observed "that in Fort Augustus
there is a very attached congregation who are now shewing their zeal

THE CHURCH AND SCHOOLS AT FORT-AUGUSTUS

The SUBSCRIBERS to the Fund for Repairs of CHURCH and SCHOOLS at FORT-AUGUSTUS will be glad to learn that the Petition of the Committee to the Commissioners of Woods and Forests, praying for a Grant of Land for Sites, has been responded to by granting said Sites under the Sign Manual of her Majesty, dated at Osborne, 24th July 1866.

The Committee, in the attempt to restore the old fabric of this Church, found the building in such a dilapidated state that they were compelled to take it down and raise a new structure. The funds are inadequate to meet this increased expenditure, and the Committee are again obliged to appeal to the generosity of the public to assist them with the means to liquidate the debt that has been incurred by this necessary change in their plans; and they hope that those interested in the Church and District will lend their generous aid, as the resources of the districts in which this Mission Church is placed are exhausted, and very few additional subscriptions can be looked for in the immediate neighbourhood. The Church is in a forward state, and will be opened for Public Worship about the end of November.

Any Contributions will be thankfully received by the Treasurer, Francis T Rufford, Esq., Prescott House, Stourbridge; or by Captain Ewen Ross, Fort-Augustus.

[Advertisement: Inverness Courier, 18.10.1866]

for, and attachment to the Church of Scotland by erecting a new Church and Schoolhouse there."[164]

There is a report suggesting that other fund-raising initiatives were under way. In an article in the Daily Telegraph in 1871 the unknown author described his passage on a steamer through the locks at Fort Augustus and states that beside them "was erected a booth fitted up as a fancy fair. It contained, besides the ordinary inutilities of such bazaars, a lot of the huge long sticks with a hook at the end which are affected by Highland gentlemen in imitation of the shepherds, to whom these Scottish alpenstocks are really serviceable implements. The proceeds were, if I remember rightly, to be given to the Established Church of Scotland; but if the Kirk depended much upon this source of income, it would be, I opine, in very great straits."[165]

Financial matters dominated the next meeting in February 1867. Clearly the committee was anxious to take over the new building as soon as possible to boost its income. It was proposed by Mr McDougall, presumably the newly-appointed minister at Fort Augustus who bore the same name as his predecessor, that "if the Architect took the Church off the hands of the Contractor that the Church should be opened immediately ... it would increase this Congregation and [be] finally handed over by the Presbytery

Committee." On a vote it was "decided that the Church should not be interfered with until the Presbytery Committee should formally hand over the Church to the proper authority and arrange the Church sittings."

The final entry in the Committee's notebook, sadly undated, records "that Mr Rufford the Treasurer should have the arrangement of decorating the Church. Unanimously agreed to. Mr Rufford proposed that Mr John McBain should arrange for the … fencing and procure the material and an iron gate for the South entrance to the Church. Unanimously agreed to. Mr Grant called attention to furnishing the School Room. The Committee resolved to finish the fences and Church painting &c. first, and when the balance was known furniture would be purchased for the School Room." The meeting closed with a vote of thanks.

In July 1867 the Presbytery recorded that the new church was completed, and in August it received a certificate of completion from Henry Burrell. The building had seating for two hundred and sixty, and "is in all respects suitable and comfortable as a place of worship." The school was also in good order. In September the Presbytery met at Fort Augustus to inspect the buildings. The minute reads that "Capt. Ross … in the name of the Committee formally handed over both the Church and Schoolhouse … to the

Presbytery of Abertarff as the property of the Church of Scotland ... The Presbytery instruct their Moderator to convey to Capt. Ross and the Committee ... their sincere thanks for the great and successful exertions which they have made in carrying on the work now so happily completed. And the Presbytery considering that F T Rufford Esq. ... now residing at Inchnacardoch in this neighbourhood has shewn great liberality in contributing to the funds of the Building Committee and has given much time and care to the Superintendence of the works, instruct the Moderator to convey to him likewise their sincere thanks."[166]

Thus ended a twelve year period which saw the fabric of both church and schoolhouse in poor condition, the momentous failure of the East gable of the church, and a variety of schemes to restore both buildings. Finance was a continuing concern, and only the timely intervention of generous benefactors and the Presbytery, not to mention the fortunate provision of a ready-made roof, ensured that Fort Augustus Church was rebuilt. An ordinary notebook, thankfully preserved within the archives, explained why a building that was new in the mid-1770s, and described as "snug and comfortable" in 1831 needed to be replaced just thirty years later!

" ... the Parish fully equipped"

" ... bearing fruit in every good work,
growing in the knowledge of God ... "
[Colossians 1:10]

With the encouragement of its new building the congregation at
Fort Augustus moved towards a new independence. This did not
prove to be straightforward, however, because Presbytery was very
quickly made aware of some disagreement among the congregation
as to the seating arrangements![167] Perhaps because of this, Rev
Robert McDougall, who was at the mission from November 1866
preached on only four occasions and resigned due to ill-health in
April 1868. In a welcome change to form he was quickly replaced
by Rev James McDonald. However, the new incumbent brought a
matter to Presbytery which revealed that "the house formerly
provided for him as well as an annual sum of £10stg" had been
withdrawn, quite possibly because he could not reside at the Fort
which had finally been decommissioned and sold to Lord Lovat.
Presbytery noted that his reduced income of £60pa was "utterly and
obviously inadequate for his support; and in these circumstances
they most earnestly recommend to the congregation to provide in
such manner as they may deem just, a sum which will at least

compensate him for what has been withdrawn; and they hope that the congregation will show their liberality in raising their Minister's income to such an amount as will afford not only the bare means of subsistence but to such an amount as shall be suitable for his position, and thus help to promote his usefulness in his ministerial charge. They direct that an Extract of this Minute should be read to the congregation at Fort Augustus."[168]   A few weeks later Presbytery informed the Royal Bounty Committee of "the great importance of that Mission, and the peculiar circumstances which render it impossible to obtain the usual accommodation from the landed Proprietors in the neighbourhood (some of them being Roman Catholics)" and requested additional financial support from the Home Mission Committee of the Church of Scotland.[169]

The Royal Bounty Committee again floated the idea of merging the Glenmoriston and Fort Augustus missions in 1878, and once more the Presbytery asked what salary might be paid for such an appointment, but nothing was heard from the Committee.[170]   This may have been an effort by the Committee to reduce its financial commitments to the Great Glen area, but it did stimulate a new initiative, for in November 1880 the Minister of Boleskine and Abertarff came to Presbytery with a Statement and Appeal to provide an Endowment and Manse for Fort Augustus, "and to have the District of Abertarff erected into a separate Parish." The proposal received the approval of Presbytery who determined to "recommend the same to the favourable consideration of the Endowment Committee, the Baird Trustees, and all friends of the church." The following year it was reported that the minister at Fort Augustus had been making progress "towards the endowment of the district."[171] The following year the Endowment was secured.

A list of Communicant Members at Fort Augustus in 1880 is reproduced in Annex 4, where twenty-nine names are recorded. This is not, however, an accurate measure of the size of the congregation since it was common in Highland churches to draw a distinction between the Members who had been admitted to partake of the Lord's Supper or Communion, and the Adherents who where often the majority associated with the church family. The numerical strength of the congregation was thus far greater than the membership alone might suggest.

In November 1882 the Presbytery received a petition from Mrs Ellice of Glengarry, Francis T Rufford, Esq., Inchnacardoch, George Malcolm and others, craving leave to take the necessary steps to have the district recognised as a parish by the law of the land."[172] Over many years the Factor of the Glengarry Estate, George Malcolm, had been a good friend to the congregation, and in 1882 he circulated information about a "mission in which I am greatly interested – viz. Fort Augustus. We hope to have the village and District erected and endowed <u>quoad</u> <u>sacra</u> ere long but we require more money to provide a manse and so have the Parish fully equipped." He added the comment that "the circumstances at Fort Augustus are very peculiar": he was alluding to the creation of the Benedictine Abbey in 1876.[173] At the end of 1882 the Endowment Fund had reached £3140, "more than the sum required," so the surplus was put towards the building of a manse. The necessary legal documents were assembled, and the following March the Deed of Constitution had been approved, and the appointment of James Robertson as the first Minister of Fort Augustus was confirmed. He was inducted on 9 May 1883.[174]

There was still no manse for the new parish. In February 1884 James Robertson was residing at "Rose Cottage" in Fort Augustus[175] and perhaps it was the lack of a manse that encouraged him to accept a call to Lanarkshire later that year: he ended his ministry in Glasgow twenty years later. A Congregational Committee was appointed to elect a new minister, comprising Mr Aichison, Session Clerk; Andrew Brown, Culachy; Duncan Campbell, The Locks; James Chisholm, Mail Contractor; George Douglas, Merchant; Mr Macrae, Borlum; Hector Monro, Supervisor; and Alexander Munro,

Beadle.[176] The Committee chose William Flint who would become the second-longest serving minister in the parish.   Born in Northumberland he was ordained to the English Presbyterian Church in Manchester; later he joined the Church of Scotland and was inducted to Fort Augustus in 1885. Like his predecessor, Mr Flint still had no manse.   He told Presbytery of "the great disadvantage under which he labours in consequence of not having a Manse – a circumstance which materially injures the position of the Church in Fort Augustus."   The Presbytery appointed a committee to work with local parties to raise the necessary funds. It was only in 1892 that Mr Flint brought plans for the new manse to Presbytery, whereafter building work began on the site of the old schoolhouse alongside the church.[177]   The Church school had become redundant following the 1872 Education Act when the new public school was built on Bunoich Brae. In 1894 the Manse was ready for occupation.

Although the new parish no longer required a missionary, as in the past, a new sort of lay missionary was obtained in 1897 to serve the workmen building the Invergarry and Fort Augustus Railway.[178] In 1898 Fort Augustus was described as "this growingly important and peculiarly-situated parish,"[179] a comment certainly made in the light of the growth and increasing stature of the Benedictine Abbey and its school. During Mr Flint's tenure the Manse was built, he married, the railway arrived, a third Presbyterian denomination was established, and an organ was installed in 1911. Mr Flint retired in 1921. These were thirty-six eventful years.

The village grew during the years straddling 1900, with improvements to buildings and the provision of community facilities.   One now-forgotten facility was the Inverness-shire Sanatorium, built in a lonely setting a mile south-west of Auchterawe. Funded by public subscription and opened in 1907, it had accommodation for twenty-two patients, with a staff of around nine. The Fort Augustus doctor served as Medical Superintendent. The hospital was intentionally remote, with road access from the south rather than Fort Augustus: indeed the headed notepaper gave Aberchalder as the nearest railway station! The Sanatorium finally closed in 1951 and was demolished by 1959,[180] although in recent years the site has been reclaimed from the forest overgrowth and a picnic site created.

The longest ministry in Fort Augustus was that of Hugh Gillies who served for forty-one years from the outbreak of war in 1939 to 1980. During these years the porch was added, and the interior of the church was re-ordered by removing the central pulpit and the elders' pews. Mr Gillies also served as a County and a District

Councillor for some years, years which witnessed the coming of mains electricity and the building of many new houses for the Forestry Commission, the North of Scotland Hydro-Electric Board and the County Council. He was preceded by August Kesting, who was born in Inverness, had been a missionary in Nyasaland for three years at the turn of the century, and during the First World War had been minister at the Scots Kirk in Paris. In 1934 he oversaw the Union of his Abertarff congregation with that of the Inveroich congregation, the former United Free Church congregation, and thereafter the UF building became a much needed church hall which was named The MacKay Hall to commemorate the Free Church minister who went into the Union of 1900. Fort Augustus was Mr Kesting's last charge, from 1925 to 1939.

Gilbert Cameron followed Hugh Gillies, having served for six years in the Church of Scotland charge of St Andrews, Nassau, in the Bahamas. He retired in 1986. Following complex negotiations, Fort Augustus was linked with Glengarry on 26 March 1987, and George Charlton was appointed the first minister of the linked charge. Whilst the two parishes had been associated in various forms for at least two hundred years this formal linkage has been sustained to the mutual benefit of both parishes. With the sale of The Mackay Hall, the old United Free Church, in 1988 a new hall was built alongside the church in 1992, and this facility has been a boon to the congregation and the community alike: it was substantially modernised in the early years of the new century.

"… four bonnie kirks"

> *"… holy brothers and sisters,*
> *who share in the heavenly calling"*
> *[Hebrews 3:1]*

Having charted the succession of the four parish churches of Abertarff from the first on the shore of Loch Ness, to the church at Borlum, to the new one built in the 1770s, and then the most recent built in the 1860s, it is instructive to review the three other congregations that have existed within Fort Augustus, the Free Church, the United Free Church and that of the Abbey Church.

"But seeing we've four bonnie kirks,

It is plain we're not quite heathen Turks;

And think you our faith is a phantom or wraith?

No, we don't hold with "faith without works." [181]

The Free Church

The short-term ministries of the Established Church must have contrasted poorly with the zeal and promise of the Free Church: the impact of the Disruption upon the Church of Scotland has already been alluded to. Whilst there were only four male members who adhered to the Free Church in 1843, three of them resided in Glenmoriston. Nevertheless the missionary, William Lauder of Glengarry, did a sterling job in building up the new congregation in Fort Augustus which worshipped at first in a malt-barn. With great speed he oversaw the appointment of the four men as elders and he obtained a site for a church to the west of the River Oich as early as July 1843. Not surprisingly Mr Lauder received a Call from over two hundred communicants and adherents to be their minister, but he declined, having accepted a Call to return to his native Argyll.

The following year Francis McBean was called by four hundred and ninety people to be the minister for Fort Augustus and Glenmoriston. Until his death in 1869 Mr McBean worked tirelessly for the congregation, raising money for the church and a manse. The church at Fort Augustus was finished quickly, although the manse, now Morag's Lodge hotel, was not completed until 1870. The first occupant of the Free Church manse was Alexander

McColl, who served from 1870 to 1877, whereupon Glenmoriston became a separate charge.   Thereafter Donald MacDonald ministered from 1878 to 1888, during which time the established Church of Scotland at last became a charge in its own right, some forty years after the Disruption.[182]

The following Free Church minister, John MacKay, was to play an important part in the evolution of presbyterianism in Fort Augustus. He accepted the Call in 1889 and oversaw an increasing membership which rose to more than two score by 1900. However, the plans for a union at national level between the Free Church and the United Presbyterians, who had no local presence, led to much debate in Highland Free Church circles.   The Free Church Presbytery of Abertarff voted 8:5 in favour of the Union in September 1900, Mr MacKay having seconded the motion in favour. Later that month, although the Fort Augustus Kirk Session expressed doubts about the proposal, both congregation and minister entered the Union. The doubts remained: by 1903 it was clear that two Elders and just over half the members had adhered to the continuing Free Church. This group, being debarred from using the Free Church for worship, met in the school on Bunoich Brae.[183]

It was 1906 before the Free Church regained its buildings, and it has been suggested "that the Free Church never really recovered from this period."[184] The immediate effect was that the Free Church congregations of Fort Augustus and Glenmoriston were once again linked together. Thereafter there were six inducted ministers who served until 1983. The last ministry, that of Rev John Fraser, commenced in 1965 with just five members in Glenmoriston and ten in Fort Augustus; during his ministry the Fort Augustus manse was sold and that in Glenmoriston was brought back into use. Following Mr Fraser's retirement the congregation was linked with Glenurquhart. The first minister of the new grouping was Rev Ian Allan: his history of the Free Church "West the Glen" is a valuable source of information.

The United Free Church

Whilst Rev John MacKay and the congregation of the new United Free Church got off to a good start using the Free Church and manse, the subsequent legal challenges resulted in the continuing Free Church repossessing their buildings following the 1904 judgement of the House of Lords. The United Free congregation then built their own church beside the canal, one of the distinctive "Tin Tabernacles" that were commissioned by the UF Church to meet the needs of their congregations across Scotland.[185] It was opened just before Christmas 1906. A new manse, now "The Dell" in Fort William Road, was built in 1909.

Following Mr MacKay's departure in 1907 there were five subsequent ministries. The last, that of Angus MacIntyre which commenced in 1929, coincided with the discussions between the Church of Scotland and the UF Church, which resulted in the Union of 1929. Because Mr MacIntyre had a status as an inducted minister, a second Church of Scotland congregation was created. The established church revived the name of Abertarff, whilst the UF Church took the name of the river at its back and was named Inveroich Church of Scotland. This duality persisted until Mr MacIntyre left in 1933, when a Union was effected and Abertarff Parish Church reverted to the name of Fort Augustus. As has been recounted, the UF Church became a church hall and was named after Rev John MacKay who had led his congregation out of the Free Church in 1900. Following the construction of a new hall adjacent to the church, the "Tin Tabernacle" was then sold and it became a retail outlet.

The Catholic Church

The New Statistical Account of 1831 records the presence of a Meeting House used for Catholic worship at the "farthest west" farmhouse, adjoining the Glengarry march. A map of 1796 shows a "Meeting House" at Aberchalder, in the vicinity of Newton, so this may have been set apart following the Catholic Relief Act (Scotland) in 1793.[186] A new chapel was erected there in 1820, holding up to 500 worshippers, with a door at one end for those from Fort Augustus and one at the other for those from Glengarry.[187] This building was replaced by St Peter's Church on Fort William Road in Fort Augustus in 1842.[188]

The small token garrison at the Fort was withdrawn in 1854, leaving only the barrack-master, Capt William Spalding and a couple of veterans as caretakers. Spalding died in 1860, and in 1867 the Fort was sold to Lord Lovat who in turn gifted the property and sixteen acres of land to the English Benedictine Order along with a farm, rent free for nineteen years.[189] What was described as "a college for the sons of Catholic gentlemen" was commenced at the Abbey in 1878 with just fifteen scholars. At that time the Abbey community comprised five priests, four juniors and three lay brothers. During the severe winters the boys enjoyed skating on the loch, but there were protests from the local protestant ministers when they were observed skating on the Sabbath. The practice was stopped for the sake of peace![190]

The Monastery was formally opened on 24 August 1880. The Scotsman reported on "the restoration of one of their most ancient and cherished orders in a land from which it had long before been to all intents thrown out." The report suggested that this was a good solution to the Fort's annual drain on the national military budget! J A Hansom, the noted architect, had been appointed to prepare plans to adapt the Fort to its new use. With accommodation for twenty monks, eighty school students and thirty guests in the Hospitium, and the former parade ground adapted to create cloisters, a church would follow when funds permitted. All this, wrote the correspondent, would complete "an edifice which will throw far into the shade the Established and Free churches which rear their plain and modest heads on either side." Commenting that the local Catholic congregation numbered up to three hundred "coming mostly from the outlying districts" it was reflected that this community had "suffered greatly in consequence of what is termed by the Church the oppression to which, it is alleged, they were subjected by the soldiery at Fort Augustus and elsewhere, and which determined many of them on emigrating."

Amongst the guests on this occasion were Mr and Mrs Rufford of Inchnacardoch, who had been generous benefactors of the Church of Scotland twenty years earlier.[191]

During the latter part of the century the local priest was Coll (Colin) MacDonald serving the area as far as Glenquioch: he "was no less popular with Protestants than among his own scattered flock." He resented the establishment of the Abbey and "had no love for the monks whom he saw as interlopers poaching ... in his special field of labour." There was a contrast between the priests who "were welcomed with joy in the glens ... and slept under the thatch with their people. Gentlemen with tonsures knew nothing of hard travel on mission and traditions going back to Columba."[192]

Following the death of Father Coll, St Peter's Church became a convent for first one and then a second religious order of nuns. Later it provided staff accommodation for the Abbey School and is now private accommodation known as the "Old Convent". A farmhouse at Markethill was adapted to serve as a hospital under the auspices of the Abbey in the 1880s, and after 1897 it served the railway contractors until 1904. The Abbey itself became a Voluntary Aid Detachment (VAD) hospital during the First World War, receiving first Belgian soldiers and then casualties from the Gordon Highlanders. Local fundraising helped to support this venture through the local branch of the Red Cross whose chair was Mrs Ellice of Invergarry.[193]

The construction of the Church for Fort Augustus Abbey commenced in 1953, and thus it became the place of worship for the Catholic community in the village; priests from the Abbey served the smaller places of worship at Invergarry and Glenmoriston. Following the closure of the Abbey School in 1993 and then the Abbey itself in 1998, the Gate Lodge was retained and converted into a place of worship, and a resident priest covered both Fort Augustus and Stratherrick. By that time the church building at Glenmoriston had been abandoned and that at Invergarry was served from St Margaret's in Roy Bridge. More recently the congregation at Fort Augustus has been served by priests from both Inverness and Beauly.

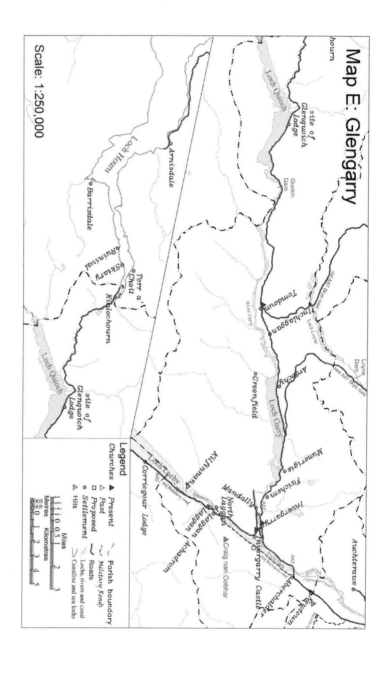

Map E: Glengarry

Scale: 1:250,000

Chapter 3:

GLENGARRY

*"There the Lord will be our Mighty One. It will be like
a place of broad rivers and streams"*
[Isaiah 33:21]

"Strong on the rock of faith" [1]

"The Lord is my rock, my fortress and my deliverer"
[Psalm 18:2]

Invergarry Castle is built upon Creagan an Fhitich, the Raven's
Rock, on the shore of Loch Oich. It was the stronghold of the
Macdonell's and the clan's war-cry. It was also a refuge of Catholic
missionaries and, later, a nursery of reformation influence. Across
the centuries it was destroyed and rebuilt and the gaunt ruin seen
today bears testimony to its strong foundations. The spiritual
foundations of the district, however, pre-date the castle because, as
elsewhere, local place names bear testimony to the activities of
various Celtic saints or their followers.

Kilfinnan may recall Finnan, from Iona, who became Bishop of
Lindisfarne in 651AD. Donan, whose name is given to Kildonan,

near Munerigie, lost his life on the Isle of Eigg in 617AD. Then Creagan Sagairt, the rock of the priest, at Faichem suggests an ancient preaching station. There is little doubt that there was a church at Kilfinnan until 1460 when it was destroyed by the Chief of Clanranald, although it is interesting to note that a map by Robert Gordon of circa 1640 shows a church at the northern head of Loch Lochy.[2] There MacDonnell's Mausoleum continued to be used, with "The Last Great Chief" Alastair Macdonell being interred in 1828.[3] Clearly the Kilfinnan area was considered to be a valid location for a church because in "1651 the Commission for the Plantation of Kirks decreed that there should be two kirks in Lochaber, Kilmallie and Kilmonivaig, with another at Laggan Achadrum to be served alternately with Kilmonivaig." This was at a time when both Kilmallie and Kilmonivaig were without ministers for a century following the Reformation. Perhaps because of this the third kirk was never created despite the unfulfilled proposal for a church beside Loch Oich, as will be related. It would be 1820 before the long-ruined church of Kilfinnan would be replaced by the small church at Laggan.[4]

There is less evidence for early churches elsewhere in the area. A legend about churches founded by Allan Cameron, the twelfth Chief of Clan Cameron, during the Fifteenth Century includes one at

Kildonan, but this may not refer to the Glengarry site.[5] It could have been a restoration of Donan's cell, but the site now lies below the expanded Loch Garry and today it is the small cemetery beside the main road that perpetuates the name of the Celtic saint. Invergarry Castle was clearly a safe place from which Catholic missionaries worked, and there may have been a small chapel within its walls. Local sources also suggest that Aldernaig may be derived from words suggesting a place of worship, and may refer to a chapel close to Craigard, below Creagan Sagairt.[6]

With important drove roads crossing Glengarry the area became a link between west and east, north and south: the name of Greenfield testifies to one of the transit grazing sites beside Loch Garry. Cattle were a valuable commodity, so it is not surprising that the predations of raiders both in the glen and from the glen continued well into the Seventeenth Century. It was not an easy territory for Christian outreach, and yet the spiritual need was all too clear.

"... the most important mission"

preach the word; be prepared in season and out of season"
[2 Timothy 4:1,2]

The progress of the Catholic Church in Glengarry has been reviewed earlier, with accounts of the priests who sustained a substantial flock during the years of "Underground Catholicism." Like the early Protestant missionary-ministers, the clergy shared the same poor conditions as the local population. It is reported that some priests lodged at Invergarry Castle, others lodged with their parishioners. The protection of the Chief of Glengarry ensured a degree of safety for the priests, although in 1677 it was reported by the Church Elders at Abertarff that "severalls of My Lord McDonalds familie doeth of late come to the ordinances" at Abertarff. Four years later Inverness Presbytery heard that a priest named Francis McDonald was resident in Glengarry.[7] As will be recounted later, the Chiefs of Glengarry had a varying Christian commitment.

In the years following the '45 "Glengarry was the most important mission in the Highland Vicariate" comprising fourteen hundred Catholics.[8] Bishop Hugh Macdonald, who had returned to the Highlands having accompanied the fugitive Prince to France, moved to Aberchalder in 1761 where he kept a low profile, dying there in 1773. He was buried at Kilfinnan, and although his resting place is now below the waters of Loch Lochy a memorial was placed nearby in 1900.[9]

Glengarry was not without a Catholic priest or a place of worship, no matter how inadequate: in 1832 the Rev Donald Macdonald reported that "at present the place of worship is a most miserable hovel, incapable of defending the people, when assembled, from the inclemency of the weather. It is in so ruinous a state that it can scarcely be used with safety. To this may be added, that the clergyman has no house of his own, and is under the necessity of living with such families as are willing and able to receive him."[10] In 1835 Bishop Scott wrote of the need for six chapels, including one at Glengarry: "In every one of these missions the walls have been built with dry stone, thatched with turf and heath. Part of the walls have fallen down and half of the roofs are blown away. There are now neither doors nor windows, and the roof being open, there is no possibility of getting a candle to burn ..."[11] Whether or not these two descriptions refer to the early chapels at Aberchalder, Kilfinnan or Munerigie cannot be determined. In 1848 it was reported that "though the Roman Catholic population be the most numerous class in [Glengarry], their nearest place of worship is at Fort Augustus – a distance of twelve miles from the greater number of them."[12] Blundell[13] tells of parishioners walking thirty miles from Glenquoich to Fort Augustus, leaving home at 4am!

It will be related that Lord Ward, who owned the Glengarry estate from 1840 to 1860, refused to give a site to either the Roman Catholics or the Free Church, and it was only later that a Catholic Church, Our Lady of Perpetual Succour, was erected at Mandally in 1891. This was extended in 1892 and then replaced in 1938 by the present St Finnan's chapel at the Mandally road end.[14] During the presence of the Abbey at Fort Augustus this congregation was served by priests from there, but after the Abbey's closure in 1998 St Finnan's came under the care of St Margaret's in Roy Bridge.

Given the progress of the Catholic Church "it was generally considered that Glengarry was untouched by the Reformation."[15] So in 1725 the newly-formed Synod of Glenelg, prompted by the Presbytery of Abertarff, wrote to the Laird of Glengarry to express to him "their confidence in him that he will evidence his zeal for the Protestant interest, particularly by countenancing and strengthening the hands of the missionaries to be sent to his bounds to carry on a Reformation."[16] In a review of the spiritual needs of the district in 1760 the Royal Bounty Committee recorded that the Minister of Kilmonivaig preached in five places including Auchadron, but that the minister had no church, manse, glebe or school in the parish. They recommended that Glengarry should be joined with Fort Augustus "for it lies very discontinuous from the rest of the parish of Kilmonivaig"[17], but this amalgamation was never enacted. There were, in fact, no missionaries directed exclusively to Glengarry prior to the creation of a "Mission District of Knoydart and Glengarry" in 1811, although as early as 1776 John M'Kilican was named as a Missionary-minister serving Boleskine, Urquhart and Kilmonivaig, the vast territory of into which Glengarry fell.

The Church that never was

"Like a dream ... no more to be found,
banished like a vision of the night"
[Job 20:8]

In 1784 Presbytery expressed their opinion to the Royal Bounty Committee that a "preaching house" should be sited on the south side of Loch Oich, "immediately opposite to Invergarry House".[18] This made some sense at the time, given that the Military Road ran on the east side of the loch, and the site was convenient to the settlements of Aberchalder and Laggan Achadrom to the north and south. Loch Oich was at its narrowest at this point so a ferry could give access to the glen to the west. The Presbytery was "assured that early next season a Preaching house will be erected, wherever they direct, and till then Glengarry offers one of his barns to accommodate the congregation." This signalled a significant change on the part of Duncan Macdonell, the fourteenth Chief of Glengarry, who had been warming to the Protestant cause for some years. Both his second son, Lewis, and his daughter Elizabeth were baptised by James Grant the missionary minister at Fort Augustus in1774 and 1775.[19] As early as 1776 the missionary, John M'Kilican, was conducting a service at Invergarry House[20], and in 1784 the Governor at Fort Augustus hinted that the missionary based there was spending too much time in Glengarry. At the same time Presbytery noted that Macdonell was "the first protestant Laird of his family … and he pays all due respect to the Protestant religion and her ministers."[21]   In May of 1785 two representatives of the Presbytery met for a site-visit with Glengarry himself: the site was chosen, agreed, and the Laird "positively engaged that it should be built forthwith; and that till it was ready Weir's house should be put in such order as to receive the minister and congregation."[22] Alas, the Laird did not fulfil his promise: he died in July 1788 and it is significant that Rev Patrick Grant, minister of Boleskine, officiated at his burial.[23]

Even before the death of the fourteenth Chief, the family and their lands had faced financial problems. The fifty years after 1782 saw major changes in Glengarry and there were successive clearances following the creation of sheep farms across the estate. Hundreds emigrated to Canada and elsewhere. Alistair Ranaldson Macdonell, who succeeded his father as the fifteenth Chief, was despised by Robert Burns "for his arrogance and his indifference to the true condition of the people", but he inherited his father's debts, and that fact drove the evictions.[24] Thomas Gillespie took out a lease for sheep in Glen Quioch in 1782, but "it was a typical beginning, the sheep grazier moving first into the upper reaches of the glens and then putting pressure on the lower reaches, which were appreciated for their shelter and arable land."[25] For whatever reason the preaching house never materialised, at least not beside Loch Oich. Right up to 1792 the Presbytery continued to enquire about progress, but to no avail.

As has been related, the first record of a Church of Scotland missionary labouring in Glengarry is that of John M'Kilican who had been appointed to cover Fort Augustus, Glenmoriston and Glengarry in 1776. He served this vast territory until 1785 when he accepted a call to Dores. His successor, John Macdonell covered the same territory, but in 1786 Presbytery was concerned that in

Glengarry he was "unable to pay that strict attention that is necessary to defeat the intemperate zeal of the Roman Catholic Clergy on account of his avocations in the other parts of his extensive mission." They agreed to appoint Thomas Campbell "to discharge the duties of a Minister of the Gospel within the bounds of Glengarry and the contiguous parts of Abertarph."[26] In 1789 there is the first reference to services being held at Glenquoich. Between 1760 and 1806 the Abertarff Register of Baptisms contains details of many children baptised in Glengarry. Apart from two members of the Laird's family there are records of the children of the incoming sheep-farmers in the upper part of the Glen and, intriguingly, the baptism of a child of "a blackman in Glengarry" in 1787. These entries bear testimony to the wide territorial ministry exercised by the missionary-ministers.[27]

As if in recognition of the demands of a vast mission district the Royal Bounty Committee created a new district of Glengarry and Locharkaig, but no appointment seems to have been made before 1806 when Alexander McIntosh was recruited, with his stipend coming from the Committee and the ministers of Kilmallie and Kilmonivaig.[28] McIntosh had no accommodation provided, despite the two parish ministers pleading with the Heritors over a few years, and he resigned in 1811. The Laird of Glengarry thereupon offered to provide accommodation so long as the mission was redesignated as Glengarry and Knoydart to serve his own property, something to which the Royal Bounty Committee agreed.[29] McIntosh moved to this new station and Macdonell assured Presbytery that the accommodation was ready. At the same time he told the Presbytery that he had provided quarters "for a Society Schoolmaster ... in the Village of Ball-Alasdair Laggan-Achendroume." McIntosh, however, had left under a cloud by the end of the year.[30]

Such were the demands of Glengarry and Knoydart that Presbytery sought to appoint a missionary in 1814, the candidate John Ross "having pledged himself to accept of one of the most laborious, extensive, and difficult missions in this church ... a district of above sixty miles intersected with dangerous rocks, rapid rivers and lofty mountains." They licensed Mr Ross "in consideration [of] the lamentable state of the extensive and populous Mission of Glengarry and Knoydart, with respect to religious instruction and their total privation of all the ordinances of religion, and finding that it is utterly impossible for the Ministers of the Parishes concerned in that District to pay the necessary attention on account of the vacancies in their bounds."[31] The Presbytery was censured for making an irregular appointment, and it was 1821 before another appointment was made to the western extremity of the district.

The eastern part of Glengarry, centred in the Great Glen, continued to be served by the missionary ministers at Fort Augustus, although John Macintyre, once tutor to the fifteenth Chief of Glengarry and later to become the minister of Kilmonivaig in 1828, had a special interest in the spiritual welfare of the area. In 1834 he created six Elders' Districts within his vast parish, two of them to serve Glengarry north and south of the river. Two men, Donald Macintyre of Laggan and Alexander Cameron of Drynachan were ordained as the Glengarry Elders.[32] The early years of the Nineteenth Century saw a succession of missionary ministers working in Glengarry, including William Lauder, who adhered to the Disruption in 1843. He was replaced by Patrick Grant, but John McIntyre the minister of Kilmonivaig stated that "the Gaelic which he speaks being somewhat different to that spoken in Glengarry, and from other considerations, he is resolved not to continue in the charge of the Mission, and that he accordingly resigns it henceforth."[33] When James MacNaughton was called to Dores in 1848 both Lord Ward and Edward Ellice, the new proprietors of the Glengarry lands, offered to contribute towards the raising of a missionary's allowance to £100pa.[34] This generosity, on Mr Ellice's part at least, signalled the moves towards the establishment of Glengarry as a parish in its own right.

Although the preaching house beside Loch Oich promised by the Laird of Glengarry in the 1780s never materialised, when Glengarry became a parish in 1867 the Presbytery noted that there had been a mission church in Glengarry "for around sixty years."[35]   The Kilmonivaig Kirk Session met at "the Church at Oldground of Glengarry" in 1838, described in the New Statistical Account as a "thatched cottage"; this perhaps locates the building to the west of the present church, but apart from a reference to a meeting "within the Church of Invergarry" in 1861 the details of this building remain elusive.[36] It must be recognised that Alasdair MacDonell eventually did build a church at Laggan where he planned a new village. He also set aside land for resettlement of his tenants at Balmaglaster and Mandally.[37]

Destitution and Development

"They will rebuild the ancient ruins and restore
the places long devastated"
[Isaiah 61:4]

Harvest failure in 1836 added to the destitution of those who had not emigrated, and the effects of the failure of the potato harvests in 1846 and 1847 lasted for some years. In 1841 the people of Glengarry were in a wretched condition, with one third of the population described as destitute.[38] Another report stated "the cotters and crofters are in an equally destitute condition. In one instance eleven cotters had been kept from starvation by the kindness of a large sheep-farmer." The Minister of Kilmallie, the adjoining parish, reported that "more than half of his parish … three thousand people were in need of urgent aid."[39] Such destitution became an impetus for further emigration, but most noteworthy was the clearance in Knoydart in October 1853, which was not only cruel in its execution, but also involved forcible removal of those who lost their homes to emigrant ships without their consent.[40]

Whilst Glengarry's population was vastly reduced by the clearances and emigration to Canada, it was wealth earned in North America that brought a revival in the fortunes of the Glen. In 1840 Edward "Bear" Ellice bought the estate of Glenquoich for £32,000, his family having made their fortune from the Hudson Bay Company and other ventures in America and Canada. In his role as a Member of Parliament he made "important contributions to the expansion and survival of the British Empire in North America."[41]

Once established in Glenquoich, Ellice was clearly alive to the social needs of the district. He sent blankets and food to the dispossessed, and using his political clout he challenged the effectiveness of the parochial relief system.[42]   His concerns contrasted with his neighbour, Lord Ward, later to become the Earl of Dudley, who had bought Glengarry in 1840.   When Ellice purchased the Glengarry Estate from Lord Ward in 1860 the Inverness Courier commented that: "This information will be received with much satisfaction in the glen; for though Lord Dudley was not unpopular, he did little in the way of improvement, regarding his Highland estate chiefly as a shooting-ground or place of temporary residence. Mr Ellice, on the other hand, has constantly had people at work, draining, trenching, planting, &c., and his liberal hospitality has every season brought crowds of visitors to the country. Mrs Ellice has been no less assiduous in attending to the wants of the poor, and providing means of education for the children."[43]

With the purchase of the Glengarry Estate the Ellice family embarked upon further improvements to the local community. Their principal mansion, completed in 1869 and now the Glengarry Castle Hotel, was built on the shores of Loch, along with sporting lodges at Aberchalder, Ardochy and Glen Quoich. Across the estate Ellice created a series of sheep farms, with well-built houses and steadings at Kinlochourn, Glen Quioch, Greenfield, Tomdoun,

Ardochy, Invergarry, Aberchalder and South Laggan.[44]   In Invergarry the family built estate houses, alms-houses, a school, a hospital[45], a laundry and a gasworks. Furthermore they built the small church at Tomdoun as well as the larger one in the village that would become the parish church in 1867. Their contribution to both church and community cannot be underestimated. It is reported that the Ellice family invested over a quarter of a million pounds in their property prior to 1892, and that Lord Burton, who tenanted Glenquoich, not much less.[46]

The evolution of the Glengarry Estate from extensive cattle-rearing, to sheep-farms, then to sporting estates and forestry is graphically represented in a series of maps within David Turnock's book. He charts this process thus: "Invergarry was certainly used for stalking by the Macdonnells even if it was not officially constituted as such until after it passed into the hands of Mr Ellice in 1860. Afforestation for letting begins in the 1870s with a successful sheep farmer in Glen Quoich giving up his lease in favour of a sporting tenant around 1874".[47]

"... the root of religious toleration"

"Remove the obstacles out of the way of my people"
[Isaiah 57:14]

The Disruption affected Glengarry inasmuch as its Missionary, William Lauder, was the only ordained minister in the area to adhere to the Free Church. Celebrated in a popular song written by the local schoolmaster, Mr Lauder's preaching "had substance and was wholesome."[48]   Lauder had been "a solid supporter of the Disruption"[49] and it fell to him to organise the new church for Fort Augustus and Glengarry.   As has been related, progress in Fort Augustus was swift, but after Mr Lauder accepted a Call to Argyll at the end of 1843 those adhering to the Free Church in Glengarry decided to disengage from Fort Augustus and to seek pastoral oversight from Kilmonivaig which was under the care of Rev. Dugald Shaw of Laggan in Badenoch. Shaw tried to get a site for a church in Glengarry but came up against the implacable opposition of the landowner, Lord Ward.

Shaw wrote twice to Lord Ward, and later sent Ward's reply to the second letter to the Inverness Courier. In its comment the newspaper admits that the "style of Mr Shaw's letters was impudent and arrogant, but Lord Ward's answer ... is still more indefensible,

for it strikes at the root of religious toleration. It is unbecoming a
British nobleman to bandy incivilities or disputes with a poor
Missionary. His concern should be with the people resident on his
property, and his lordship will seek in vain to improve their
condition or secure their regard, if he does not concede to them in
this matter of religious feeling.[50] The letter from Lord Ward to Mr
Shaw was printed in full:

"Rev. Sir, - I returned no answer to your first letter to me,
because it was not written, I conceive, in a respectful tone. You
now press for an answer, and I will give you one. As long as the
law of the land upholds the Established Church of Scotland I
shall countenance no other; nor will I do any thing for a body
whom I hold to be Dissenters, stirrers-up of strife, and most
unchristian in spirit. Do not suppose that this is an opinion
hastily formed. I was in Scotland when the question was first
raised, and was thoroughly instructed in its moaning and
tendency by a clergyman who has now seceded; but as I did not
adopt my views hastily, neither shall I be induced to alter them.
One word more, and I have done. You reside in this Glen by
sufferance on my part. If there was a clergyman of the
Established Church here to take care of my people, I should not

permit you to stay here to thwart his labours. There is none at present, and I prefer your teaching to the knowledge that there is no pastor in the Glen. You may forward this letter to the committee of the Free Church if you will, and express at the same time my determination to grant no site to the authors, aiders, and abettors of this movement on my property; and I am, Rev. Sir, your very obedient servant WARD, Glengarry, Oct. 9, 1847"

The laird's reply underlined some of the reasons that lead to the Disruption: his antipathy to the Free Church may have been influenced by his father-in-law, Sir Thomas Moncreiffe, of Perthshire, and his attachment to the established order was emphasised when the following week the local paper reported that Lord Ward had commenced an annual payment of £20 for "the erection of school accommodation for the General Assembly's teachers in Glengarry."[51] Later in his life he was to pay for extensive restoration work at Worcester Cathedral. Within the local community it is noted that Ward "resurrected the spirit of Alistair Ranaldson … he also introduced the flavour of squirearchy, organizing ploughing matches among those few tenants who remained between his sheep walks."[52] There followed correspondence both supporting and criticising Lord Ward's comments. The first, from "XYZ" stated that out of a local population of five hundred, just sixty-one adhered to the Free Church, but recognised that the Rev Mr Macintyre at Kilmonivaig "has not been able to furnish ministration and pastoral superintendence ... during the last four years; the whole duties of that large parish devolving on this one minister, where there used to be two missionaries ..." The correspondent concluded: "I do believe that the desire for a Free site is limited to a very small fraction of the population, and that the impulse is from without. We have, at length, through the Divine blessing, procured a worthy man to discharge the missionary duties in the glen, and that fact materially alters the state of matters."[53]

A week later another correspondent put this point of view:

"besides the members of the Free and Established Churches, there is also another class of religionists, viz., the Roman Catholics, who always formed, and still form, the majority of the whole population on Lord Ward's property. ... it is an undisputed fact ... that the Rev. Mr Chisholm, the Catholic clergyman, performed, during the year of 1847 alone, fifteen baptisms ... on Lord Ward's property; and, I have no doubt, that the Free Church missionary has performed more than one baptism."

The letter continued:

"on the last Sabbath-day, the 26th December, on which Mr Macintyre preached in Glengarry, the whole of his audience amounted to thirteen individuals, inclusive of all the schoolmasters and elders. Hence the state of matters is not as your correspondent tells you ..."

This letter reveals that the Catholic priest "has frequently made application for a site whereon to build a chapel" and concludes that "the great majority of this population on Lord Ward's property have as yet been unable to procure from the proprietor sites for churches."[54] Despite this publicity the laird held to his views, and consequently a Free Church was never built in Glengarry although, as will be related below, worship was conducted at Laggan.[55] When Lord Ward became the Earl of Dudley he sold his estate to Edward Ellice in 1860 and then there was a new policy towards both the Roman Catholic community and the Free Church which was later to establish a school at Laggan.[56]

"... the benefits of a fixed parochial charge"

"He is the one we proclaim, admonishing and teaching everyone with all wisdom, so that we may present everyone fully mature in Christ"
[Colossians 1:28] [57]

Much of Glengarry fell within the vast parishes of Kilmonivaig and Kilmallie and after 1811 it was served by missionary-ministers who were appointed to minister across areas greater than the parish. There was the place of worship in Invergarry, as well as the church at Laggan built in 1820. In 1818 the Presbytery heard that contact had been made "with the Lords of the Treasury urging the need for new churches in the Highlands not only on spiritual grounds but for the general well-being of the country." The costs were outlined as follows: "To build a church £800, a manse £800, to purchase a pasture glebe ... £1500, together with a stipend of £200 per annum, which stipend would partly come from the Royal Bounty." Glengarry was one of five new parishes envisaged within Abertarff Presbytery.[58]

The absence of progress, however, meant that the nature of the pastoral ministry within the area was somewhat patchy. With the creation of the Mission District of Glengarry in 1811 there were four missionaries serving before the appointment of William Lauder in

1840, and their sojourns were not lengthy. In 1854 we learn that the Fort Augustus missionary preached in Glengarry every fourth Sabbath, alternating between Invergarry and Glenquoich, whilst John McIntyre visited once a month.[59] McIntyre clearly had a deep concern for the Glengarry area, having been Tutor to Aeneas Macdonell, son of the last chief, at Invergarry House: he was presented by the Laird to the charge of Kilmonivaig in 1828.

After William Lauder's departure to the Free Church in 1843 there was a steady succession of missionaries serving Glengarry, their impermanence emphasising the need for a continuity of pastoral care. The initiative for the endowment of Glengarry, the first step towards the creation of a parish, came in 1848, although John McIntyre pointed out that the General Assembly's Endowment Committee had long set its sights on such a status for Glengarry.[60] However, the final push for parish status was to come from Edward Ellice in 1865. Following the death of his father in 1863, it fell to Edward (1810–1880) to continue the work of developing the Estate. This included the building of the mission church at Invergarry in 1864 on the site overlooking the Skye road. The architect was Alexander Ross, the noted Inverness architect who designed many Highland churches, most notably Inverness Cathedral. Ellice lobbied to have his Estate lands created as a parish, something achieved in 1867 by taking territory principally from Kilmonivaig, but with portions from the parishes of Boleskine, Glenelg, and Kilmallie.

In May 1865 John McIntyre brought a letter to Presbytery from George Malcolm, Factor to Edward Ellice, "intimating that it is the resolution of Mr Ellice to disjoin, endow, and erect into a Parish quoad omnia, said lands of Glengarry and Glenquoich ... and praying the Presbytery to give their sanction ..." Needless to say, Presbytery gave their wholehearted approval.[61] The family provided a large proportion of the stipend and provided a Seventeenth Century farmhouse, the present Glengarry Lodge, for the manse. Financial support also came from the Provincial Endowment Fund of the national Church. It was reported that the new church seated one-hundred and fifty, and that attendances were around sixty, double at Communions, all to serve a population of six hundred.[62]

The Missionary-Minister, Donald Cameron, was admitted as the first minister of Glengarry in August 1867. At the service:

"The Moderator [Mr Macintyre of Kilmonivaig, and once tutor to Aeneas Macdonell] preached in Gaelic from Matthew xxviii, 18-20, and Mr Cameron [the minister of Urquhart parish] in English, from Col. i, 28. The Moderator, after putting to him the usual questions to Mr Cameron, and receiving satisfactory answers, inducted him to the pastoral charge of the parish, and thereafter addressed him in an earnest and impressive manner as to his new position and duties. Mr Cameron, Urquhart, delivered a most suitable and affectionate address to the people … inculcating upon them their duty towards their pastor, now in a more exalted position through the Christian generosity of their landlord."63

The Presbytery minute of that occasion concluded with a note of gratitude to Mr Ellice:

"The Presbytery in bringing to a close the services of the day feel it at once a duty and a privilege to inscribe permanently on their records an expression of their high admiration of, and deep gratitude for, the Christian munificence of Edward Ellice Esquire, M.P., proprietor of the district, in endeavouring and erecting it into a Parish; to his great liberality the good work of conferring on the former Mission District all the benefits of a fixed parochial charge is principally due; and herein he has laid not merely the Presbytery, but the whole Church of Scotland under lasting obligation to him. The Presbytery hope that his excellent example may be the means of inducing others to whom God hath entrusted wealth to go and do likewise. They fervently pray that abundant Christian fruit may result from the ministry which he has instituted in this parish – that he may be long spared to witness these fruits in the improvement of the moral and religious condition of the people – that he may be continually enriched more and more with Godly spiritual blessing, and finally receive the reward of a faithful servant of Christ."[64]

Edward Ellice died in 1880, and his second wife, Eliza, carried on many of the local improvements. Hers was the vision to enlarge Glengarry Church built just thirty years earlier which was "inconveniently small for the requirements of the neighbourhood, especially in the summer when there is a considerable influx of strangers."[65] The project was completed in 1896. The annual influx of visitors included those who were guests at the various big houses and and shooting lodges. None were to prove more controversial than two particular visitors in 1871.

The Glengarry Affair

*"How good and pleasant it is when God's people
dwell together in unity!"
[Psalm 133:1]*

Glengarry Church made the newspaper headlines when, on 3 September 1871, the Rt Rev the Bishop of Winchester, Samuel Wilberforce, preached and conducted public worship in the Parish Church. A week later the Rt Rev Dr Thomson, Archbishop of York entered the pulpit: both services were reported to have been conducted "according to the forms of the Church of Scotland."[66] The Prelates were guests of the Ellice family at Invergarry House, autumn house parties being common at Highland estates. Reaction within the Episcopal Church in Scotland and the church south of the border was swift. Letters were written to all the principal newspapers and yards of column inches of comment filled their pages, as well as those of various denominational journals. The Inverness Courier endeavoured to collate and summarise them all. Some hailed the two events as a welcome indication of Christian unity, whilst others saw the two Prelates as slighting their sister Episcopal Church. Others again felt the Prelates were denying their own episcopal ordination vows, or were giving recognition to the ministry of the Presbyterians. The controversy rumbled on to the end of the year and then surfaced again in 1883 with a mixture of grievance and grace and not a little humour; thus was Glengarry firmly planted in the consciousness of the nation. Abstracts of the letters and reports are contained within Annex 3.

Since about 1860 there had been a "strong 'Anglicanizing' Movement" within the Scottish Episcopal Church with the aim of achieving a complete identification with the Church of England.[67] This had been emphasised in 1866 when Bishop Eden, by then Primus of the Episcopal Church, invited the Archbishop of Canterbury to lay the Foundation Stone of the new Cathedral in Inverness. At that time this event created some controversy since the Archbishop claimed that the Episcopal Church was the Church of England in Scotland, thus side-lining the Church of Scotland and its status as the Established Church north of the border. Such presumed empire-building on the part of Bishop Eden drew the ire of one who asked "why then, is Dr Eden so exceedingly anxious, as he ever shows himself, to sow divisions among the English Churchmen, resident or visitors, who prefer a Church openly protesting all Romish or Greek superstitions and errors, to a Church giving, to say the least, a very uncertain sound."[68]

Beyond the affairs of bishops and humble Christians there were other events in 1871 which were relevant to "the Glengarry Affair." In Europe the end of the Franco-Prussian War and the tumultuous events of the Paris Commune earlier in the year had raised fears of revolution. At home Parliament had enacted the disestablishment of the Church of Ireland and had introduced important trade union reforms: these too were seen as threatening the stability of church and social order. It was little wonder that the debate about the events at Glengarry were said to raise the spectre of atheism and communism!

It is against such background circumstances that the two English Prelates preached in Glengarry Church. According to the contemporary accounts both services comprised the singing of Scottish metrical psalms or paraphrases, prayers, Bible readings and a sermon. It is clear that both the Bishop and Archbishop used the scripture readings prescribed in the Church of England Prayer Book, and that their main prayers at least used words and phrases from the Liturgy. The parish minister was absent from the first service on 3 September since he was conducting worship at Glen Quoich Lodge, but he was present the following Sunday when the Archbishop of York conducted the service, at the close of which Mr Cameron baptised the son of the Estate Factor. The Archbishop returned the compliment on 17 September by sitting under Mr

Cameron's ministry. So it was that Glengarry became the arena in which several contests were staged, none of them having any real relevance to the Highland parish. It was as if concerns and controversies that belonged elsewhere had alighted at Invergarry to play out their contests: Mr Ellice was the unwitting promoter and Mr Cameron, the parish minister, the bemused spectator.

The "Glengarry Affair", as it came to be known, highlighted five areas of controversy current at the time. The appearance of two English Prelates almost on the doorstep of the Primus of the Scottish Episcopal Church generated the first area of concern. Following the Archbishop of Canterbury's declaration of full identification between the Church of England and the Scottish Episcopal Church in 1866 the fact that two senior English Prelates led worship in a Presbyterian church was seen to be something of a breach of trust. Bishop Eden had come from England to take the Bishop's Chair in Inverness in 1851, with a substantially smaller stipend but an ambitious zeal to encourage landowners and other well-wishers to build a Cathedral for the Diocese along with a number of new churches across the Highlands. During his tenure he quadrupled the income of the See, he enhanced the standing of the Scottish Episcopal Church, and became its Primus in 1862.[69] Described as "a learned Moderate High Churchman"[70] Bishop Eden worked hard to secure the status of his clergy vis-à-vis those of the Church of England: the recognition of his church by the Archbishop of Canterbury in 1866 served to emphasise the mutuality of the two churches. Events at Glengarry threatened to undermine Eden's ambitions.

Bishop Eden may have seen Samuel Wilberforce as a natural ally; they had been at Oxford University together, and the Bishop of Winchester was a fellow high-churchman, despite his evangelical upbringing as a son of William Wilberforce MP.[71] Previous to his appointment to Winchester, as Bishop of Oxford Wilberforce had been invited by Eden to be present at the opening service at Inverness Cathedral in 1869. His high church leanings notwithstanding, Wilberforce did retain a great respect for his low-church colleagues, and thereby gained the nickname of "Soapy Sam." He had been translated from Oxford to Winchester in 1869, and by taking the service at Glengarry he not only emphasised his own broad-mindedness, but also his independent spirit. The subsequent claim that the service he had conducted was, in fact, a "mission-service" adhering to Anglican forms was a belated attempt to reclaim a modicum of reconciliation between Winchester and Inverness. It is interesting to note that the service conducted by the Archbishop of York attracted less comment, perhaps because of his more senior status, and perhaps because Wilberforce had been the first to enter the Glengarry pulpit.

The second controversy settled around the differing churchmanship of the two Prelates. Whilst both Winchester and York were seen to be high-churchmen they had their differences: Wilberforce in Winchester was seen to be more broadminded, whilst Thomson was a stickler for ecclesiastical legislation within the Archdiocese of York.[72] Thus whilst Wilberforce's visit to Glengarry might be forgiven, Thomson was setting a bad example of apostasy. Thomson had disciplined his clergy for lesser shortcomings: how then could he now exercise discipline within his own realm of York? Wilberforce came from a much respected family with a strong Christian pedigree, but Thomson, the son of Scottish parents, came from an industrial background in Cumberland. The two Prelates represented different traditions, and their supporters and critics lined up to stress the divisions between them.

A third controversy focussed upon the debates about Church Establishment. Given the fact that the Irish Church Act, securing the disestablishment of the Anglican Church in Ireland, had come into force in 1871, the issue of further disestablishment in England and Scotland was a live topic: when two English prelates conducted services in a church of the Established Church of Scotland were they seen to be strengthening the case for the status-quo? If the two national Established churches were seen to be recognising each other's ministry such a case was reinforced. At the time there was much pressure from those lobbying for disestablishment.   In England the nonconformists were gaining ground and resented the privileges afforded to the Church of England. In Scotland there were moves towards a union between the Church of Scotland and the United Presbyterian Church, and disestablishment was likely to be a pre-condition.[73] Reunion with the Free Church, a more distant hope, would most certainly have depended upon disestablishment. The Glengarry services were therefore seen by both sides of the debate as indicative of the issues to be resolved.

The Glengarry services highlighted a fourth area of controversy, that of issues of church governance and styles of worship. Antipathy to bishops ran deep in the history of the Scottish Reformation, so should any bishop at all have occupied the Glengarry pulpit? There was much coverage in the press as to how the Prelates dressed on those Sundays, and whether Mr Cameron would be invited to take services in their own dioceses. Then, what was the nature of those services: were they Presbyterian, Anglican or Episcopalian? Much was made of the fact that an order of service had been laid out for the guests, but there was debate about the nature of the prayers and the degree to which they relied upon the Prayer Book form. The readings and the sermons had been guided by the Church of England Prayer Book Lectionary, but there were questions as to whether the sermon was read or extempore.

Bishop Eden, however, in a letter dated 16 September firmly claimed the service for the Episcopalians: "I was very much obliged to the Bishop of Winchester for thus affording to Mr Ellice's family and household, and many other Episcopalians in the neighbourhood, the opportunity of enjoying the services of our Church, which, for want of clergy, I cannot supply. The ordinary service of the Church was slightly abbreviated, and as the Bishop concluded his service with an extempore prayer, this probably gave rise to the statement that the services had been conducted according to the forms of the Established Church of Scotland."[74] Then the Bishop of Winchester claimed the service for the Anglicans: "I beg to explain to you that the service referred to was a mission service, there being no English service in the village that day, and many strangers and others. It had of course nothing to do with the orders, &c. of the Presbyterian body. The kirk, as a building, was offered for an English Bishop's service in it, and accepted readily by me. I believe that I did what St Paul did at the place where prayer was wont to be made. Nor can I conceive that such a mission service has any tendency to increase the difficulties of our beloved sister, the Church of Scotland. What I did met with the full approval of the Primus."[75] When referring to "our beloved sister", did the Bishop of Winchester mean the Church of Scotland, or was he referring to the Scottish Episcopal Church?

Those present at both services wrote to claim the service for the Presbyterians: "Besides the prayers and sermon, to which the Bishop of Moray, &c., confines his attention, the service in question included the singing of portions of three or four psalms in the Scottish metrical version, the reading of two portions of the Scriptures from the Old and New Testament respectively, and the pronouncing of the benediction; in short, with the slight difference that the first prayer – which was, however, not read, but spoken from memory – contained some portions of the Church of England form, the whole service was conducted, as was originally announced in your columns, strictly in conformity with the usual Presbyterian order."[76] Another correspondent tried to settle the dispute with this simple test: "Were the Psalms sung … the Scotch metrical version or the English version of Tate and Brady? If the former, the service, according to the facts admitted on both sides, squares substantially with the forms of the Establishment; if the latter, it may fairly be styled an Episcopalian Mission service."[77]

Finally, across the whole controversy there rang a note of optimism versus orthodoxy: were those two services harbingers of better relationships between the churches, or evidence of compromise or even apostasy? After all, it was argued, Queen Victoria worshipped at Crathie Kirk whilst at Balmoral, and many Anglicans, Edward Ellice included, were happy to worship within the Church of Scotland when sojourning north of the border. With such examples, why should the Prelates' presence at Glengarry draw any comment? Bishop Eden, whilst he "lived at peace with his ecclesiastical neighbours" he nonetheless "would not commend that easy intercourse in which some Episcopalians delighted, whereby those who, in England, would not enter a Presbyterian church did, when they came to Scotland, worshipped in the parish kirk. The Faithful Remnant must remain faithful and defend the truth …"[78] Eden's neighbour, Alexander Ewing, Bishop of Argyll and the Isles, however, approved of the events at Glengarry: in a letter to the Archbishop of York he said: "your Grace's officiating in the Parish Church of Glengarry gave me well-founded pleasure; for I looked upon it as a step towards that great goal to which I hope all Churches alike are tending, where the distinctions of their various ministries shall be lost and swallowed up in the common objects for which they exist."[79] He had elsewhere written of "the scandal of refusing to join in common worship with fellow Christians."[80]

Throughout the autumn months of 1871 the debate rumbled on, occupying acres of column inches in the local, national and religious press, highlighting each of these five areas of controversy. That, however, was not the end of the affair. The publication in 1882 of the third volume of a biography of Bishop Samuel Wilberforce included reference to the events at Glengarry along with some associated correspondence giving the Bishop's account thereof.[81] The volume generated various comments in the press. Dr Archibald Clerk, the minister at Kilmallie, wrote to The Times to restate the facts as understood by the Presbytery of Abertarff, and this drew a riposte from Rev J Brodie Innes who had moved the resolution at the Episcopal Diocesan Synod in Inverness shortly after the Prelates' visits to Glengarry.[82] The Glengarry Affair took some time to reach a conclusion! Its lasting legacy may be seen in the range of denominational backgrounds represented within the local congregations in the Great Glen today and the good relationships which exist between all the churches.

"... living stones"

> *"... you also, like living stones,*
> *are being built into a spiritual house"*
> *[1 Peter 2:5]*

When Edward Ellice died in 1880 the Presbytery sent a Memorial to his widow recalling that "in his consistent deportment, his regular attendance with his people on the parish church and his liberal contributions towards every Christian scheme – he furnished a powerful incentive to Christian living. Mr Ellice has thus left behind him a bright and illustrious example of the great good a Christian and enlightened landlord may do – an example which, if generally followed, would speedily unite the bonds of mutual good-will ... and go far towards permanently securing the safety and prosperity of the land."[83] His widow, Eliza, continued her husband's policies towards the Estate and the parish church: she enhanced the finances of the church and announced her plans to extend it, as has been mentioned above.[84] The Presbytery noted her "large-hearted generosity displayed in these gifts which are only fresh instances of a long and loyal devotion to the good of the Church."

On 20 September 1896 the extension to the parish church was dedicated. It comprised the transepts, chancel, tower and vestry,

with the granite pulpit, a heating system and new pews. An organ
was installed at the same time powered, initially, by a hydraulic
system fed from a nearby burn. This increased the seating of the
church to one hundred and sixty: there were fifty-three
communicant members in 1891. The work cost £2000, "entirely
defrayed by Mrs Ellice." The service of dedication was conducted
by the minister, John Macgilchrist, and the preacher was Rev Dr
Cameron Lees of St Giles Cathedral, Edinburgh. According to the
Inverness Courier Dr Lees had "been the guest of Mrs Ellice during
the past month, conducting the services in the Schoolroom."
Indeed, this was a close friendship for Dr Lees was to dedicate his
"History of the County of Inverness", published in 1897, to Mrs
Ellice. Following a prayer of dedication, Dr Lees preached on the
parable of the widow's mite, and concluded with an earnest wish
and prayer:

"that this house may ever be the house of God and the gate of
heaven to many souls; that this place may be a source of spiritual
influence in the district where it stands; that here the pure gospel
of Jesus Christ may be preached in charity and in love; that here
as the generations go on, a succession of good men and holy men
may stand to declare the whole counsel of God; that here sinful

men may be awakened to the beauty of eternal life in Christ; and that here the sorrowful may find rest and the afflicted comfort."

He concluded with the hope that all would see the quality of the lives of Christians, rather than that of the building itself:

"see what manner of men and women are here, living stones fashioned after the similitude of Christ."[85]

Referring later to the creation of Glengarry Parish the Third Statistical Account notes that:

"By this happy measure a large, intelligent and active congregation were brought together, and entered upon separate parochial work, which they have since, with every increasing posterity, carried on, contributing also to every scheme and mission of the church."[86]

The Baptismal Register charts the changing social structure of the parish over the last century and a half. In the 1870s the occupations of the fathers recorded therein were largely connected to the local estates – shepherds, gamekeepers, foresters and farm workers, along with those of teachers, policemen and the Estate Factor. The recorded places of residence stretched well into the remote arms of

Glengarry, Glen Quoich and Glen Loyne. Signs of change followed the construction of the Fort Augustus railway, with the baptism of children of railwaymen and a "hut-keeper" for the navvies. Then in 1916 the child of a chauffeur betokened the dawn of the age of motorised transport. The 1920s and 30s saw the growth of occupations connected with the Forestry Commission's activities.

Mrs Eliza Ellice, widow of Edward who had died in 1880, continued the beneficence of the family and she was actively involved in local affairs, serving on the School Board from 1888 until 1903. Upon her death in 1910 Sir David Hunter-Blair, later to become Abbot at Fort Augustus Abbey, was able to testify that the "Highland Catholics resident on her estate … had always found in her a most friendly, kind, and considerate neighbour."[87]

The Great War brought its sadness to Glengarry as to most Highland communities. Twenty-two men lost their lives, including three of the Ellice family: they are commemorated at a unique War Memorial opposite the old bridge across the River Garry.[88] Family fortunes declined and Invergarry House was sold in 1923: the Ellice's heirs moved to Aberchalder Lodge where they still reside. The family's munificence continued, however, for in 1947 the Manse was gifted to the Church of Scotland.

Glengarry Church [89]

There was a little hill where long ago
the birches spread their springtime green
Then drew a golden cloak around when autumn came,
and there a woman dreamed a daytime dream

The willing workers came, their masons dressed the granite blocks
And carved the warm brown sandstone holding a towering spire that lifted
hearts and minds to higher spheres

Out to the singing birds and whispering leaves an organ rolled its many
coloured tones
Leading the voices on in hymns of thanks for Beauty, Life and Love

The generations came and passed away, sharing in fellowship their griefs
and joys
Until beneath the heavy load of years the organ faltered as it led the praise

Strong on the rock of faith, help flooded in from all around and far across
the seas
And now once more the aged rafters ring the echo of a woman's daytime
dream

Alistair Grant

After World War II Glengarry was transformed by the Garry-Moriston hydro-scheme which, within the parish bounds, required the damming of Loch Quoich and the flooding of various cottages and two lodges; the damming of Loch Garry, thereby doubling its length; the creation of two power stations in Glen Quoich and at Invergarry; and the building of what was then the largest salmon hatchery in Europe just west of Invergarry. There were camps for the labour-force at Inshlaggan and Invergarry.[90] The creation of a tunnel from Glengarry dam to Invergarry power station had the unexpected effect of robbing the Manse of its water supply: the Hydro Board installed an electric pump to maintain the supply![91]

The temporary influx of workers did little to arrest the continuing population decline, and thus it was inevitable that the independence of Glengarry parish should have been questioned. Over its one hundred years as a Parish Church, Glengarry was served by eighteen ministers, two of them destined to become Moderators of the General Assembly; Norman MacLean in 1927 whilst minister at St Cuthbert's, Edinburgh, and Alexander MacDonald in 1948 whilst minister at St Columba's, Glasgow. With the demission of John Dale in 1967 the Presbytery of Lochaber considered readjustment. From April 1968 Glengarry joined Kilmallie under a "Special Area of Readjustment" which lasted until 1974 and two Associate ministers served during this time. Thereafter Glengarry was linked with Kilmonivaig for thirteen years under the ministry of Grahame Henderson, the manse at Glengarry having been sold. Further adjustment followed in 1987 when Glengarry was linked to Fort Augustus, a happy association which has now lasted for over thirty years.

A Family Memorial

"… like a tree planted by the water that sends out its roots"
[Jeremiah 17:8]

In 1820 Col Alistair Macdonell of Glengarry built the church at Laggan at the time that the Caledonian Canal was under construction nearby. This would have followed the raising of the water level of Loch Lochy which obliterated any remains of Kil Finnan, the ancient church of the district. Macdonell had plans to create a new settlement named Balalister beside the Canal, and he reports that he had built and endowed a Chapel "for the accommodation of the people and the convenience of the neighbourhood."[92] It seems that this building was also built as a memorial to the Chief's six sons lost in infancy, since it contained a large plaque recording their deaths between 1804 and 1818.[93]

Initially, at least, it appears that the building was dedicated as an Episcopal Church because the family adhered to that denomination. It is clear that Macdonell had "a somewhat relaxed attitude to denominational matters – an Episcopalian at Oxford and a Presbyterian in the Highlands – at least until around 1809 when the evidence for his Episcopal connection seems good."[94] However, Macdonell's son, Aeneas, was baptised by a Presbyterian minister in 1808, and was educated by tutors amongst whom was John MacIntyre, then a Church of Scotland divinity student.[95] MacIntyre was later nominated by MacDonnell, as heritor, to the Parish of Kilmonivaig in 1822, but this was contested by Commissioners for the Duke of Gordon, with the consequence that MacIntyre was not ordained and admitted to the charge until 1828. In the meantime he served as Missionary at Fort Augustus[96], marrying the daughter of Thomas Clark, a farmer at Auchterawe and an Elder at the Abertarff church, in 1826. In passing, it is worth noting that it was such control of ministerial appointments by heritors that was just one factor that lead to the Disruption of 1843.

The church at Laggan could have been served only very occasionally by Episcopal clergy. In 1824 there were just eight Episcopalians in the vast parish of Kilmonivaig and since, as has been related, the Chief's son had an aspiring Presbyterian minister as a tutor and his daughter had a Presbyterian governess it is not surprising that the family was open to many religious influences.[97] In 1842 John MacIntyre, by then the minister of Kilmonivaig, reported that there were only two Episcopalian families within the whole of the parish.[98] Laggan Church both mirrored the family's open-mindedness and anticipated the inter-denominational co-operation of later years.

Following the death of the Chief in 1828 and the sale of the Estate it has been suggested that Laggan Church was unused until 1843 when the Free Church took it over.[99] However, the Church of Scotland's Kilmonivaig Kirk Session certainly met there between 1837 and 1862[100], and given the hostility of Lord Ward to the Free Church after he took the Estate over in 1840, it is unlikely that Laggan Church was available to the new denomination. It is more probable that James MacIntyre, described as "missionary at Laggan, Loch Lochy" in 1839, may well have used the church as his base, along with successive missionaries. The picture, though, is not entirely clear, for it is recorded that in 1847 the Free Church minister of Kilmallie preached there on a Sunday morning, at Gairlochy in the afternoon, and at Laggan "where he took an evening service in an abandoned episcopal church." There he stayed the night, walking the twenty-one miles back to his home in the morning.[101] It is also reported that prior to 1860, when a church was opened at Gairlochy, the congregation often met in the open air.[102]

Once the Ellices took over the estate the Free Church held regular services at Laggan until the beginning of the Twentieth Century. A plaque above the door of Laggan Church suggests that the building was renovated by Eliza Ellice in 1887. Later it was used by both the Church of Scotland and the Free Church until 1970 when the Church of Scotland Presbytery of Lochaber stated that it had fallen into disuse. The Free Church, though, seems to have used the building thereafter, with services being held between 1990 and 1996. The building, which had come into the guardianship of the Forestry Commission when South Laggan Farm was taken over, has since been sold, and the memorial plaque relating to the Macdonell family has been removed to the Clan MacDonald Centre at Armadale in Skye.[103]

"… deprived of the benefits of civilisation"

"Do not be afraid, for I am with you:
I will … gather you from the west" [Isaiah 43:5]

There is no doubt that the western extremity of Glengarry Parish is isolated and remote. The essayist Richard Cobden, who visited the area in 1862, called it a "dreary glen, without a neighbour, or even the primitive resources of butcher, baker, grocer or tailor ... deprived of the benefits of civilization ..."[104] Even today it is a lonely district threaded by a road which has been called the longest cul-de-sac in Scotland! It is commendable that the Royal Bounty Committee administering the appointment of missionaries within the Church of Scotland had appointed someone to serve both in Glengarry and the adjoining Locharkaig area in 1811. The Committee insisted that the landowners provided suitable accommodation, and without that: "the consequence to the religious interest of the population of an extensive district within the bounds would be fatal."[105] Col MacDonell of Glengarry proposed that he would provide a house if a missionary were to be appointed to Knoydart and Glengarry, thereby serving his own Estate. Within a year this new mission was established, described as "one of the most laborious, extensive, and difficult missions in this Church – a district of above 60 miles."[106] The population was scattered: the Glengarry Baptismal Register bears witness to shepherds and gamekeepers living in very remote places amongst the hills, and so pastoral work was intermittent. It is reported that "in the nineteenth century a boy of five or six at Kinloch Hourn was to have been baptised. He did not know what baptism involved, but ... as the minister's boat drew in to the shore the boy took to the hills."[107]

The Ellice family were noted for their hospitality. Edward Ellice, who purchased Glenquoich in 1840 "entertained all his old friends, though his house was then small and the facilities for travel none too good. Here every season wearied politicians, keen sportsmen, artists and literary men came to visit their old counsellor, to stalk, to shoot, to fish, and, when wearied of the sport, to discuss and mature plans for the welfare of their fellow-men...Glenquioch played no mean part in the history of the Empire."[108] It has been said of Edward Ellice, who died in 1863, that "At his highland estates of Glengarry and Glenquoich he exercised famous hospitality to a great number (over 1000 in one season) and variety of guests." The same generosity continued when the estates passed to his son, also Edward, who died in 1880.[109] Amongst the guests over many years was the painter, Sir Edward Landseer, whose famous "Monarch of the Glen" painted in 1851 is supposed to have been inspired by the scenery of the Glenquoich Estate.[110] In 1873 Michael Arthur Bass, of the brewing dynasty, took the lease of Glenquoich and later engaged Alexander Ross, the architect, to extend and improve the Lodge. At the same time new roads and bridges were built, and over one-hundred miles of pony-paths engineered and constructed.[111] Mr Bass was knighted in 1882 and was ennobled as Lord Burton in

1886: he held the lease of Glenquoich until 1905, and during those years he entertained many illustrious persons including King Edward VII in 1904 and 1905, when two-hundred stalkers and gamekeepers came from a wide area to assist.

Papers held by the Glengarry Heritage Centre reveal that there were missionaries working in the area before 1873, and the Ellice Estate provided accommodation and fuel, free of charge, at the Lodge at Kinloch Hourn for six summer months each year: services were held at Glenquoich, probably at the Lodge, every second Sunday. In 1881, the then Mr Bass started renovations at the Lodge which precluded use by the missionary. Prior to the 1882 season a correspondence commenced between George Malcolm, the Estate Factor, and others, regarding the location of a missionary in the area. In letters over a twelve month period to Mr Bass, the Rev Norman MacLeod, the Secretary of the SSPCK, and the landowner of the Glenelg Estate, it becomes clear that the district had been ill-served by missionaries in the past. Mr Malcolm and his employer had a poor opinion of the work undertaken by these men and had proposed terminating such appointments. Writing to Mr Bass in April 1882 he recognises that the people in the area "seem sincerely sorry that they are not to have the services of a missionary", but he expresses concern about "a missionary stationed at Loch Hourn or

Glenquoich spending his time in reading, smoking and sleeping." He enclosed a letter from the minister of Glenelg who suggests sending a Colporteur, a lay person engaged to distribute Christian literature and to hold cottage meetings. "If such a labourer really penetrated to every cottage [this] would open a way out of the missionary difficulty."[112]

Four days later a letter to Rev Norman MacLeod, later to be Minister of the Old High Church in Inverness and clearly influential within the SSPCK, Mr Malcolm stated: "I trust the Director of your Society will see that if a missionary is hereafter to be stationed in the Loch Hourn and Glenquoich district, he shall stick to it and not leave home except for reasons of unavoidable necessity. I trust that he will not limit his missionary labour to preaching merely, with more or less regularity on Sundays. In all districts as this there are always a certain number of people who cannot leave their families to walk a number of miles across the hills to church – who cannot be reached or receive any benefit from the missionary except by house to house visits. To all who know these districts and live within them the pressing importance of this is well known."[113]

In May Mr Malcolm informed Mr Bass that a missionary had arrived "in spite of us and although his appearance this year received no encouragement from Mr Sinton our Minister, he now lives at

Skiary and now at Tomdoun and has not preached at Glenquioch."
Later he told the now Sir Arthur that the "Edinburgh Church people
are most persistent about the missionary's accommodation." Mr
Malcolm suggested creating a building between Loch Hournhead
and Loch Quoich to accommodate both a school and a place of
worship. "I think Mrs Ellice might contribute to this, if it met your
approval." In December the SSPCK had been pressing the Factor
about accommodation at Loch Hourn, which was not forthcoming,
though in reply Mr Malcolm referred to the idea of new premises, if
suitable funding was forthcoming, especially from the Society.[114]

The small church at Tomdoun predates these concerns. It was
built in 1865 as a single meeting room[115] but was extended in 1883:
it is perhaps significant that the extension might have been designed
to accommodate a single missionary, although it is not known if it
was ever used as such. However, in April 1883 Mr Malcolm again
wrote to Sir Arthur with some cautionary advice: "A Missionary
goes up tomorrow. I believe he is to lodge at Glenquioch at first
and move to another district afterwards. I think he goes to Grant's
first. I don't know what you will say to that but if he does not live
there when you come down – which can easily be arranged – I would
advise your not making any great objection as the people are all for
the missionary." The letter ended with an insight into the religious

arrangements for the summer season at Highland lodges, as Mr Malcolm states that "Mr Sinton, our Minister, tells me that he hopes to get a Minister of standing, a good preacher from Edinburgh or Glasgow to come to the district for August and September and that he, and not the Missionary, would go to Glenquioch then to preach."[116]

By contrast, Mr Malcolm's letter to the SSPCK in December 1882 addressed a very different social and spiritual concern. He drew attention to the herring fleet which visited Loch Hourn in force: "I think it is of much importance that an earnest, active and fully competent minister of our church should be sent to labour amongst the many thousand of fishermen, who every season (unless when the fishing fails), are located [there] during the summer and autumn months. Hitherto all the churches have, I think, been much to blame in neglecting this obvious duty not to say golden opportunity." He continues "that if good work – and not positive harm – is to be done, a really able, well-educated preacher must be sent and not a raw, conceited boy, who has not yet learnt his own feebleness."[117]   Strong words, but a timely reminder of the Christian's call to outreach!   There was good reason for such concern.   It is recorded that such was the size of the herring fleet in 1882 that the catch in Loch Hourn amounted to 90,000 crans, about sixty million fish! Furthermore, in 1891 there was a local population of fifty-four living around the head of the Loch.[118]

Concern for ministry in the area cannot have diminished, for in 1897 Presbytery commented on a General Assembly report that "as to Glenquoich, an effort is being made to put the Mission on a better footing by securing the services of a Missionary for the greater part of the year; and the Presbytery are of the opinion that deputies [*i.e. divinity students*] are not required." Again in 1899 the Home Mission Committee of the General Assembly recommended that there should be a Mission Hall at Glenquoich along with "Better provision for services at Loch Hournhead – A Licenciate is to be appointed for the whole year." The latter may have happened, but the former never materialised.[119] Indeed, in 1904 the Home Mission Committee suggested that Lochournhead should be served by the Arnisdale missionary from Glenelg Parish, with the Glenquoich missionary conducting services alternately at Glenquoich and Tomdoun.[120] There is no record of these appointments because they were typically divinity students employed from May to September.[121] By 1920 it was reported that in addition to the Sunday service at Invergarry Church there was an afternoon service at each of the four mission stations, presumably Laggan, Tomdoun, Glen Quioch and Kinlochhourn; Sunday Schools were being held at

Invergarry, Tomdoun and Glen Quoich.[122]

Whilst earlier missionaries had served Knoydart as part of their duties in Glengarry, the parish created in 1867 did not encompass Barrisdale: it is a sign of continuing depopulation on the west coast that the mission house in that lonely place was closed in 1934. Meanwhile, Loch Hourn was still served by the missionary at Arnisdale, at least prior to the Second World War.[123] A resident at Loch Hourn recalls that church services were held there every two to four weeks, the missionary arriving by boat. Around thirty would be present, worship being conducted in the schoolroom, later the hay loft, at Kinlochhourn Farm. "The folk would come from all around … from the Glen Quoich Estate houses, the staff in the three neighbouring Lodges and from Skiary, Runival and Torr a'choit."[124] It is not known when the last services were held at Kinlochhourn.

The centenary of the extension to Tomdoun Church was marked by a Songs of Praise service in 1983. More recently the building has been enhanced by improved access, thorough maintenance and the installation of a wood-burning stove. The Church continues to serve the upper Glengarry area with a monthly service at Tomdoun known locally as The Glengarry Gathering.

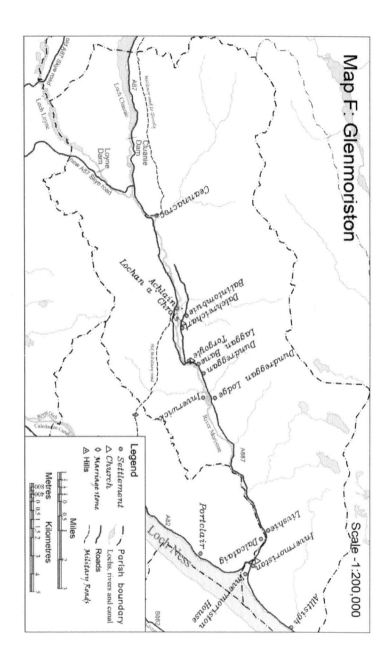

Chapter 4:

GLENMORISTON

"… a land of mountains and valleys that drinks rain from heaven.
It is a land the Lord your God cares for …"
[Deuteronomy 11:11]

"ane litle parish Church"

"… you have little strength, yet you have kept my word
and have not denied my name"
[Revelation 3:8]

There is a tradition that during the Fifth Century Erchard, a disciple of Ninian, "was the first who preached the gospel in Glenmoriston, and to him the ancient church of that glen – Clachan Mhercheird – was dedicated." The saint's name is recorded in various ways including Erchard, M'Erchard, Irchard and the English equivalent of Richard. It is told that Erchard and two companions found three bells in Strathglass and, taking one each, they travelled in different directions until each bell rang three times of its own accord. This led to the founding of churches in Broadford in Skye, Glen Convinth in Kiltarlity, and in Glen Moriston at Balintombuie. This last bell was preserved at the graveyard at Balintombuie until it went missing in the mid-Nineteenth Century.[1] By all accounts Erchard was a good preacher and much loved by the local population. Indeed it has been suggested that the name of the "patron Saint of the Glen" may be preserved both in the name of the glen and in "Invermorchen" as Invermoriston was described in 1345.[2]

The graveyard at Balintombuie is dedicated to St Merchard, but it was probably not the site of the church. There is some evidence that the church may well have been a short distance to the east, located on an island within Lochan-a'Chrois, "the loch of the cross", which is now largely drained and afforested. In the 1880s it was reported that "the only vestige …is a stone rudely hollowed into the form of a basin, which was at one time probably used as a Holy Water Font at the Chapel door."[3]

Mackay describes this place of worship as "The Abbey", having the function of a sanctuary, its "Kirklands" extending over a wide area, the bounds marked by stone crosses.[4] The label of "Abbey" does not denote a religious house of mediaeval proportions, but suggests that it was a significant centre of early Christian mission. This may be the church referred to in an early Seventeenth Century account which states that within Glenmoriston "there is ane litle parish Church of timber in this country called Millergheard."[5]

Timber buildings leave little evidence of their presence, so there are no tangible remains of the church on this site.

At Invermoriston the remains of another church may be detected in the kirkyard, known as Clachan Cholumchille, below the main road east of the road junction. Nearby the St Columba Well is another reminder of the travels of Columba or the Iona evangelists who carried on his ministry. At first these Christian centres were not so much places of worship, but hubs from which hermits shared the gospel in word and deed with the surrounding population.[6] "The old Celtic cells …continued till the Reformation to be used as chapels for prayer and devotion", their environs became burial grounds, and the "kirklands" in Glenmoriston were recognised as late as 1574. In that year the Register of Assignations for the Ministers' Stipends tells that the stipend of the "Reidar at Glenmoreistown" was to be paid "wt the Kirklands, to be payit out of the chancellarie of Murray be the takkismen or parochinaris of Glenmoreistown, or be the chanellare, as the reidare sall choose."[7] From this we discover that there was a "reader" in the glen holding a clerical office at the behest of the Diocese of Moray 550 years ago!

Whilst offering a route to the west coast, the long sinuous glen always had a scattered population and a focused parish ministry was never straightforward. Prior to the Seventeenth Century the nature

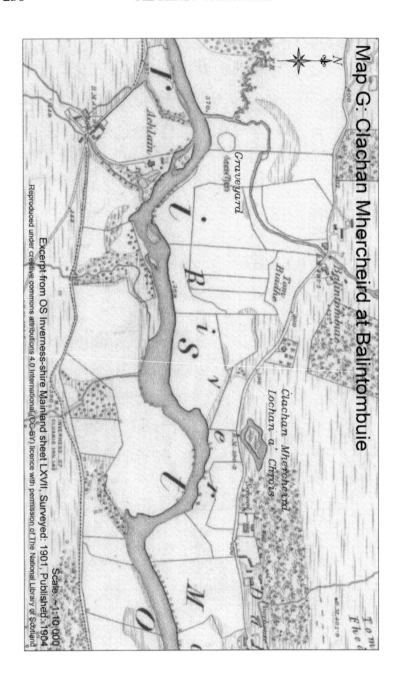

Map G: Clachan Mhercheird at Balintombuie

of this ministry cannot be determined, but although the glen "had its chapels and its clergy during the periods of the Celtic and Roman Catholic Churches, [it] was in a state of ecclesiastical desolation for many years after the Reformation. It had no clergymen of its own, and the parish minister only paid it an occasional visit."[8]

The parish of Glenmoriston was united with Glenurquhart around 1600[9], and in 1624 the minister, Rev Alexander Grant, was "ordained to proceed in building of his kirks off Urquhart and Glenmoristoun". Interestingly, in 1626 he was called before the Synod to be "rebuked for malpractice concerning a wedding" and was "called to make public repentance at Glenmoriston Kirk." The location and condition of this kirk can only be guessed, because three years later a Presbytery visitation ordered him "to forder the building of ye old foundations of ye Kirks of Urquhart and Glenmoriston." However, it is recorded that the Glenmoriston fabric "fell into utter ruin before the end of the century."[10] The Kirk that was to be rebuilt may have been the timber building at Dalchriechart, mentioned earlier, or it may have been at Clachan Cholumchille at Invermoriston.

The local economy, however, was reported at this time to be very healthy: "it is a verie profitable and fertill little glen, or countrie both plenteous of corne and abundance of butter cheese and milk and great and long woods of firr trees doeth grow in that countrey and the river doeth transport big Jests and Cutts of timber to the fresh water Loghnes."[11] Part of the problem in providing suitable church buildings was due to the fact that ancient church lands had been appropriated by the lairds, meaning there was no glebe or income for building churches or manses. Little wonder that the clergy became disheartened: Mr Grant's successor, Duncan Macculloch, was reported in 1651 as being "verie negligent of his charge." He was deposed in 1658 and restored in 1664, but again the parish was said to be in a "sad and lamentable state." Another Presbytery visitation noted his lack of parish visiting, his failure to pray in the houses, to catechise, and to celebrate the sacrament "ever since his entrie to ye ministrie there."[12] He demitted in 1671.

James Grant was admitted as Minister of Urquhart in May 1673, but the vastness of the parish, and the difficulties of travel were no less. Glenmoriston and its people "were left in a state of spiritual starvation: there was no priest or parson in their own glen, and the visits of the minister of the Parish were few and far between. The adjoining district of Abertarff ... was in the same precarious state of dependence upon the minister of Boleskine. In 1675 an attempt was made to provide those desolate places with the means of grace." In the days before the Revolution Settlement of 1690 which restored

Presbyterian government, the ministers of Boleskine and Urquhart petitioned the Bishop of Moray to have "Mr Robert Monro settled as minister and their helper in the said bounds of Abertarfe and Glenmoriston."[13]

In the spring of 1676 Robert Monro was introduced at Kilchuimen to the charge of Abertarff and Glenmoriston, an association which lasted until 1688. This new and innovative ministry had mixed fortunes. At the Presbytery visitation to Abertarff on 25 September 1677 it appears that there were five Elders in Glenmoriston, one in "Inver", and the others in the middle part of the glen – two in Livishie and two at "Invervuick". However, during the visitation the Elders of Glenmoriston expressed the opinion that they regretted that their minister "did not keepe with them every Sabbath *per vices*", on alternate Sundays. The reason became clear later in the minute when, it was recorded, the minister "regrated that there was not a boat to transport him to his charge upon the water of Glenmoristonne. Mr James Fraser and Master Hugh Fraser promised to speak to the Laird of Glenmoristonne for the s'd boat, as also anent the most commodious place qr the sermon may be heard each Lords day."[14] Clearly Mr Monro was expected to conduct a service in Glenmoriston every second Sunday, but the church building, wherever it was, was inadequate.

Despite the five Elders, it is reported that Mr Monro "was but poorly supported in his work ... and his success was not great, among either Catholics or Protestants. His income was insufficient to keep body and soul together, and, notwithstanding that he eked it out by acting as clerk of the Presbytery ... his poverty increased, and he was forced to beg for charity."[15] When Mr Grant, the minister of Urquhart, received a Call to Abernethy in 1685, his appointed successor was presented "to the churches of Urquhart and Glenmoristone, now vacant." At this, Mr Monro protested, "claiming that he himself was minister of Glenmoriston."[16] His claim was dismissed, thus highlighting his anomalous position, and by 1688 Glenmoriston was firmly within Urquhart parish for the next two hundred years.

"... a most troublesome and fatiguing charge ..."

"... your labour in the Lord is not in vain"
[1 Corinthians 15:58]

In the Eighteenth Century there is evidence of "two thatched meeting houses within Glenmoriston, one of which provided accommodation in the loft for the missionary." One of these was at Dundreggan and the other at Invermoriston.[17] These buildings may well have been the venues for outreach in 1725 by missionary Alexander Macbean. Robert Cumming, the minister of Urquhart and Glenmoriston since 1686, had raised concern with Presbytery about itinerant Catholic priests in Glenmoriston, and as a consequence Mr Macbean was instructed "to spend the remaining six weeks of his mission – four weeks thereof in Glenmoriston, and two in Urquhart." Furthermore, "Mr Skeldoch, minister of Kilmonivaig, and Mr Chapman, missionary, were appointed to preach on the following Sunday at Duldreggan, and Mr Macbean, and Mr Gilchrist, minister at Kilmallie, at Invermoriston on the same day."[18]

These accounts shed some light upon the work of these missionaries, who it would seem worked for limited seasons, probably just the summer months, residing in poor conditions, often working unsupervised and providing the only worship services during the course of the year. Mr Cumming was cautioned by Presbytery "anent his preaching so seldom at Glenmoriston." The ministers called to preach in the glen that Sunday in 1725 signify the fact that in 1724 Urquhart and Glenmoriston had been transferred to the newly created Presbytery of Abertarff: the journeys from Kilmallie and Kilmonivaig, even in the summer months, were not easily undertaken.

One positive outcome was that Presbytery promoted the first school in the parish: it opened in 1728 at Dundreggan under the auspices of the SSPCK. Thereafter the glen "was not without a school in Glenmoriston, except for an interval of eight years immediately after the troubles of The Forty-Five."[19] The SSPCK records further identify its Glenmoriston School as being at Livissie, although in 1732 the location is described as "Bunaldi". The school may have struggled to find permanent premises, for between 1733 and 1736 Alexander Dallas, who was later at Abertarff during the '45, is described as the schoolmaster at "St Richards", presumably at Dalchreichard: the enduring continuity of Erchard's name is hard to dismiss![20] Such schools may have been constructed from "wattles and turf" as one at Torgyle Bridge started early in the Nineteenth Century: the first custom-built schoolhouse at Dalchreichard was built about 1830.[21] The SSPCK school was moved in 1776 from "the Braes" to Invermoriston, because the population in the upper part of the Glen was in decline,[22] although the Presbytery was concerned that the Laird should provide "proper accommodation for the Schoolmaster."

The work of ministers and schoolmasters could not have been easy, for life in the glen was far from tranquil. The first Statistical Account states: "this parish was exceedingly exposed to depredation from their neighbours in the West Highlands, who came and took up their cattle and other property without ceremony, for which they made no compensation."[23] The young men of the glen were often absent in the various volunteer and full-time militia that were raised during the century: forty glen-men had joined the 1st Strathspey Fencibles recruited by Major John Grant, the Laird of Glenmoriston in 1793.[24]

Robert Cumming, the minister of Urquhart and Glenmoriston, died in 1730 and was followed by Rev William Gordon who, in 1731, was joined by Thomas Montfod, ordained as "missionary preacher" in Glenmoriston. It appears that Mr Montfod had been appointed as catechist in Glenmoriston and Abertarff at the same time, and was supported by the Royal Bounty Committee. Mr Gordon, as Parish Minister, wanted permanent provision for the needs of his distant glen. He pleaded "for a missionary Preacher to the United Parishes of Urquhart and Glenmoriston there being four stated places of worship in that Parish, besides that the country of Glenmoriston lies at a considerable distance from the minister's place of residence, and mostly inaccessible to him during the winter season."[25]

Throughout the Eighteenth Century, with the discontinuous service of ministers and missionaries, the presence of a schoolmaster was a saving grace. With the exception of the years following the '45 there is a fairly steady record of schoolmasters within the glen.[26] This was because further to his school duties "each teacher was *ex officio* the Catechist of his district. He was bound to visit the people on Saturday and vacations, and also conduct worship on Sundays, if the parish church were at a distance. He was forbidden to preach, but allowed to explain the Scriptures."[27] Not for the first time, the commitment of lay Christians, working as "salt and light" in their local communities was pivotal.

It is important to record that following the Battle of Culloden "the district of Glenmoriston ... suffered much. Officers and men forgot their humanity, and revelled in blood, plunder, lust and brutal horse-play."[28] There were accounts of "unspeakable treatment of men, women, and children at Dundreggan, Inverwick, and elsewhere; the harrying of the Glen from end to end; and the treacherous betrayal of some seventy of its male population, who, after imprisonment in Inverness for some weeks, were sent to London, and eventually shipped off to Barbados, whence only eight or nine returned to their native country; while among numerous ravages destructive to property, Invermoriston House was again burned down."[29] The famed Seven Men of Glenmoriston held out in the upper braes of the glen and gave refuge to the fugitive

Prince[30], whilst one Roderick Mackenzie, being assumed to be the Prince, lost his life at the hands of the King's troops.[31] His grave and a commemorative memorial stand either side of the A87 near Ceannacroc.

The suffering was to continue through the ensuing winter: hunger, cold, and destroyed houses meant that "a great mortality happened among them."[32] It is not known how the harried populace was ministered to, nor how the victims of hunger and cold were supported. However, William Grant, signing himself as "Missionary Minister of the Gospell att Glenmoriston", gave testimony for sixty-eight men of the Glen who had surrendered to Sir Ludovick Grant on May 5 1746, and who were later exiled. His comments regarding their conduct both before and during the "rebellion" suggests a fair knowledge of the individuals and their characters.[33]

After the depredations post-Culloden there were efforts to improve the social and economic fortunes of the area. The Board of Trustees for Fisheries and Manufactures built a linen works and training school at Invermoriston after 1753, anticipating that local agriculture would supply the raw materials. In 1769 Thomas Pennant reported with some satisfaction that "forty girls at a time are taught for three months to spin, and then another forty taken in:

there are besides six looms."[34]   Spinning wheels and reels were distributed around the district to encourage outworking, and an account of 1764 lists six recipients in the Fort Augustus area of Boleskine parish, one in Glengarry, nine in Glenmoriston, and others scattered across Glen Urquhart, Kiltarlity, Kirkhill and Dores.[35]   By the time of Pennant's visit, however, the Board of Trustees had already sealed the fate of this loss-making venture in the previous year, and it closed soon thereafter.[36]

Whilst such development had been envisaged to "civilise" and "pacify" the Highlands, the provision of Protestant ministers and missionaries perhaps had a longer-lasting, though intermittent, influence.   During the Eighteenth Century there were nine missionaries recorded as working in Glenmoriston, but six of them were also appointed to Abertarff and other areas.   Two Catechists are also recorded working in 1768 and 1788.   There are lengthy gaps in the service of these men throughout the century, when those working in Abertarff were clearly offering additional spiritual support in the Glen. The once-lost Abertarff Register of Baptisms and Marriages notes sixteen children baptised during the century, most of them when there was no missionary formally appointed to Glenmoriston.   The same register records thirteen marriages of Glenmoriston residents between 1760 and 1798 performed by the

Abertarff missionaries. Whilst the location of these marriages is not recorded, it is interesting to speculate if any of them took place at Clach a'Phosaidh, the "Marriage Stone" beside the Military Road from Fort Augustus to Achlain. The very presence of this site emphasises another traditional link between the two parishes.[37]

Amongst these diligent labourers was William Grant, previously mentioned, who served in the 1740s, and John MacDonell who was appointed from 1786 and 1788 to serve Boleskine, Urquhart and Kilmonivaig, a vast area which of course included Glenmoriston, Abertarff and Glengarry. The workload of such men is underlined in the first Statistical Account of Scotland in the 1790s where it is stated that "the missionary minister of Fort Augustus ... preaches in the glen once in three weeks; and where there are two tolerable meeting-houses. Before the establishment of this mission, the minister of Urquhart had to supply every fourth Sunday in Glenmoriston, which made the charge a most troublesome and fatiguing one; but it is now only expected, that he goes thither occasionally, except when there is a vacancy in the mission: in this event, he goes there regularly once a month. But, until Glenmoriston has a missionary entirely to itself, the people cannot be properly accommodated with the means of religion, having at present sermon only once in the three weeks, though it is admitted,

that the schoolmaster and catechist ... are great aids."[38] In 1784 the
two meeting houses at Dundreggan and Invermoriston were served
in turn. It is quite possible that these places of worship were shared
with the SSPCK schools: in 1801 the school for the upper glen was
located at Dundreggan.[39]

James Fowler served as a missionary in the Glen and in Abertarff
from 1791 until 1799 when he was presented to the Parish of
Urquhart and Glenmoriston. With his intimate knowledge of the
glen he was able to state that he "was entitled to and wanted a glebe
for the Parish of Glenmoriston" because there was not enough
pasture for his cattle. This request was turned down, but he renewed
his request in 1811 when he explained to the Factor that the parish
"including Glen Moriston is 30 miles in length and I cannot do the
duty of it without a horse, this I cannot have without a small farm
as my present Glebe is only 6 acres arable land."[40] Such were the
circumstances of local ministers.

Over the next century the glen was served occasionally by its
parish minister, or more usually by the missionary minister based in
Fort Augustus supplied by the Royal Bounty Committee. After
"1811 the Committee agreed to establish a separate mission in
Glenmoriston, and to pay the missionary a salary of £60 a year, the
proprietor furnishing him with a place of meeting and a dwelling-

house and other allowances."[41] In fact, a letter from James Grant, Laird of Glenmoriston, informed Presbytery that instead of providing a house he was offering accommodation within the "Easter house of Invermoristone" comprising two rooms and use of a kitchen.[42] The lodgings offered would have been within the servants' quarters known as "The Barracks", still to be seen to the rear of the modern mansion house. This location suggests that the newly-created mission was to serve the lower part of the glen, and that a meeting place was provided in the village. This must be the "meeting-house" in Invermoriston that was demolished in 1912, although the location of the second meeting-house at Dundreggan remains to be identified. It is interesting to note that there are references to the Kirk Session meeting at "Torgoil" on occasions between 1827 and 1835, and at Dundreggan in the 1850s, with services being held at "Torgoil" in 1842: this may locate the building to the western side of Dundreggan. There was a Sabbath School held at Dundreggan as late as 1882.[43]

It appears that the provision of one missionary for the glen, let alone two, was less than continuous, and there was much reliance upon the missionary in Fort Augustus. Colin Fraser was appointed in 1813 to serve the two stations as well as Glengarry, although the Presbytery had to gently remind the Royal Bounty Committee that

Glengarry and Glenmoriston were separate charges.[44]   It is acknowledged that Mr Fraser's "labours have been constantly exerted to instruct the people." The places of worship, however, were in a poor condition, and there was little urgency to improve them.   In 1815 the proprietor requested the principal heritor, Colonel Grant, "to contribute towards the replacement of the 2 meeting houses in Glen Moriston, which were both thatched and leaking.   The total cost was to be £150.   Colonel Grant at first declined but agreed to contribute £50 towards the cost of repairs by 1829."[45]   Within a few years it was reported that a missionary minister was settled in the glen, "who preaches alternately at Invermoriston and in the upper part of the glen, at each of which stations there is a comfortable meeting-house. Both Gaelic and English are preached in the different places of worship ..."[46] By 1827 the Royal Bounty Committee told the Presbytery that it had postponed the appointment of a missionary to Glenmoriston due to limited funds[47] and in 1841 it was announced that the Committee had withdrawn the mission. The Presbytery was not pleased and it responded by stating that the "Minister of Urquhart and Glenmorriston has had to divide his labours by preaching at four different stations in his Parish; the Roman Catholics in the District have recently opened a splendid and spacious place of worship capable of accommodating the whole population of the Glen."[48] As will be related, this new chapel at Torgyle did not have a resident priest beyond 1850.

The Presbytery continued to press the priority of posting a missionary to the Glen, but recognised that the effects of the Disruption in 1843 restricted the personnel available.[49] The Presbytery suggested that the best that could be done was to appoint a missionary to the "triple" charge based at Fort Augustus. By 1848, noting that Glenmoriston had been vacant for seven years, and Fort Augustus for four, Presbytery agreed that the two "could make a useful unit together."[50] With only short appointments and long gaps between them it is not surprising that the Royal Bounty Committee again wrote to the Presbytery in 1878 enquiring "as to the practicability of uniting the two stations of Glenmoriston and Fort Augustus."[51] It is significant that in 1818 Presbytery had identified Glenmoriston as one of five new parishes it wished to see created, although the General Assembly favoured the creation of new "chapels of ease" instead.[52] It would be 1891 before the Parish of Glenmoriston was be established. By that time Urquhart and Glenmoriston had left the Presbytery of Abertarff to join Inverness Presbytery: this move in 1884 reflected the fact that the centre of gravity of Abertarff Presbytery had shifted to the south with new parishes having been created in Fort William, Ballachulish, Glencoe, Ardgour and Strontian. However, there was still wisdom in Glenmoriston rejoining its southern neighbours, all the more so once it had become a parish in its own right: in 1896 the case was made in response to a General Assembly committee, something that was turned down in 1898.[53]

The places of worship may have been "comfortable" according to the Statistical Account, but the lodgings for the missionaries were less so. Recorded in the 1861 census, and again in 1871, the missionary Alexander Gair lived at Invermoriston with a housekeeper in a humble house with just three "windowed rooms". In 1881 George Birrell lodged with a family at Fassack, whilst the Free Church minister, Donald MacInnes lodged at Achlean Farm prior to his manse being completed in 1882.[54] Archibald McNeill, who became the first minister of the newly created Parish of Glenmoriston in 1891, is recorded in both the 1891 and 1901 census returns as living at Livishie Lodge with its eleven windowed rooms! Sometime thereafter the house standing above the Hotel was granted to the Church for use as a manse.

Despite the good intentions of the Royal Bounty Committee, missionary ministers when appointed, were usually serving for short periods, creating opportunities for itinerant preachers and Catholic priests to exert their influence. Foremost amongst the former was Dr John MacDonald of Ferintosh. Dr MacDonald made several tours in the early 1800s and preached in Glenmoriston at "An open-air chapel … in a quiet shady nook. He was fresh from scenes of revival, and preached with great power." The location was most probably near Torgyle where around 1827 a travelling evangelist names Finlay Munro gathered a crowd. He was a Cathechist with the SSPCK and was abused by a person ridiculing both the message and the preaching. He replied by saying "that as proof that what he was speaking was the truth, no grass would grow on the spot on which he was presently standing till the day of judgement!"[55] His footprints may be seen to this day in the natural amphitheatre which was ideal for such open-air preaching.[56]

A New Parish and a New Church

"…they pour new wine into new wineskins"
[Mark 2:22]

Before the Disruption there would appear to have been several gaps between the appointments of missionaries when presumably the area came under the direct oversight of Urquhart Church or was served once again from Fort Augustus: in 1844 William Sutherland was ordained to serve Glengarry, Fort Augustus and Glenmoriston. The population of Glenmoriston was, in any case, on the decline: between 1811 and 1831 it fell from nearly seven hundred to five-hundred and fifty "occasioned by emigration, consequent on the introduction of sheep-farming."[57]

It is surprising therefore that the status of Glenmoriston changed in 1891 with the creation of a charge "Quod Sacra", a parish with spiritual but no civil responsibilities. Planning for this event had commenced some years earlier, and some correspondence from 1886 and 1887 between the minister of Urquhart and Glenmoriston and officials of the Church of Scotland is preserved within the archives. Concern was expressed that the income was insufficient to cover the minister's stipend for a new Glenmoriston parish, and that the income left to Urquhart would be much reduced. Questions were also raised about the funds available for the maintenance of church buildings. Such doubts were countered by the reassurance that "the proprietor and his mother not only continue their interest in the people of this Glen, but are also prepared to make most generous provision for their spiritual oversight."[58] This pledge, which was not fully realised until 1904, must have given the encouragement necessary for the plans to come to fruition. Archibald M'Neill, who was Assistant at Urquhart, was ordained first minister of the new parish on 23 September 1891. Thereafter four ministers served until the parish was linked with Urquhart in 1980, the two being united in 1992.[59]

It was in 1904 that the generous offer came from Mrs Harriet Morrison to build a new church at Invermoriston, in memory of her husband. As a daughter of James Murray Grant of Glenmoriston she had a long association with the district. However, it was not until after her death in 1909 that Mrs Morrison's trustees were to administer a "Legacy of £5000 to be applied by them in building a Church at Invermoriston and in furnishing or completing the furnishing of the Manse there and in the provision of a garden for the Manse…"[60] The old mission church was pulled down in 1912 and building works commenced, with a Foundation Stone being laid in 1913: extensive repairs to the Manse were also reported. Perhaps because of wartime restrictions it was 1915 before the new church was brought into use. In the meantime the Kirk Session minutes note that the congregation had held its services in the Public School "for nearly three years, a very unsuitable place for adults owing to the seating being made simply for children." There had been no Communion held in 1912 "for want of a suitable place for such services."[61]

The first nine decades of the Twentieth Century saw many

changes and challenges within Glenmoriston Parish Church. One of the on-going problem was the provision of Elders within the new parish. Whilst two were appointed at the outset, it was later necessary to appoint Assessor Elders from other congregations to make up the required quorum of two Elders and the minister in the Kirk Session. Thus from 1901 to 1927 the Session met just once a year in Inverness at the time of Presbytery meetings when the Assessors would be present. The small and fluctuating membership meant that key roles were not easily filled, the minister often acting as Session Clerk. Membership was rarely above three dozen, and those communicating at the Lord's Supper could sometimes be counted on one hand.

With its new building completed in 1915 the congregation faced the uncertain post-war years, and the decline of estate-based employment was only partially compensated by the work of the new Forestry Commission. In 1929 the Kirk Session noted the appointment of perhaps the last Missionary to serve in any of the three parishes: Walter Gordon had been appointed to the Dalchriechart district by the Home Mission Board with effect from 5 May although he left in September.[62]

In the early 1930s there were significant civil engineering works in the parish to upgrade the A82 from Drumnadrochit to Fort

Augustus: the main contractor was Messrs Tawse. Mr MacKenzie, who had been a missionary in India and Nepal for over thirty years, had been inducted as Parish Minister in 1930. In 1932 he told the Kirk Session "that in accordance with instructions from the Presbytery, and with the permission of Messrs Tawse a fortnightly Sunday evening service has been arranged for at Altsigh Camp. In view of this arrangement it was decided meantime to discontinue the Sunday evening fortnightly services in the Church."[63] This special ministry was to anticipate a far larger opportunity in the 1950s.

The scattered nature of the parish meant that the new church at Invermoriston was far from central. Indeed, regular services were held at Dalchreichart School, with occasional services elsewhere in the upper part of the parish. In 1953 the minister confessed "to great difficulty in establishing contacts between the Church and certain elements of the community in and around Invermoriston" but "that nearly every house in Dalchreichart and Torgoyle area was in touch with the church."[64] It is instructive that the Free Church congregation built its church 1857 at Dundreggan, in the middle of the glen, and that remained its sole place of worship in the area until it closed in 1980.[65]

"... considerable demands"

"... the Lord thunders over the mighty waters"
[Psalm 29:3]

It was in the 1950s that significant changes came to the parish. In 1943 the precursor of the North of Scotland Hydro-Electric Board was set up to harness the power of Highland lochs. By 1944 over one hundred projects had been identified, including one to exploit the waters of Glenmoriston. Rev Duncan Turner, who came to the parish in 1940 foresaw the significance of these dramatic post-war developments. In response to a questionnaire from the Church of Scotland after the end of the war he wrote of his efforts to create a Community Association to promote social development, although he despaired of the lack of support in some quarters due to conservative attitudes. Much depended, he wrote, upon the personality of the parish minister to create a sense of community. He stated: "I do not think it is too much to say that the fostering of community life is as essential to the Highlands today as economic rehabilitation." He concluded that "there is an imperative demand for a social ministry on the part of the church. Hitherto that has been lacking. Allied to the other aspects of the church's work, a social ministry can do much to save the situation."[66] In 1949 Mr

Turner demitted to take up an appointment as Chaplain and Welfare Officer at the huge Cannich Camp established to serve the Glen Affric hydro scheme, so the likely impact of developments in Glenmoriston was vividly foreseen.

Detailed plans were published in 1948 outlining the enlargement of Loch Clunie and Loch Loyne, the building of three dams and four power stations, and the creation of miles of aqueducts and tunnels.[67] The new minister, Peter Fraser, rose to the challenge. The Kirk Session minute in mid-July 1952 notes: "The Moderator stated that there was the distinct possibility that the new Hydro-Electricity scheme taking shape at Loch Cluanie would soon be making considerable demands upon minister and congregation." As construction work commenced it was minuted that "services at Cluanie Camp had begun and there had been some response from Camp personnel."[68]

Those "considerable demands" became evident the following year. "The Session noted the continued inability of the Home Board to help with transport for ministerial services to Cluanie Camp and other new centres such as Ceannacroc, and the expressed possibility that the Home Board might … decide to equip a travelling specialist for several camps in the north. It was the unanimous view of the Session that the Church in Glenmoriston ought to have a car at its service."[69] Three months later the Moderator "said that he very much wished for a strong local witness in the face of [the schemes]" and that he had secured a donation of £50 from Halcrow's, the consulting engineers, towards the provision of a church car! Further help was forthcoming from the Mitchell Construction Company, for a minute in December 1955 records thanks to them and Halcrow's for providing transport for the minister "and at communion time for the people of the Glen."[70]

The Church of Scotland was less quick to help so Rev William MacIntyre, Industrial Chaplaincies Organiser for the Church's Home Board, was invited to conduct the Summer Communion in Glenmoriston in 1955. It is recorded that Mr MacIntyre "expressed gratitude for the contact maintained in Glenmoriston between Schemes and local personnel and promised to do all in his power to further this work ..." He acknowledged "that there was a real case for help from the Home Board in the matter of transport for the minister ... while the Hydro-Electric Schemes were in process of construction."[71] It was not until a year later that the Church and Ministry Department of the Church offered a two-thirds grant towards a second-hand car for Mr Fraser. The pastoral demands of the Hydro scheme should not be underestimated: for instance, at Cluanie camp "which at its busiest housed 1,000 workers, there were

22 fatalities in two and a half years."[72] Despite his ministrations over many years to the hydro scheme the minister was not to see electric light installed at Glenmoriston Church until 1963!

North or South?

"If we walk in the light ... we have fellowship with one another ..."
[1 John 1:7]

With the forthcoming retirement of Peter Fraser in 1980, moves were made to establish a Linkage with Urquhart. Following the ordination and induction of Bart Buell to the new linked charge it was agreed to sell the manse at Invermoriston. It became clear that repairs to the church were required at a cost of around £11000, although only limited work took place.[73] This news, however, heralded a more permanent change to the status of the parish, for in the mid-1980s there was a renewed debate about the relationship of Glenmoriston to its neighbours to the north and south.

In 1986 there was a vacancy at Fort Augustus, and Lochaber Presbytery began to explore options for readjustment. A link-up with Glenmoriston was one possibility, and Rev Bart Buell told the Kirk Session that he "was in favour of such a linkage as there is no distance between the parishes."[74] A few days later, at the

Congregational AGM there was a report from the recent Quinquennial Visitation by Presbytery. The minute[75] states:

"Their report ... recommended that ... the congregation should not accept unity with FortAugustus and the status-quo to be maintained with a view to uniting with Urquhart in the future. Mr Buell said that he had not yet been asked for his official position, but although he would be sad to leave us, it would be in our best interests in the long run. He pointed out that the distance from Fort Augustus to Invermoriston is six miles less than from Drumnadrochit and this in itself would be a big saving in time and money."

In reply to a question Mr Buell continued "it would be of mutual benefit for us to unite" although another person "expressed her concern that the Church might close eventually, like the Free Church did."

The next year Lochaber Presbytery had arranged a linkage between Fort Augustus and Glengarry, and the Kirk Session at Glenmoriston agreed the matter "should be reconsidered by Inverness and Lochaber Presbyteries."[76] The 1988 AGM was told that "no further move has been made regarding the proposed linkage." Alas, other factors were at play: the same meeting was reminded that the church membership was twenty-three with eight adherents, and on average the attendance at services was six at the church, five at Dalchreichart and nine at Communion services.[77] Two years later the congregation was facing a deficit of £900, and the Board recorded that the solution would be a union with Fort Augustus.

"Members were very aware of the effects such a union would have on the community, and gave due consideration to any possible congregational expansion or community developments in the future. But in view of all the circumstances including a steadily diminishing membership roll, the consensus of opinion was that union with either Urquhart or Fort Augustus should be considered. Local residents on the Congregational Board felt that in the case of a Union being decided on it would be more logical to unite with Fort Augustus because of other established links with the community there."[78]

A year on, the Kirk Session agreed with the Church of Scotland Parish Re-Appraisal Committee to proceed with readjustment. Then at a meeting with Presbytery representatives, the local office-bearers again expressed both their understanding that something needed to be done, and that a Union with Fort Augustus was desirable. However, the Assessor Elder felt that "a quick and satisfactory settlement" was required, and proposed "that Glenmoriston Church of Scotland seeks Union with Urquhart Church of Scotland and to facilitate this the Congregational Board would be prepared to accept closure of the Glenmoriston Church building." This was unanimously agreed[79] and the last Communion service was held in the church on 28 June 1992. The final service was on 23 August and the Union took effect four days later. The newly re-united congregation of Urquhart and Glenmoriston continued to hold services at Dalchreichart until the school there was closed in 2006, since when a monthly service has been held at Glenmoriston Millennium Hall. The Christian community that had been courted by its southern neighbours for over four centuries had returned to its northern partner.

The Enduring Footprints

"Righteousness will go before him, and will make his footsteps a way"
[Psalm 85:13 (RSV)]

The legacy of Erchard in Glenmoriston no doubt sustained those adhering to the Catholic faith for centuries, but there is no evidence of a resident priest until the 1840s: the local Catholic worshippers were served by priests crossing the hills from Glengarry or Strathglass. Indeed, it was a priest from the latter glen who raised money for the building of a chapel.[80] The first Statistical Account stated that there were eighty Catholics in Glenmoriston in 1789 and that "they are moderate, and some of them come occasionally to the Established Church": the New Statistical Account reported fifty-five in the early 1800s.[81] The chapel at Torgyle, sometimes known as Laggan-bain, with its garret for the priest, was built in 1841[82], but the area ceased to have a resident priest in 1850, whereafter the district was served from Fort Augustus or Stratherrick. After the re-establishment of the Catholic hierarchy in 1878 both Fort Augustus and Glenmoriston came within the Diocese of Aberdeen, and the monks at Fort Augustus provided a service every three weeks.[83] It is not known when the church at Torgyle was closed, but it fell into an advanced state of decay: in 1977 services were being held at the village hall in Invermoriston.[84]

It has already been recounted that in 1843 a large number of worshippers adhered to the newly-formed Free Church, with three men from the Glen being appointed as Elders in the new Fort Augustus and Glenmoriston congregation. In 1844 Glenmoriston was formally linked to Fort Augustus, and whilst a site was identified for a church at Invermoriston a year later, it was some twelve years before a new building at Dundreggan was opened. It was reported that the congregation comprised people "of the poorer class" and thus relied upon "kind friends elsewhere (to) lend their generous aid."[85] An indication of the growing strength of the congregation came in 1878 when the Free Church General Assembly agreed to its request to become an independent charge. Their first minister, Donald MacInnes, was inducted the following year. By 1882 he had built a new manse alongside the church "without placing a burden upon the congregation." After his death in 1889 the next ministry of William MacKinnon was but for five years, when another Donald MacInnes was inducted. He personally entered the Union of 1900 which created the United Free Church, but the majority of the congregation stayed with the Free Church. Despite this the church and manse were transferred to the new denomination until the House of Lords ruling in 1904, whereafter the Free Church congregation repossessed their property. In the meantime the church had been locked to prevent any party using the building, and the Free Church met in an old meal mill to the west of the church. Mr MacInnes had left the glen by 1907[86] and later ministered within the Church of Scotland in Mull and Tiree.

It was 1909 before Glenmoriston Free Church had a minister,

but once again in linkage with Fort Augustus. Services were held once a fortnight with a Communion weekend in July when visitors from other parts, notably Glen Shiel, would be present. Communion services were held in Gaelic and English until the 1950s.[87] There were five pastorates until the 1950s, by which time it was reported that: "The Free Church element in Glenmoriston is fairly strong, more so than the Church of Scotland, but we do find a number of Roman Catholics forming a community in the glen, with a small chapel at Laggan-bane."[88] However, there was a long vacancy from 1958 to 1965 by which time the Free Church membership in the glen had shrunk to five. The Fort Augustus manse, being in a poor state, was sold in 1962 and John Fraser, inducted in 1965, lived in Glenmoriston Manse which had been tenanted for many years previously. The congregation of Fort Augustus and Glenmoriston was unable to support a minister after John Fraser's retirement in 1983 and so joined up with its sister congregation of Urquhart: Mr Fraser was thus the last minister to reside in the glen. The final Free Church service had in fact been held at Glenmoriston in 1980, and the properties were sold in 1988.[89]

With the Church of Scotland building being last used in 1992 this glen, with its long Christian history, was now without a dedicated place of worship. The Church, of course, is made of "living stones" and a dedicated building is not always appropriate or necessary. A visitor to the service at Dalchreichart in the early 1970s wrote that "we were all in that shabby old school to hear a simple sincere man who had a message for the 'two or three who gathered together in His name'".[90] During a service broadcast from the parish church by the BBC in 1968, Rev Peter Fraser stated that "there is a danger all through this century so far that we have been writing off ... places and communities, and the faith of places and communities that kept them going: God help us to overcome that danger ..."[91] The churches in the upper Glen and in Invermoriston may be long gone, but the enduring footprints of Finlay Munro remain: they bear testimony to the ever-present Holy Spirit. Before he retired Mr Fraser wrote of the Glen: "May its people, whoever they may happen to be, not forget nor dismiss the faith of their worthy forerunners. That to them, will be as a 'font' that never goes dry and as 'footprints' that never fade."[92]

A Prayer Inspired by Highland Communion Seasons

Lord God, as Highland Communions were traditionally times for the faithful preaching of your Word, the powerful moving of your Spirit, the renewing of faith amongst your people, and were often held outdoors;
so may we, in our time, listen carefully to your challenging Word, be fully open to your transforming Spirit, pray earnestly for the harvest of souls, and bear witness to Christ in the public place.

Eternal God, as Highland Communions called sinners to repent, invited waverers to the table, offered your life to the lonely and your love to all;
so may we, here and now, receive your forgiveness through your Son, restore our commitment to Christ, discover fullness of life and the joy of your eternal love.

Heavenly Father, as Highland Communions often gathered people from near and far, lasted many days, heard testimonies to your saving grace, and displayed the bountiful hospitality of your Church;
so may we, for all our days, embrace our fellow believers, look for your continued blessings, speak of our faith, and share your gifts with our brothers and sisters in Christ.

This we ask through Jesus Christ our Lord. Amen

Adrian Varwell

Chapter 5:

OUR GUIDE EVEN TO THE END

"… surely I am with you always, to the very end of the age"
[Matthew 28:20]

The title page of this book carried the words of Psalm 48:12–14 which have inspired this exploration of church and community across the years in the Great Glen. The Psalmist invited the people of Zion (Jerusalem) to explore their city, to enumerate its features, to understand its strengths and weaknesses, and to appreciate what they saw around them. This, however, was not meant to be a simple inventory of their city: it was to be an account that was to be passed on to the next generation. The people of Zion were to convey their knowledge and experiences to those who would follow so that others might appreciate and apply the wisdom and the lessons of the past.

> *Walk about Zion, go round her, count her towers,*
> *consider well her ramparts, view her citadels,*
> *that you may tell of them to the next generation*
> *For this God is our God for ever and ever;*
> *he will be our guide even to the end*
> *[Psalm 48:12–14]*

Zion, of course, refers not just to Jerusalem, but is a metaphor for God's eternal city and for the on-going fellowship of the church. Thus Christians are called to take stock of the history of the church in their home community, its strengths and weaknesses, and the lessons to be learned. This should not, however, be a simple exercise in historical reportage: Psalm 48 reminds us that any review of the past is to be undertaken in the context of God's eternal sovereignty and his rightful role as "our guide even to the end." We are to learn from the past and to apply its lessons to our future plans. That has been the intention of this examination of the Christian Church in the communities of Glen Albyn, Glengarry and Glenmoriston. The story of the local church over a millennium-and-a-half should inform its ministry and mission for the years to come: there are new things to be charted and embraced and they are outlined in this chapter.

Church and Community in the Great Glen

"See, I am doing a new thing! Now it springs up; do you not perceive it? I am making a way in the wilderness and streams in the wasteland. ... I provide water in the wilderness and streams in the wasteland, to give drink to my people, my chosen, the people I formed for myself that they may proclaim my praise"
[Isaiah 43:19–21]

"... doing a new thing!"

"From now on I will tell you of new things"
[Isaiah 48:6]

Isaiah was addressing words of hope to a community exiled in Babylon: at that time their homeland had been devastated, they had been uprooted and now they faced an unknown future sustained only by the promises of their gracious God. It was time to let go of the past and move on to new experiences; but God's people were, and still are, to learn from the past. Furthermore they are to recognise in the events of history a pledge of God's faithfulness in times of challenge and a promise of his presence in times of change. Writing of these verses in Isaiah 43 a commentator reminds us that "the past can teach and illustrate but it must not bind. The Lord always has greater things in store; he is revealed in the past, but he is always more than the past revealed."[1]

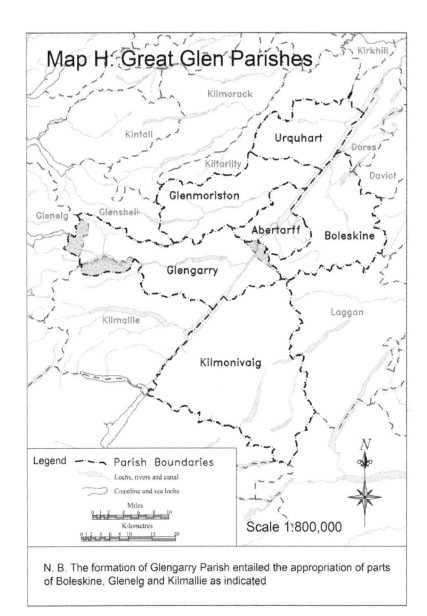

Map H: Great Glen Parishes

Kirkhill

Kilmorack

Kintail

Urquhart

Dores

Kiltarlity

Daviot

Glenmoriston

Glenelg   Glenshell

Abertarff

Boleskine

Glengarry

Laggan

Kilmallie

Kilmonivaig

N

Legend — · — Parish Boundaries

Lochs, rivers and canal

Coastline and sea lochs

Miles

0 1 2   4   6   8   10

Kilometres

0 1 2 4 6   8   10   15   20

Scale 1:800,000

N. B. The formation of Glengarry Parish entailed the appropriation of parts
of Boleskine, Glenelg and Kilmallie as indicated

Reflecting upon the story of the churches at the heart of the Great Glen it is instructive to see how the theme of God's faithfulness runs through the narrative. From the time of the earliest missionaries to this day Christians are engaged in the work of sharing the Good News of Jesus Christ in word and deed. Whilst church closures, lower attendances and parish amalgamations may indicate a decline in Christian commitment, the challenge to God's people nevertheless remains constant and urgent. Some may regret the changes to local church organisation, but it is worth noting that the pattern of a church with its minister residing in a manse in every community is a fairly minor part of the Christian record in the Great Glen. Fort Augustus was a stand-alone parish for just over a hundred years, and Glenmoriston for ninety; the parish of Glengarry, created in 1867, was independent for a century. Thus in a history of Christianity spanning sixteen centuries or more the supposed "traditional" parish model has existed in the Great Glen for only around six percent of the time. Perhaps the experience of these parishes points the way to a different and new model of Christian witness.

For many centuries the area was sustained by itinerant workers, both lay and ordained, from the early Celtic saints, to the clandestine "underground" Catholic priests, the missionary-ministers of the

Royal Bounty Committee, and on to those who served canal and railway navvies, the fishing fleet at Loch Hourn, and the construction camps for road-building and hydro-electric schemes. The dogged determination of those Catholic priests during the years of proscription, and that of the Royal Bounty missionaries, has to be both admired and emulated. They endured hardships beyond modern experience, and they exemplify a sacrificial commitment to Christian service which has at times been absent from all denominations. The laity also played significant roles, sustaining and housing the itinerants, giving pastoral support to their neighbours and, where they had the means, generously offering their wealth and talents to build churches and to support the clergy and their worshipping communities.

Across the years, Christians have had great opportunities for community engagement. Within the Great Glen they have set up schools; their ministers have catechised and conducted baptisms, marriages and funerals. Members of the congregations have been active in voluntary organisations, taken part in community affairs and engaged in local government. It has been seen how local ministers lobbied for assistance to reach out to distant areas of their parishes, and took the initiative in setting up support for railway navvies in the 1890s, the road-builders of the 1930s and the hydro schemes two decades later. The Registers for Fort Augustus and Glengarry bear testimony to their ministers travelling to the remote cottages of shepherds, stalkers and gamekeepers, and to forestry camps to conduct baptisms when home baptisms were the norm. From time to time visiting evangelists have preached the gospel across the district, both to encourage the local Christians and to share the faith. The "vagrant preachers" of the early 1800s who, according to the minister of Boleskine, "undervalued the ministrations of the established pastor"[2] may have attracted some followers but they planted no new churches. The story of Finlay Munro and his footprints in Glenmoriston in 1827 has been related, and Katharine Stewart tells of travelling evangelists in the 1920s[3] and there were others. Today, with the advent of personal transport and electronic communication much contemporary ministry has an itinerant quality, albeit sustained from a fixed base.

Every Christian, of course, is called to be "salt and light" within their communities, and the Great Glen parishes have a long record of those who were active in Christ's service both locally and elsewhere. Ian Allan's account of the Free Church "West the Glen" relates several examples[4], and the other denominations may testify to individuals making a significant contribution to both community and congregational life. Their stories and the value of their contributions quite correctly belong to a future reckoning. Whether Celtic, Viking or Pictish, the early Christians adapted to new ways of faithfulness. Monastic models of church organisation gave way to the Parochial, Episcopal to Presbyterian, yet each have brought their rich legacies to the contemporary church. Reformation and Disruption, and reunions and re-adjustment of denominational patterns have all presented their challenges, but through them all God is doing that "new" thing.

"Now it springs up ..."

> *"... a spring of water welling up to eternal life"*
> *[John 4:14]*

There is a temptation to believe that the Christian Church is somehow impervious to innovation and organisational change. However, within the Great Glen since the Sixth Century its churches and congregations have had to adapt to change, sometimes imposed from without and sometimes emerging from within. Political, economic and social influences have required different church structures. From the Sixteenth Century the local churches have been part of a constellation of administrative structures stretching from the Moray Firth to the Atlantic. Whilst the distant abbeys and cathedrals had lost their influence by the time of the Reformation, the Great Glen parishes have been variously associated with their neighbours in every direction through presbytery, synod and diocesan structures. More locally the parish groupings have been reorganised so that at various times churches as far away as Moy and Ballachulish, both way beyond the Great Glen, have been grouped with Glenmoriston, Glengarry and Abertarff/Fort Augustus. In more recent times the growth of Inverness and Fort William as population and service centres have stretched the affinities of the residents of the central Great Glen, and have played a part in defining church governance. The boundary between Inverness and Lochaber Presbyteries lies at Invermoriston Bridge. The Episcopal Dioceses of Moray, Ross and Caithness and Argyll and the Isles, and the Catholic Dioceses of Aberdeen to the north and Argyll and the Isles to the south, both meet at Aberchalder Bridge. At present the Free Church Presbytery alone embraces the Great Glen end to end.

Organisational change, however, is not the only response to the huge changes within society over the last century, and more recent events have put these changes into sharp focus. The outbreak of the Coronavirus pandemic in 2020 frustrated the completion of this study, with access to libraries and archive centres and some local fieldwork being denied. The disruption to the tourist trade had a devastating effect upon the economy of communities in the Great Glen as elsewhere, and the closure of churches forced congregations to find new ways of worship and outreach. It may be thought that on-line services produced in a distant place might threaten the viability of the local church, but a church rooted in its community is vitally placed to act as "salt and light" amongst its neighbours.[5]

This means that the Christian family has to undertake a radical re-assessment of their role within their locality. New circumstances have "sprung up" that demand new responses; the status-quo is no longer appropriate. The Chief Executive of the Bible Society has commented that we need to realise that "much of our institutional infrastructure was created for a world that no longer exists ... my conviction is that God is mobilising the Church for a new wave of mission ... I have been struck by the changes: a renewed appetite for Scripture, a fresh conviction about evangelism, a sustained commitment to unity, and a growing confidence in the gospel and to talking about it in public."[6] In response to a declining number of ministers the Church of Scotland is facilitating the reorganisation of parishes to create "hub" churches served by one or more workers serving the surrounding area. With the creation of the roles of Ordained Local Ministers, Parish Development Workers and

Worship Leaders there are more opportunities to release the gifts of full and part-time trained personnel, as well as those of congregational members. With imagination and sensitive nurturing there are many possibilities for "Fresh Expressions" of the church-life.[7]

Such an emphasis on church as community is vitally important in a society that is increasingly disconnected. This requires a new form of leadership, described by Alan Roxburgh as "leaders who listen to the voices from the edge. This is where the apostle, the prophet, and the poet are found. These are the metaphors for congregational leadership today. The pastor's ears must be attuned ... to those who recognize that marginality is the church's reality."[8] Roxburgh sees the pastor-as-poet as "living within the congregation's experience and giving voice to its desire for transformation and renewal", the pastor-as-prophet as giving "a new vision and fresh definition" of what it means to be the people of God, and the pastor-as-apostle as one who "must lead congregations as witnesses to the gospel in lands where old maps no longer work." He concludes, nonetheless, that the work and calling of a congregation belongs not just to a pastor, but to all the people of God.[9] For pastor and people alike, the rural church especially must be shaped by imagination that is informed and inspired by the Holy Spirit.

There are those who claim that investment in buildings and clergy has not produced authentic Christian communities, nor effective disciples, and that there should be a new emphasis on creating strong fellowships of believers. At the same time others remind us that buildings are essential as bases from which these fellowships might offer spaces for services and worship.[10] The very presence of a church building "bears witness to the vision and creative spirit of the disciples of Christ, and to the fact that the Gospel message is as important to the little hamlets nestling among the hills as it is to a metropolis ..."[11] Indeed, new centres of worship may be appropriate in some rural areas although every church building requires a committed congregation since: "We build churches in vain if, when the building is finished, we lift not our voices in praise and bring our gifts to the altar. We need places of worship, but we need much more a clear idea of the place of worship in life, and a better understanding of the real purpose of worship."[12] It is sobering to be reminded of Robert Pont, appointed in the Diocese of Moray in 1567 as a "Commissioner to plant kirks"! The role of the full-time Minister may be changing, but the call to ministry by the whole people of God has not diminished and may need to be rediscovered.

"... do you not perceive it?"

> *"... ever hearing, but never understanding:*
> *... ever seeing, but never perceiving"*
> *[Isaiah 6:9]*

New circumstances require new responses, both from local congregations and from their denominational structures; the need is urgent. The Chief Executive of the Bible Society again states that since the 1960s "The Church has largely retreated before a wave of hostility and indifference. Sadly, there has been a loss of confidence in the gospel, we have grown ignorant of the Bible and vulnerable to ideological capture by the attractive narratives of our culture"[13] The former top-down patterns of church organisation are no longer fit for purpose. A sense of Christian community must be rediscovered and re-energised, and lessons from the early church must be revisited. The author's research and work experience prior to entering the Christian ministry convinced him that the local resolution of community affairs was both beneficial and constructive. This was a perspective carried into his various ecclesiastical responsibilities, and he believes this to be a Biblical perspective which is so often ignored by decision-making within centralised denominational structures.

Steve Aisthorpe's research "shows that forms of Christian community that are highly organised are declining and that most [committed Christians] who move away from church congregations are involved in fellowship that is informal and highly relational." Of those flourishing churches within the historic denominations he observes that they have developed "ways of working within an institutional framework, while avoiding it becoming a straightjacket."[14]   More recently he has suggested that by "maintaining congregational models that require certain functions and roles, we forgo a community that emerges from the gifts of its people, shaped by the context of their lives and the realities of the wider community." He speaks of the liberating discoveries that await every Christian, "knowing ourselves to be beloved, putting our roots down deep into Christ, allowing our self-identity to be reshaped in the light of Scripture, discerning his purposes and stepping out into the adventure of faith." We are reminded that our "love for Christ, for one another and for the communities of which we are members need to be greater than our love for any institution."[15]

It is one thing to hear and to see, as Isaiah observes, but quite another to understand and to perceive the signs of the times. This is all the more urgent not just because the church has lost its place within the communities it is called to serve, but because the Church of Scotland, for one, is faced with a radical restructuring of its ministry and mission. The 2021 General Assembly was told that it faces a reduction of one-third of its ministers, alongside a pruning of its buildings and administrative structures. At the same time there was a call to equip every congregation for a mission-focussed role within each parish. Such a restructuring will require every congregation to make an honest appraisal of its work and witness to the local community.

The General Assembly was reminded of the long-standing Five Marks of Mission which have been adopted by many denominations since the 1980s. These marks are (1) to proclaim the Good News of the Kingdom; (2) to teach, baptise and nurture new believers; (3) to respond to human need by loving service; (4) to transform unjust structures of society, to challenge violence of every kind and pursue peace and reconciliation; and (5) to strive to safeguard the integrity of creation, and sustain and renew the life of the earth. They are as relevant to rural congregations as to those in urban areas. The Church of Scotland's Theological Forum, in a paper published in

2020[16], emphasised that the Five Marks "serve as a theological vision statement for Christian mission. They include essential aspects of the missional work of the church: evangelism, discipleship, pastoral care, social justice, reconciliation and care for creation. This combination echoes the teaching of Jesus, the practice of the early church, the message of the biblical prophets, insights from the experiences of poor and oppressed people, and openness to science and ecological awareness. Their language and emphases are agreeable to our Reformed understanding." The Forum continued with the assertion that "Proclaiming the Good News of the Kingdom necessarily involves transformation in the lives of individuals and societies; loving service does not stop with care for individuals but aims to reach their community and environment; Good News is not only for the salvation of individual people, but for their lived experience within families, communities, conflicts and creation."

In its conclusion the Theological Forum comments that to maintain its integrity and credibility the Church of Scotland must embrace a concern for social justice, reconciliation and the environment as essential parts of mission alongside evangelism, discipleship and pastoral care. To use the Five Marks as a vision for mission the Forum recognises that they must be used "to frame pragmatic decisions over priorities," which require "a practical wisdom, with an awareness of specific local, regional and national contexts." Awareness, understanding and perception are called for everywhere, and specifically amongst the church within the Great Glen. As we reflect upon the real challenges facing the church in the Great Glen, as elsewhere, do we not perceive God's call to see that He is doing a new thing in our midst?

"...a way ... and ... water in the wilderness"

> *"... he leads me beside quiet waters,*
> *he refreshes my soul"*
> *[Psalm 23:2]*

Fundamental to a renewed understanding of the Christian community and its place in its locality is the realisation that we inhabit places that God has created and Christ has redeemed; thus we are reminded that nowhere is off-limits. That is one of the strengths of a parish-based church: there is, or should be, a pastoral concern for everyone and everything within its boundaries. A parochial system is valuable because it reminds minister, congregation and the wider community that the church is present to reach out and to serve the locality. In the Old Testament, and initially in the Covenant revealed in Genesis 15–17, there is outlined "a three-way relationship between God, his people, and place" and the consequences of ignoring this inter-relationship "are disastrous for the wellbeing of God's people."[17] At times Christians have been guilty of ignoring the precious inter-dependence of people and place with the Creator of all things, and there is much to be reclaimed and restated. Across the Christian era there are "powerful interdependent connections between the wellbeing of the natural environment, the security and health of the people, and the depth and fidelity of the people's walk with their God."[18] Within the Great Glen, given its strong sense of community, its small population, its natural beauty and its ambitious conservation projects, there are ample opportunities for the church to emphasise the connection between God, people and place.

Turning to the New Testament this three-way relationship is emphasised less, and yet the Gospels have been summarised as the Good News (*Matthew*), for all people (*Mark*), in every place (*Luke*), at all times (*John*). Luke's geographical emphasis is evident in that "He gives the names of more places than any of the other evangelists, and never loses his sense of direction … all the points of the compass are covered. Jesus goes everywhere. He turns his face in every direction. He sets his feet on every highway, and makes time to visit out-of-the-way places. There is no place too small, and none too large for him to enter. He covers the whole country."[19] As the Son of God walked the lanes and streets of the Holy Land, sailed on a lake, preached on its hillsides and prayed on its mountains, so he has hallowed the land, the lochs, the glens and the bens of Scotland as much as anywhere else. Jesus is described as "Immanuel", God *with* us, and his incarnation claims our communities and embraces our environment: in his paraphrase of John 1: 14 Eugene Peterson reminds us that "The Word became flesh and blood, and moved into the neighbourhood."[20]

Because Jesus has "walked the land" we know it is holy, it has been claimed as his own, it is to be treated with reverence and taken on trust. We are to be good stewards of the land, using it wisely, and sharing its blessings with others. "Scripture has a lot to say about land. The land which God gives to Israel so that they might flourish is tied to ideas about ethical holiness. Land is to be cherished as a gift for which we must always be thankful. To be so gifted by God is to impose a duty of hospitality, mutuality and roominess so that the stranger might also find a home."[21] As we stand and live and work on these blessed acres we must remind ourselves that "God relates *to* people *in* places, and the places are not irrelevant to that relationship but, rather, are integral to divine human encounter."[22]

A sense of place is essential to human wellbeing. To be uprooted from any place is to lose something valuable, even sacred. To be connected to our environment and our neighbours is an important dimension to our humanity and our spirituality, and Christians must bear witness to this truth. Anne Richards, National Adviser in mission theology to the Church of England, asks "What can we do to show people how important our shared space and communities really are to our spiritual health and general wellbeing? I think that churches, especially rural churches, can be sites of common ground for their communities, both physically and spiritually." She reflects that too often those outside the church "see invisible walls and fences where there should be none."[23]

The history of the Christian church in the Great Glen, and in Glen Albyn, Glengarry and Glenmoriston in particular, displays a close connection between place and people. The earliest sites of missionary outreach were well chosen, and the Celtic saints engaged with the land and the locals through their farming and educational activities. Later, churches were located amongst the scattered communities and became the locus for worship and sacrament. The reaction of some to the closure of Fort Augustus Abbey in 1998 demonstrated the depths of tangible sentiment and a sense of attachment to a spiritual place. Such places bear witness to the fact that God *has* acted in history, *is* acting in the world, and *will* act in history.[24] Given the history of conflict and confrontation within the Great Glen and its district, the Christian community must bear witness to God's presence even in the wildernesses of human experience.

"... streams in the wasteland"

> *"This is the gate of the Lord through which the righteous may enter"*
> *[Psalm 118:20]*

The Great Glen sits on the boundaries of many regions, geographical, cultural and ecclesiastical: that fact should be seen as an experience that informs and refreshes the future of the Christian community there as elsewhere. It has already been suggested that the changing demands of ministry and mission raise issues that cannot be addressed by rigid bureaucratic structures. The lessons of a millennium and a half of Christian witness in the Great Glen is that flexibility and creativity is of the essence. Once at the centre of the Province of Moray, and then shunted around various combinations of parishes which placed the area on the periphery of administrative structures, "the most centrical point of the habitable part of the Highlands", to use Edmund Burt's phrase, must be seen as having a potential for Christian ministry. Existing borders should not be viewed as obstacles to divide, but rather as unifying meeting points. Steve Aisthorpe, a servant of the Church of Scotland working in the Highlands has written: "The chronicles of the Christian movement remind us that, while attempts to harness, steer or exploit the Church may have stifled the life of the Spirit, it cannot be extinguished. God is God and will break through and do the unimaginable – whenever and however."[25]

Looking beyond the Highlands one might consider those border areas distant from the seats of power which nonetheless share ethnic, linguistic and cultural identities with their neighbours across the boundaries that separate them. Very often those boundaries become the stimulus for creative and innovative institutions and new forms of social activity. The borders which once divided create bonds which unite. This is nothing new, of course. The account in Genesis 28:10–22 tells how Jacob met with God on the borderline or threshold between his old life and his new. For him it was a time of crisis: he was at a dark place between past failure and a promised future, but there at Bethel, significantly the "House of God", he was able to recommit himself to his journey of faith, to service and worship, and above all to God. It proved to be a place where he experienced the presence of God, illustrated by the stairway between heaven and earth, and God's promises for the future: God pledged his presence (*"I am with you"*), his protection (*"I will watch over you"*) and his provision (*"I will bring you back"*).

Jesus walked and tested such boundaries, and his parables and his social engagements showed how they might be crossed with positive effect. "The world Jesus knew was criss-crossed by powerful, even if often invisible, barriers: religious, ethnic and gender barriers for starters, and throughout the Gospels we find Jesus treating those fences with indifference."[26] The parable of the Good Samaritan and Jesus' conversation with the woman at the well, to note but two, illustrate this graphically.[27] As Jesus probed those ethnic and cultural divisions he highlighted a spiritual loneliness in his hearers, yet he offered healing and fulfilment through faith in his transforming love. Jacob's borderline experience was by no means unique, and it brings encouragement to those who still experience the uncertainties of such physical and spiritual borders. A former Moderator of the Church of Scotland has written: "There is something spiritual about the ... borderlines. We need to open our eyes to see the mystery and recognise God in the lonely places where visions are caught."[28]

The Christian faith centres on the crucifixion which took place outside a city wall; the Ethiopian official came to faith at a desert roadside; it was on the Damascus Road that Paul met with Jesus who broke down his implacable opposition to the Christian faith; a Roman soldier was converted when Peter crossed an ethnic and religious divide: then, later, Paul met with Lydia and other women as they did their laundry by the riverside, thereby breaking cultural taboos.[29] Social and spiritual differences are so often seen to shrink into insignificance where the boundaries are crossed and meaningful dialogue takes place, even more so where Jesus Christ is present to heal and reconcile. When Christ calls us to open the door[30], when the barriers are dismantled, the boundaries ignored and the borders removed, then the way is clear for Christ to cross the threshold and to engage with his people in creative ways. The initiative, though, lies with his people: their Lord's voice must be heard loud and clear, and be responded to before change can be initiated.

In recent years the concept of "liminality" has been explored by many, theologians included, to show that it is on the thresholds, the boundaries, the borders, that creative exchanges may take place. These are places of encounter, of discovery and of new relationships. For individuals, as much as for worshipping communities, such liminal or "threshold" experiences are both embedded in their faith and expressed in their outreach to those

around them, or at least they should be. "Celtic Christians had –
and still have – a strong sense of living on "edges" or "boundary
places" between the material world and the other world. The natural
landscape was both a concrete reality where people lived and, at the
same time, a doorway into another, spiritual world."[31] With a
renewed awareness of the interaction amongst the material, natural
and spiritual dimensions of creation, today's Christians are well
placed to assist the streams of God's healing and renewing Spirit to
water the wastelands.

Such awareness is not confined to rural areas alone. Writing of
her experience of working with urban parishes Ruth Harley suggests
that "the places we have thought of as 'edges' become holy ground
on which, together, we discover the glory of God, and therefore
become new 'centres' ... of our listening, learning, discerning,
gathering, sharing, worshipping, deciding and world-changing –
through the power of the Spirit in our midst."[32]

Because every threshold, whether physical or spiritual, is a place
of transition from one place to another, there is an element of risk.
"Characteristic of liminal experience is that we are free of previous
structures and ways of being. We feel a sense of freedom, but also
of uncertainty and anxiety."[33] Christians, though, are not on their
own: as Dietrich Bonhoeffer has written, Jesus Christ is ready to

welcome us and to come alongside us in our service for him: "He stands on the boundary of my existence, beyond my existence, yet for me."[34] Like the residents of the Great Glen, those who live on many boundaries are well equipped to reach across geographical, social and ecclesiastical boundaries: they may as a consequence experience a spiritual transformation both for themselves and for those with whom they engage. "The whole Christian life is supposed to have the quality of sustained liminality as we journey through the world, leaving behind the sinful nature, its desires and 'worldly' ways of being and thinking, and yearning for the coming kingdom and its fullness of life, joy and peace in the Holy Spirit. This is not a journey from earth to heaven, but rather a life that cries out for the kingdom to come 'on earth as it is in heaven' and keeps moving towards that fullness."[35]

Christians should not see this calling as something that is new and radical. The early church "was a new social reality formed out of a liminal experience ... It took the form of a group existing on the edges of the social worlds of its time. It was a distinct and peculiar people with a strong sense of belonging to one another."[36] The contemporary church should seek to bring refreshing streams of the spirit to the wastelands of the communities in which they are placed. Every Christian, every church family, every church building, and every church worker should be seen to act as a threshold between time and eternity, doubt and faith, self-centredness and service.

"my people ... my chosen ... the people I formed for myself"

"... you are a chosen people... God's special possession ..."
[1 Peter 1:9]

Isaiah has reminded us that the God of new things has a plan for the renewal of wastelands as well as wasted lives. Broken landscapes and defeated people can be restored, and his refreshing streams are there to effect the changes. More direct and personal is the reminder that God recruits his people to be the agents of change; that commission starts with a fresh encounter with Jesus on the thresholds of our lives. God's people belong to the One who claims his people as his own, who choses them and binds them in a close relationship. His people, his privilege, his promise, all bound together to promote worship and service.

It has been instructive to see the various ways in which the Christians within the three glens worked to promote worship and service within the community. Many examples have been outlined in the preceding chapters. There were those who worked "beyond the threshold" to lobby for the provision of clergy or more helpful solutions to local needs. There were the local residents who pledged gifts in cash or kind to advance the Kingdom of God. There were clergy and laity who "went the extra mile" to bring relief to the poor and comfort to the sick. There were the unsung saints who tramped the roads and endured the rain to share the Gospel in word and deed. There were those who welcomed and worked with the incomers to the area even when some might have been identified with military oppression. There were those who, moved by the Holy Spirit, left the district to make new lives and to pursue ministries elsewhere. Above all, there were the ordinary people who worshipped in their homes and church-buildings, raising the praise of Almighty God and bearing faithful witness to his sovereignty. All these, known or unknown, were God's people, chosen and called to make a difference with their Spirit-given gifts. They were the people formed by the landscape of the three glens and moulded by the grace of God.

Despite the many boundaries that have divided Glen Albyn, Glengarry and Glenmoriston over the centuries, it has been demonstrated that they have had, and still have, more to unite them than would separate them. In the Eighteenth and Nineteenth Centuries the agencies of the Royal Bounty Committee and

Presbytery worked to promote the three mission districts at the heart of the Great Glen, thereby loosening their ties with, and oversight by, the parishes of which they were a part. At various times, by default or by intention, the three were seen as one, and many voices championed their union. Indeed, for more than half of the years between 1725 and 1855 the missionary-ministers of Abertarff had a pastoral responsibility for at least one of the neighbours to the north and south.

It is instructive to look at the external boundaries of the three mission districts, and to discover the distances between the last habitation within each of them and the first in their parental parishes. On the southbound A82 there are three miles between Laggan and Corriegour Lodge; northbound there are four between Primrose Bay and Achnahannet, and there is a similar distance between Glendoebeg and Knockcarrach on the B862. Going west on the A87 it is nine miles from Bunloyne to Cluanie in Glenshiel. By contrast, the distances between "first and last houses" at Aberchalder and Invermoriston, where the internal boundaries of the three districts march together, may be measured in yards. The three glens belong together and they stand distinct from their neighbours.

If geography underlines the sense of unity and identity within

Glen Albyn, Glengarry and Glenmoriston, then the scene is set for a rediscovery of a common purpose for Christian work and witness in the area. Geography creates a sense of belonging which helps to embrace the local Christians within a common fellowship in which they may understand all the more deeply what it means to be the "people of God". It is surely significant that Robert Pont, the pioneer Commissioner appointed in 1563 to plant new kirks within the Diocese of Moray had a grasp of the territory he served. He clearly passed this understanding to his son, Timothy, who as a minister and a topographer created the first comprehensive maps of Scotland. Timothy's map of the Great Glen and Glen Garry[37] shows the "K of Kilchuma" at the centre of a constellation of settlements from Glenmoriston to Glengarry and Loch Lochy. The map graphically portrays the juxtaposition of church and community, something that Timothy Pont no doubt intended to impart.

For Christians today that juxtaposition of church and community remains a significant impetus for work and witness. The knowledge that their residence within the area is part of a Divine Plan serves to emphasise the privilege and the responsibility that rests upon the shoulders of God's people, "the people I formed for myself". The promise of God's eternal presence and power will inspire His people to serve with faithfulness and effectiveness. The place in which a

Christian community lives can be the threshold of new and creative initiatives, and that is true wherever that place may be. It is no mistake that God's people are living where they are! As Paul said when addressing the Athenians, God "marked out their appointed times in history and the boundaries of their lands. God did this so that they would seek him and perhaps reach out for him and find him, though he is not very far from any one of us."[38]

Steve Aisthorpe challenges every Christian when he asks if "it is possible to refocus our attention and energies on Jesus, to rediscover our first love and reignite a passion for living wholeheartedly for him."[39] Paul Williams suggests that we need "to understand our present experience as part of the permanent characteristic of Christian identity, to be in the world but not of it. Jesus' prayer [for his disciples[40]] suggests that by virtue of our allegiance to Jesus, we are no more of the world-as-it-is than he is, but we are, nonetheless, sent into it. This is what characterises Christian pilgrimage – perhaps best put in the language of the ancient Celtic missionaries – a voluntary exile for Christ."[41]

"… that they may proclaim my praise"

"Lift them up, you ancient doors, that the King of glory may come in"
[Psalm 24: 9]

A people called to proclaim God's praise: that is the calling of Christians. Worship is a sacrifice both of praise and the starting point for our work and witness[42]: it is the mainspring of the Christian's service to others. The act of worship is the point at which the desire for change, within and without, is sparked. It is the time for confession, consecration and commitment. It is the opportunity to see the world as God sees it, the lens through which we understand how God's own Son has redeemed and refreshed the world. In worship, God's people are energised and equipped to do great things, no matter how impoverished or marginalised or remote they may be from the centres of influence and power. As in worship, so too in service: "congregations must now learn how to live the gospel as a distinct people who are no longer at the cultural center. The emerging experience of the churches is indeed that of being on the culture's margins."[43]

The Scottish poet Charlotte Runcie, recalling a visit to Holy Island set between the North Sea and the Northumbrian coast, tells of "this in-between place [where] something real and solid can grow from the intangible."[44]   The spiritual heritage of Holy Island continues to bear fruit on its geographical threshold between land and sea, and it bears testimony to the truth that places "on the edge", at the interface of different regions, may have a valuable role in Christian witness and Kingdom-building. Such places are certainly vulnerable in the face of their larger neighbours, but they may also be crucibles for innovation and change.

Joyce MacMillan, the Scottish cultural commentator, has written "that negative attributes of poverty and 'remoteness' have been imposed … on many landscapes … by people and their power structures, **and can be changed by them** …"[45]   The Christian Church, which gathers together those who testify to changed lives and attitudes through Jesus Christ, should certainly have the boldness to embrace a new approach to the places and communities in which they reside. Sadly, "What began as a Spirit-empowered movement has become hindered by excessively complex and risk-averse institutions. The Christian way has been domesticated and it is time to rediscover the adventure of faith."[46]

The call to the contemporary church, and to the church in impoverished, marginal and remote settings especially, is to embrace new patterns of ministry. There is an urgent need to move from traditional forms of ministry to transformative models. The parish ministry must become a pioneer ministry. The congregation must no longer be the sole focus of ministry, but instead the focus should be on the community as a whole. The denominational labels have to take second place so that each local church may be a lively demonstration of the diversity and unity of God's people. The church, so often perceived as being self-absorbed, must become a channel of grace to the locality. A readiness on the part of all Christians to embrace such transformations is essential if the Good News is to make an impact in the current century. The adventure awaits, but a new mind-set is required: "having heard [Jesus'] call afresh, we need to respond by culling what is unhelpful, live lives of simple and courageous obedience, and trust God that what emerges will reflect the splendour of his kingdom."[47] This will not be straightforward, for "experience of the margins causes a group to feel very vulnerable": however such a liminal place "is also a place of opportunity, creativity, and transformation." It is at this place, it is suggested, that the Spirit may be found "inviting the church to rediscover its missional heart in unimagined and unexpected places."[48]

The Church of Scotland's *Church without Walls* report challenged the congregations to "turn again to the people with Jesus at the centre, travelling wherever Jesus takes us."[49] This challenge is as relevant to rural churches as to larger urban congregations. A contemporary observer has stated that "Some smaller churches, having grasped the tendency of God we find in Scripture – to champion the needy and to use what is weak to show His power and glory – are full of faith. They are a joy to visit. They are a band of brothers and sisters, full of hope and love, who are up for anything so long as it is biblical and will promote Christ's name."[50] More than ever the church will prove its effectiveness through the creation of a real sense of community, both within its congregations and also in the communities in which those congregations live and work. The local church must always be an example of the Kingdom of God and a source of transformation for those amongst whom it is placed. Small rural communities are ideal "seed beds" in which Christians may share the love of Christ in word and in deed. The rural church of tomorrow may be very different from the church of the past, but this study has shown how God's people may respond and adapt to changing circumstances.

The Celtic Christian heritage of the Great Glen still offers both a challenge to and a channel for today's Christians. After all "their spirituality was that of those on the edge. They were groupings of Christians clinging onto faith at the edge of the known world ... It is a spirituality and theology of the insecure ..."[51] The Celtic prayer, recorded by one who lived "on the edge" in the Uists, takes us back to the saint who played a part in establishing the Christian faith in northern Scotland:

> May the herding of Columba
> encompass you going and returning,
> encompass you in strath and on ridge,
> and on **the edge of each rough region**;
> may it keep you from pit and from mire,
> keep you from hill and from crag,
> keep you from loch and from downfall,
> each evening and each darkling;
> may it keep you from the mean destroyer,
> keep you from the mischievous niggard,
> keep you from the mishap of bar-stumbling
> and from the untoward fays.
> The peace of Columba be yours in the grazing,
> the peace of Brigit be yours in the grazing,
> the peace of Mary be yours in the grazing,
> and may you return home safe-guarded.[52]

The prayer evokes both the creativity of the periphery and the peaceful homecoming when the "boundless boundaries" are recognised and then crossed.

Therefore, my dear brothers and sisters, stand firm
Let nothing move you
Always give yourselves fully to the work of the Lord,
because you know that your labour
in the Lord is not in vain
[1 Corinthians 15:58]

Let us not become weary in doing good,
for at the proper time we will reap a harvest
if we do not give up
Therefore, as we have opportunity, let us do good to all people,
especially to those who belong to the family of believers
[Galatians 6:9,10]

May our Lord Jesus Christ himself and God our Father,
who loved us and by his grace gave us eternal encouragement
and good hope, encourage your hearts
and strengthen you in every good deed and word
[2 Thessalonians 2:16,17]

A Prayer for the Great Glen

Father God, in this place of beauty and blessing,
    may we behold your mountain heights,
    and may our eyes of trust embrace your true delights
May we discover your well of love as deep as the loch,
    and may our feet of faith be planted upon you, the rock

Lord Jesus Christ, along with your people of failure and faith,
    may we reflect upon your life so cruelly riven,
    and may our thanks be humbly given
May we see your life-blood so lovingly outpoured,
    and may our attention be focussed upon you, our Lord

Holy Spirit, attended with your power of wind and flame,
    may we experience your Spirit, steady as the breeze,
    and may our hope be as sturdy as the trees
May we be cleansed by love's forgiving stream,
    and may our lives be changed by your transforming gleam

                                  Amen

Adrian Varwell

ANNEX 1:

SETTLEMENT AT KILCHUIMEN, 1676

The Supplication, presented by the Ministers of Boleskine and Urquhart and others to the Bishop and Chancellor, patrons of their parishes, is engrossed within the minute of the Presbytery of Inverness of 22 March, 1676. The same minute records a report of the introduction of Mr Monro at Kilchuimen on 12 March. [Scottish History Society Publications, Vol 24, "Records of the Presbyteries of Inverness and Dingwall, 1643-88, 68-71]

Supplication of Abertarff and Glenmoriston

"Unto the Right Reverend Father in God Murdo Lo. Bishope of Morray undoubted Patrone of the Kirks of Boleskine and Abertarfe, and to the Reverend Mr. James Stewart, Chancillour of Morray, undoubted Patron of the Kirks of Urquhart and Glenmoriston, Wee the under- subscryving heretours, gentlemen, and Elders of Abertarfe and Glenmoriston, humblie supplicatethe,

THAT Whereas upon mature and serious consideration we the said Ministers and respective Parishioners have unanimously agreed and condescended with Mr. Robert Monroe, Expectant, to serve hereafter *per vices* at Abertarfe and Glenmoriston with the benefice and office according as our said condescendence subscryved mutually be us at more length beares, and that we have before our eyes the glorie of God, the propogation of his Gospell there, the peoples necessity of constant inform'n and reformation, with repression of popry upon the growing hand neer these bounds, which wee cannot punctually wait on so frequently as wee would wish in respect of the distance of these places and the dangerous waters interjected betwixt them and our usual residence in our other congregations: Herefore wee humblie and cordially supplicat your Lo. and Mr. James Stewart, the other Patrone, to homologate and ratifie this our reasonable, mutuall, and just desire, that thereupon your Lo. may passe ane order to the Moderator and [Presbytery] of Inverness for settling [presently] and speedily the said Mr. Robert in the function of the Holy Ministrie there, seeing wee have had divers tymes of great satisfaction of his doctrine in the said congregations: And in answeiring this our lawful desire as your Lo. will doe good and great service to your Master the Lord Jesus Christ, and be instrumentall to settle further illumination and knowledge in these dark and remote corners of your dioces, So you will move us allwayes in our severall statione to beg that the Lord may continue you long above us in your most holy function, and to remain, as we still are,

Your Lo. most humble affectionat Servants and Supplicants,

J. GRANT of Glenmoriston

Mr. JAMES GRANT, Minister at Urqhart

Mr. T. HOUSTON, Minister at Boleskin

Jo. FRASER of Little Glendo

Jo. FRASER of Borlume

M. FRASER of Culduthell

ALEXr. FRASER in Carngodie"

There follow consents from both the Bishop and Chancellor of Moray as Patrons of Boleskine and Urquhart.

Introduction at Kilchuimen

"Mr. Thomas Huison and and Mr. James Grant reported that according to the Bishopps order they were at Kilchuimen upon the 12 of March, being the Lords day, and Mr. Thomas Huison did preach [text left blank] and after sermone delivered to the said Mr. Robert Monro the sacred bible, and the keys of the Churches doors, with the books of discipline, as is usuall in such cases, seriously exhorting him to humility, fidelity, and sedulity in his future ministeriall function, and immediately, thereafter all the gentlemen and elders [present] did cordially and unanimously, by reaching furth of their hands, signifying and declaring by this their acceptance of the said Mr. Robert Monro for their future Minister in these respective bounds of Abertarfe and Glenmoriston, promising obedience, faithfulness, and assistance to him, according to their severall power and charge.

Sicklyke the said Mr. Thomas declared that he gave the said Mr. Robert reall possession and infeftment in the manse and gleib by delivering to him timber, stone, and earth, as is usuall in such cases."

ANNEX 2:

FORT AUGUSTUS CHURCH SEATING

1862		
GROUND	PROPRIETOR	OCCUPANT
1	Kirk Session	Messrs Ryle, Douglas & Burton
2	Mr Murdoch Grant	Mr Murdoch Grant
3	Dr McDonnell, Glenurquhart	Mr Fraser, Kinlochunigan
4	Mr George Harrower	Mr G Harrower
5	Mr Angus Fraser	Mr A Fraser
6 & 7	Kirk Session	Mrs Gillespie
8	Rev J McIntyre, Kilmonivaig & Mr George Masson	Mr McKenzie, King's Inn
9	Mr Duncan MacDonald	
10	Mrs McIntosh	Mrs McIntosh
11	Kirk Session	Mr Joseph King
12	Mr John Fraser	Mr John Fraser
13	Kirk Session	
14	Kirk Session	
15	Kirk Session	Mr Robert Grant
16	Kirk Session	Mr Purdon
17	Kirk Session	
18	Don McKenzie	Mr Fraser
19	Kirk Session	
20	Kirk Session	
21	Kirk Session	Choir
22	Kirk Session	Mr Rufford
23	Kirk Session	Mr Martin
24	Mr Wm McRimmon	Mr Bisset
25	Kirk Session	Miss McDonald
26	Kirk Session	Capt Ross
No reference to the Galleries, perhaps because they were reserved for the Fort?		

1863		
GROUND	PROPRIETOR	OCCUPANT
1	Kirk Session	G Douglas
2	Kirk Session	A Kyle
3	Mrs Grant	Miss Grant
4	Dr McDonald	Thos. Fraser
5	Geo. Harrower	Geo. Harrower
6	Mr Angus Fraser	Mr Angus Fraser
7	Kirk Session	Mrs Gillespie
8	Kirk Session	H Munro
9	Geo. Mason	George Mason
10		McRae - Fort
11	Mrs N McIntosh	Mrs N McIntosh
12	Kirk Session	Joseph King
13	John Fraser	John Fraser
14	Kirk Session	John McBean
15	Kirk Session	Robt. Grant
16	Kirk Session	J Purdon
17	Kirk Session	Campbell
18	Kirk Session	Mrs Fraser
19	Kirk Session	Mr Shaw
20	Kirk Session	Mr Bain
21		Choir
22	Kirk Session	Mr Rufford
23	Kirk Session	Mr Martin
24	W McRimmon	Mr Bisset
25	Kirk Session	Miss McDonald
26	Kirk Session	Capt Ross
GALLERY		
West	1 Front	Mr C Campbell/Miss McBean
West	2	Robert Munro
North	1 Front - west	Sejs Anderson & Harrison
North	Front - east	Mrs Rufford for Servants
North	Back - east	Ewen McIntosh
East	Front	Mrs Cameron
East	2	Brown, John Dewar
East	3	Lawrence & J Park
-do-		Mrs Hutchison

ANNEX 3:

THE GLENGARRY AFFAIR: 1871/1883

The following are but a selection of reports, letters and comments in contemporary journals and elsewhere. Scottish and English dailies carried the story, along with titles as varied as John Bull and the Western Morning News in Plymouth! Denominational papers such as the Independent (non-conformist) and the Church Herald (Church of England) carried their own partisan comments, and the weekly Inverness Courier did its best to collate the reports. Not all of these organs are contained within the British Newspaper Archive, so the Inverness paper becomes the principle source of reference. So far as is possible, especially given the time-lag inherent in weekly publications, the items below are laid out in real-time order to chart the unfolding of what became known as "The Glengarry Affair."

3 September: Bishop Wilberforce writes to his wife
[Reproduced in "Life of the Rt. Rev. Samuel Wilberforce," A R Ashwell and R G Wilberforce, New York, 1883, 519]

"There are no services here today, so I am going to give one in their kirk, of my own, to this party this afternoon."

12 September: Protest against the Bishop of Winchester
[Letter from Charles Hartley of Hertfordshire, published in John Bull, 16 September]

"I read this day in the *Standard* with profound sorrow that the Bishop of Winchester has lately been preaching in a Presbyterian Kirk in Scotland. There is a limit to the principle, "All things to all men;" and I venture to say that the Bishop has in this instance transgressed it. It is a yearly subject of sorrow to good Churchmen to hear of their *Queen* worshipping in a kirk. But it is with far deeper sorrow and more unmixed amazement that they hear of a *Bishop* worshipping with those, and (unless he is misrepresented) helping to take a lead in the worship of those who deliberately reject Episcopacy."

12 September: Account of the Archbishop's Service
[Extract of letter from 'M', Glengarry, Daily Telegraph, 15 September. Was this George Malcolm the Glengarry Estate Factor?]

"... last Sunday he conducted the Presbyterian service and preached the sermon in the Established Kirk. The occasion was the afternoon service: that of the forenoon having been conducted in Gaelic by the resident Presbyterian minister, Mr Cameron. It was known that the Archbishop was to preach, and the little church was filled. His Grace entered the pulpit dressed in his ordinary walking garb. In true Presbyterian style he commenced the service with the usual words of unwritten liturgy which does exist in Scotland – 'Let us begin the worship of God by singing to His praise the Hundredth Psalm.' Then the Archbishop read the Scottish metrical version, beginning with the words 'All people that on earth do dwell.' Next came the usual prayer which it is the custom of the Scottish clergy to respect as if it were called forth by the inspiration of the moment, and which some, no doubt, do utter with the unpremeditation of pious fervour. Dr Thomson, however, was unequal to the accomplishment of that highest feat of Scottish invocation. He used the words of the English Prayer Book. He so strung one prayer to another as to form a whole, and he cast the Litany into a continuous invocation by placing the words 'Deliver us' before each set of petitions. Of course, no petitions came, or were meant to come, from the congregation. The Archbishop repeated the words 'Deliver us from all blindness of heart, from pride, from vain-glory, and hypocrisy; from envy, hatred, and malice, and all uncharitableness. Deliver us from all sedition, privy conspiracy, and rebellion; from all false doctrine, heresy, and schism; from hardness of heart, and contempt of Thy word and commandment.' His Grace vigorously tried to repeat the words without looking at the book. He strenuously endeavoured to equal the Presbyterian ministers at their own work. But his memory failed to carry him completely through the task of repetition, and now and again he was forced to cast furtive glances at the printed page. Next, in Presbyterian fashion, he read a chapter from the Old Testament and the New; and then came a plain, practical sermon on the several classes represented by Felix, Agrippa, and Paul, when the Apostle to the Gentiles was brought before the judgement seat, and confounded the Roman potentates by the dignity of his bearing and the force of his personality. The chapters were the English Church lessons for the day; but of course the fact was unknown to the Presbyterian worshippers. Perhaps the Archbishop wished to give a sly hint that the English and Scotch services were linked together by some points of likeness. His Grace concluded by uttering a prayer of his own composition. The prayer was written, but he tried to conceal the fact that he was forced to aid his memory by occasional glances at the paper. Finally came the announcement from archiepiscopal lips that the minister was about to administer the rite of baptism. Dr Thomson, in a word, went through the whole service with admirable fidelity to the Presbyterian model."

14 September: Guests at Invergarry
[Report in Inverness Courier, 14 September]

"The Bishop of Winchester and the Archbishop of York have this season been the guests of Mr Ellice at Invergarry. On the 3d. inst. the former conducted divine service in the parish church at Glengarry, and last Sunday his Grace the Archbishop officiated. The former preached from the words in St Luke's Gospel, eleventh chapter and tenth verse, "For every one that asketh receiveth." The discourse, we are told – and we can well believe it – was a masterpiece of touching eloquence. Dr Wilberforce gets the credit of being High Church in his views, but however that may be, he conducted worship, in the present instance, according to the simple forms of the Presbyterian Church. Last Sunday the Archbishop of York occupied the same pulpit, and conducted worship in the same manner. He preached an impressive sermon from Acts 26th chapter, verses 27th to 29th. The courtesy of the parish minister, the Rev. Mr Cameron, in asking these distinguished prelates of a sister Church to officiate, is just as much deserving of praise as their ready and cordial assent."

15 September: "... these rather notorious prelates"
[Letter from Mr Stuart of Broughty Ferry, published in The Scotsman, 21 September]

"Sir, The announcement that the Archbishop of York and the nicely-plastic Bishop of Winchester have been officiating in a Presbyterian kirk, and according to Presbyterian usage too, will no doubt puzzle many Christians of various communions who may be endeavouring, according to their light, to be legitimately consistent and loyal to the principles they profess ... we all know that the late and present Archbishop of Canterbury have left it on record that the Anglican Church was in communion alone, in Scotland, with her Scottish Episcopal sister. ... can it really be that these rather notorious prelates deliberately intend to ... forswear their professed instincts as Bishops of the Church Catholic, in favour ... of Scottish Erastianism and moribund Calvinism?

Do they intend ... to reciprocate the courtesy of the Rev. Mr Cameron ... and place their cathedrals' pulpits ... at his disposal?"

16 September: Comment by the Daily Telegraph
[From the Editorial, 16 September: a pawky exploration of the events at Glengarry, and their implications for the Church of England]

" ... on Sunday last, in the Scotch kirk at Glengarry, a distinguished ecclesiastic of the English Establishment not only conducted a Presbyterian service, but preached a sermon from the pulpit of Nonconformity, and announced the administration of the rite of baptism to a parcel of laddies and lassies who were no more "sheep of the flock" than Cheviots are South Downs. Does it matter that the guilty man dovetailed the Book of Common Prayer with the Kirk Service in a most ingeneous manner? He compromised matters, we know, as to the opening "screed," by giving out the

Hundredth Psalm; he transformed the Litany into a Scotch prayer by working the responses into the invocations; he picked out the lessons for the day for his reading, and when he pronounced the extempore "bethankit" at the close, he cunningly hid his MS. under the cushion. But do all these sinister strokes of cleverness alter the complexion of the proceeding? And, above all, how about those Glengarry babies? Has not an alarmed Church Militant the duty and the right to inquire, "Into whose baptism were they baptised?" Cross-bred lambs, christened in a kirk, under a rite sanctioned, at least, if not administered, by an Episcopalian – whose are they? and to what pastures do they appertain?"

[It was the son of Mr Malcolm, the Factor, who was baptised on 10 September: the Register was signed by Mr Cameron]

" ... when we come to look more closely, it is no other that the Archbishop of YORK who gave out that hymn at Glengarry last "LORD'S DAY," and preached to an audience of shrewd Presbyterians! Shades of SPOTTISWOODE and LAUD! What is to be said or done about such a dilemma as this? The Metropolitan of York – "Ebor" himself – tucks up his robes and "loups" the wall which divides the schism of the Covenant from his own communion, and then, "dressed in ordinary walking garb," goes through the service of the Kirk ... worse still remains behind. ... The startling tidings are added that only one "Sabbath" before the Bishop of WINCHESTER, of all Prelates in the world, officiated in the same Kirk ...
       ... it were indeed difficult to over estimate the significance of such startling events. If Archdeacon DENISON and his party have any idea of prosecuting the Archbishop and the Bishop under the Act of Uniformity, it must be, we warn them, their own affair. We may have been astounded at this "Highland Fling," but our surprise is that of pleasure to find the leading dignitaries of the National

Church thus playing the part of the Missionary, and nobly doing what in them lies to convert our countrymen, on both sides of the Tweed, from Sectarianism to Christianity. A genuine movement towards something far better than wranglings of High and Low Church, and bitter memories of war to the death between Covenant and Prelacy, really appears to be in progress at last…"

16 September: Explanation by the Primus
[Letter from Bishop Eden, Scotsman, 19 September]

"On Sunday, the 3d of September, the Bishop of Winchester, being on a visit to Mr Ellice at Invergarry, was kindly allowed the use of the Parish Church, as the incumbent was absent, having to conduct services of his church on that day at Glenquoich. I was very much obliged to the Bishop of Winchester for thus affording to Mr Ellice's family and household, and many other Episcopalians in the neighbourhood, the opportunity of enjoying the services of our Church, which, for want of clergy, I cannot supply. The ordinary service of the Church was slightly abbreviated, and as the Bishop concluded his service with an extempore prayer, this probably gave rise to the statement that the services had been conducted according to the forms of the Established Church of Scotland."

17 September: The Archbishop in the pew
[The Inverness Courier, 21 September, carried the news that the Archbishop had worshipped at Invergarry]

"On Sunday last his Grace the Archbishop of York, who had the previous Sunday officiated in the parish church of Glengarry, was among the worshippers in the Glengarry congregation. … The Rev. Mr Menzies, Fort Augustus, officiated. The Archbishop and Mrs Thomson left next day for Skye."

18 September: Explanation by the Bishop of Winchester
[Copy of letter published in the Inverness Courier, 28 September. There is some confusion within the press as to whether this letter was addressed to Dr George Mackness, St Mary's Parsonage, Broughty Ferry, or to the Bishop of Oxford, Dr Mackarness. In a letter to The Times (29 September) the Bishop of Oxford states that he had had no communication with the Bishop of Winchester on the subject]

"In reply to your letter, I beg to explain to you that the service referred to was a mission service, there being no English service in the village that day, and many strangers and others. It had of course nothing to do with the orders, &c. of the Presbyterian body. The kirk, as a building, was offered for an English Bishop's service in it, and accepted readily by me. I believe that I did what St Paul did at the place where prayer was wont to be made. Nor can I conceive that such a mission service has any tendency to increase the difficulties of our beloved sister, the Church of Scotland. [*Did he mean the Scottish Episcopal Church?*] What I did met with the full approval of the Primus."

18 September: A step in the right direction
[The Scotsman Editorial copied a comment from The Echo]

"We cannot doubt Dr Thomson has taken a step which will hereafter be noted as an early one in the right direction. The walls of prejudice which have so long stood up between the various Churches of Christendom … are beginning to crumble away; and blessed is the man who pulls down a stone of them."

19 September: Protest from Archdeacon Denison
[Letter to the Daily Telegraph published 21 September]

He writes of "the ridiculous and indecent spectacle of prosecutions of clergy by Bishops … for alleged breaches of the law of the land before courts of law. Archbishops and Bishops can hardly do such things as we have seen done in Scotland, and proceed the next day to send "letters of request" to the Court of Arches that one of their brethren may be tried for breaking the law.

It may, however, be as well for the Archbishops and Bishops to consider a little that, by conducting the worship of a Presbyterian chapel, they forfeit their own claim to the exclusive privileges, endowments, and position of a Bishop in the Church of England."

20 September: Riposte to the letter from the Primus
[Part of a letter from "Veritas", published in The Scotsman, 22 September, writing as one having been present on both Sundays]

"On the Sunday on which the Bishop of Winchester officiated … in Glengarry Church, Mr Cameron, the incumbent, had occasion to go to the further end of his parish to preach, and as no other minister had been provided to officiate in Glengarry Church, the Bishop of Winchester, who had only arrived at Mr Ellice's house the previous evening, most kindly and frankly offered to do so, and his offer gladly accepted. The Bishop of Moray, &c., says 'the ordinary service of the Church' (meaning, I suppose, the Church of England service) was slightly 'abbreviated,' and that 'the Bishop concluded his sermon with an extempore prayer,' for the rest meaning all to understand that there was no further conformity to the established Presbyterian forms. Nothing, however, could be more incorrect than the Bishop of Moray's version of the proceedings. The Bishop of Winchester was quite willing, if he did not also express the wish, to conform to the order of worship statedly following in Glengarry

Church, and that he might be able to do so quite accurately, he had supplied himself with a memorandum or kind of programme of the order of worship followed in this and all other parish churches in Scotland, which memorandum every one in the church must have observed the Bishop making frequent use of as he passed from one portion of the service to another. Besides the prayers and sermon, to which the Bishop of Moray, &c., confines his attention, the service in question included the singing of portions of three or four psalms in the Scottish metrical version, the reading of two portions of the Scriptures from the Old and New Testament respectively, and the pronouncing of the benediction; in short, with the slight difference that the first prayer – which was, however, not read, but spoken from memory – contained some portions of the Church of England form, the whole service was conducted, as was originally announced in your columns, strictly in conformity with the usual Presbyterian order. Not even the sermon was read, and had it not been so well known who the distinguished prelate was, few or none in the large congregation could have guessed otherwise than that he was one of the neighbouring clergymen come, as their manner is, to fill a brother minister's pulpit for a day.

It may be added that on the following Sunday, when his Grace the Archbishop of York officiated, exactly the same order of worship was adhered to; and as the correspondent of the *Daily Telegraph*, who was present, says, the Archbishop 'went through the whole service with admirable fidelity to the Presbyterian model,' excepting only that his Grace, for the most part, *read* his prayers – not furtively, as the *Telegraph's* correspondent unbecomingly and erroneously avers, but openly enough, and with much elocutive power.

The Bishop of Moray, &c., rather patronisingly expresses his obligation to the Bishop of Winchester for 'affording Mr Ellice's family and household, and many other Episcopalians in the neighbourhood, the opportunity of enjoying the services of our

Church, which, for want of clergy, I cannot supply.' Probably this want is not found indispensable, for it is observed that Mr Ellice and his household never omit attendance on the usual service within the church of the parish, which he, with great liberality and consideration for the wants of the district, has himself endowed, and seem quite satisfied with the ministrations there afforded. What the Bishop of Moray, &c., means when he speaks of the 'many other Episcopalians in the neighbourhood' I cannot tell. I ought, however, to have a good means of knowing this, and I cannot, save those to be found in Mr Ellice's house and neighbouring shooting lodge, who are only temporarily resident in Glengarry, put my finger on one within many miles of the parish church of Glengarry."

20 September: "Dissenting Ritualists"
[Extract of letter from "F.A." published in The Scotsman, 25 September]

"Dr Eden is however especially thankful because Mr Ellice and his family and household had an opportunity of enjoying services which he, "from want of clergy," cannot supply. Was he ever requested to make supply for Glengarry? He may be poor in clergy, in more senses than one, but it is very well known that Mr Ellice is not poor in any sense. I take it that Mr Ellice is very well able to supply himself with the sort of clergyman he likes best ... Instead, however, of applying for any of the Edenic clergy of Moray, he built and endowed a parish church, and presented thereto a clergyman of the Established Church of Scotland, and therein worships from Sunday to Sunday with praiseworthy regularity, evidently little regretting Bishop Eden's "want of clergy." I have the happiness of meeting many Church of England people from year to year in Scotland, and, so far as I have observed, they do not consider that public worship or devotion is linked to any special "forms," and as a rule they enjoy the simple and Scriptural worship of the National Church, and prefer to uphold the established, time-honoured institutions of the country, to connecting themselves with a set of Dissenting Ritualists, mostly foreigners, who call themselves Bishops in Scotland."

21 September: Reply from Rev Alexander Cameron
[From Glengarry Manse, 21 September to The Edinburgh Courant, reproduced in the Inverness Courier, 28 September]

"A letter from Bishop Eden, of Inverness, appears in your columns. The letter relates to services held in the church of this parish. On the occasions referred to the Bishop of Winchester and the Archbishop of York were kind enough to officiate for the benefit of my congregation at large, and it was understood that the usual order of Presbyterian worship would be observed. This was the case on both occasions. Those who were conversant with the Liturgy of the Church of England recognised in the first prayer of the service a compilation from the prayers of that Liturgy, but to the great majority of the congregation the service was precisely the same that they are accustomed to every Sabbath. While neither wishing nor intending to enter into any further correspondence on the subject, I think it is incumbent upon me, as minister of the parish, thus to guard against the different inference which Bishop Eden's letter might, by some, be considered to convey. I avail myself of this opportunity to express on my own part, and on that of my congregation, our grateful acknowledgements to the right rev. prelates, who in thus so kindly and readily giving us their services displayed an amiable and brotherly feeling towards our sister Church. The impressive simplicity with which they urged the great truths and precepts of our common religion will long be remembered in the glen. May I venture to express a hope that on some future occasion Bishop Eden may himself favour us by following their Christian and beneficial example."

21 September: "the courtesies of ... Christian fellowship"
[Part of an undated letter from "T"; The Scotsman, 21 September]

The incident "shows that when men – even Church dignitaries – are out of the atmosphere of religious formalism, they allow themselves to be guided by Christian good sense and the courtesies of that Christian fellowship which is so much deeper than any religious differences ... and is combined with any breadth of intelligence."

21 September: What is the difference?
[A letter from "A Minister of the Church of Scotland"; The Scotsman, 21 September]

"Sir, - If, as Bishop Eden says, the service at "the Church" was "abbreviated," and the English Bishop "concluded his sermon with an extempore prayer," wherein did the services materially differ from those "conducted according to the forms of the Church of Scotland?""

25 September: The Scotsman Editorial
[Occupying nearly two full columns the Editorial reviewed the "affaire Glengarry", from which extracts are reproduced]

"It is not easy to assign a cause for the sudden storm of Bishops that has been prevailing during the last fortnight. Here we have had the Bishop of Brechin, the Bishop of Winchester, the Archbishop of York, the Primus Bishop of Moray, and the Bishop of St Andrews, successively or conjointly demanding attention, and more or less painfully troubling the minds of men. ...

The *affaire Glengarry* is originally chargeable to the Bishop of Winchester. It was he who first threw the firebrand of ecclesiastical strife into that peaceful vale and made its modest parish church the centre of a sectarian warfare ... It is he who is responsible for the rage of the *Guardian*, and the raptures of the *Telegraph*, for the meek chidings of the *Record*, the Cassandra-like screaming of the *Church Herald*, and the sulky growling of Archdeacon Denison, for the Jesuitical plot patent to the detectives of the *Independent*, and the millennial vision vouchsafed to the seers of the *Echo*. The Archbishop of York is but a secondary performer in this matter. He merely developed the idea of his daring and original predecessor. ...

The High Churchmen regard him [YORK] as little better than Dean Stanley or even Bishop Colenso, and would have thought it exactly what was to be expected. The Broad Churchmen, for much the same reason, would have thought much the same thing, though in a kindlier spirit. But that Winchester, the High Churchmen's own redoubtable Samuel, should have administered the so-called rites of a schismatical and outcast sect, was enough to make Broad Churchmen stare, and High Churchmen grow black in the face ... the Marquis of Salisbury toasting "Home Rule" at a Fenian banquet, could not be a more unexpected and staggering event ...

Those who have been taught by the Bishop of Winchester and his fellow-Churchmen to regard the Apostolic Succession as all in all, may well feel scandalised at his latiduninarian behaviour; while those who regard the said succession as a superstitious figment ... will be in a like manner gratified. ...

Of all the cases of distress originating from Bishop Wilberforce's escapade, perhaps the most to be commiserated is that of Bishop Eden ... His misery has expressed itself, however, in such a curious form, that many hard-hearted persons may be inclined to laugh ... Yet if anyone has more cause than another to mourn over the lapse of the southern Prelates it is their brother of Moray. He gives himself out as virtually Archbishop of Scotland, and the rightful head of Christianity in Scotland, and, though supported by only two per cent of the population, does not hesitate to unchurch the remaining ninety-eight, and treat them as ecclesiastical rebels, and all on the ground of possessing this same Apostolic Succession. Yet here comes a successor of the Apostles from one of the few Churches which Bishop Eden recognises as such, and practically declares that the Succession does not much matter, and that he will preach and pray with and for the unapostolic ninety-eight as readily as the apostolic two. ...

Accordingly it is not surprising to find Moray rubbing his eyes, and asking whether it can be possible that Winchester has actually knocked the legs from below him. In the end, the Primus is persuaded by himself, or his inquiries, or both, that all his Glengarry excitement is groundless, that it has no root in fact, that it was not a Presbyterian service at all which the Bishop of Winchester performed in the Parish Church, but a pure Church of England service for the exclusive benefit of Episcopalian residenters ...

In his view, the erection called the Parish Church of Glengarry, is not a church in any true sense, but a kind of shed, in a remote part of the diocese of Moray, for the protection of a number of persons who meet for the transaction of certain irregular and unauthorised religious ceremonies. This shed, being more convenient to sit in that Mr Ellice's coach-house, or even drawing-room ... was used by them as an unlicensed place of Episcopal worship in strict accordance with the canons of the Scottish Episcopal Church. ...

The Glengarry shed, it must be remembered, not only protects schismatics from the weather, but is itself protected by the law from all but certain uses ...

Altogether, the Primus does not appear to be in an agreeable predicament, and we fear not many out of his own two per cents will much pity him. The general feeling will probably be that the southern Prelates have set an example of good sense and liberal feeling, and that the Bishop of Moray has done his best to place his Church before the country in the light of an insignificant clique of pretentious sacerdotalists, which, as to the general body of its members, is placing that Church in a false light."

27 September: Diocesan Synod of Moray, Ross and Caithness, at Inverness Cathedral

[Report in Inverness Courier, 28 September: there follow extracts from a long debate on the events at Glengarry]

Rev J Brodie Innes: "My Lord, Reverend Brethren, and Brethren of the Laity, we have lately heard of the Bishop of Winchester and the Archbishop of York having on two several Sundays in this month conducted the services in the Established kirk of Glengarry. It appears that this is a matter of importance which can hardly be passed over in silence at this Synod. Of how great significance the occurrence is deemed to be by the public, appears from the large number of articles in the public papers, which, differing widely on the question of the merit or demerit of those articles, agree in ascribing great importance to them. So far as the acts of the two bishops of what has been supposed a Church in full communion with ourselves, can be supposed to represent the mind of their Church, they are undoubtably most important to ourselves, as bearing on our mutual relations. I will not trouble you by reading the accounts which those present have given of the services. I believe they amount to this – That, on the 3d September, the Bishop of Winchester, in the absence of the parish minister, conducted the service in the parish kirk; that he did not appear in his robes; that the prayers used were not the order for service of the Church of England as laid down in the Book of Common Prayer, so that, as one present declares, unless the congregation had known who the officiator was, they would have supposed it was some Presbyterian minister who supplied the place of the regular one. On the following Sunday ... the Archbishop of York is reported to have followed the same course, appearing in the pulpit in his ordinary walking dress, and conducting the service according to Presbyterian use, making together with some of his own composition, use of some Church prayers, altered and adapted for the purpose. There is said, however, to have been this difference, that on this occasion the minister was present, the Archbishop acting as his substitute or assistant or curate, and announcing at the close of the service that the minister would then proceed to administer the rite of baptism. On the following Sunday (17th), it is reported his Grace returned the compliment, by attending the service conducted by the minister. It is hardly possible to imagine (as there was not a communion) a more complete fraternization between the kirk of Glengarry and the Archbishop of York."

He continued by outlining the importance of maintaining fixed principles, pointing out that English clergy were not allowed to officiate in non-conformist places of worship, and that the Archbishop had composed a judgement of the Privy Council which stated that "every vestment, every word, every gesture, was strictly defined by the Prayer-Book, and conformity in the most minute points required in all ministration. It is a matter of simple amazement that the same prelate, having travelled a few miles into the diocese of a brother in full communion with himself, should violate every rule of his own judgement, should conduct a service in the manner reported, and by presenting in the place a part of the extempore prayer of the minister a parody of the Prayer-Book add insult to injury. With what consistency these prelates can in future enforce on their clergy, conformity with the Prayer-Book is a matter in which we are not concerned ..."

There followed reference to the historical trials of the Episcopal Church, having been disestablished, dis-endowed and persecuted, and yet it was now showing signs of growth: the Church had a great future, it was free from State interference, Privy Council judgements and appointments by the Prime Minister. We are, he said "well assured that the acts of the two bishops we have been considering have damaged our position in an infinitely greater degree than any assistance they can have given has advantaged it."

Mr Brodie Innes then moved a resolution "expressing deep regrets at the acts of the Archbishop of York and the Bishop of Winchester in conducting or taking part in public worship at Glengarry without the services of their own Church: and that the Synod considered such a recognition of a body not in communion with their own Church in Scotland by the English bishops as inconsistent with the unity established between the Scottish and English Churches."

The Primus: Whilst agreeing with his colleague upon "the principles and views which you have enunciated," the Primus wished to take "very considerable care" before adopting the resolution. He did not wish to rely upon newspaper reports, so he had written to the Archbishop for words of explanation, but had not yet received a reply. Similar reports about the Bishop of Winchester "were not correct" because "the explanation which he gave to me was perfectly satisfactory. The Bishop came to my house from Glengarry, and he then stated to me what he had done. He had not time to communicate with me before officiating, or he certainly would have done so, to obtain, so to speak, my permission. Whether he was in robes or not, I cannot tell, for it did not occur to me to ask, but what he told me was this – that in the first instance Mr Ellice had asked him to officiate in the schoolroom, which the bishop consented to do. Mr Ellice afterwards, remembering that the parish church was vacant that Sunday, because the minister had to go to Glenquoich to conduct service there, asked the Bishop if he would object to having service in the church instead of the school. The Bishop said he would not object. We therefore had it in the church, using our service, but not in its entirety, and looking upon it as a mission service. He concluded the sermon with an extempore prayer."

The Primus then disputed contrary accounts and continued: "Anxious to comply with Mr Ellice's request to provide service on that Sunday, the Bishop did provide a service, acting, so to speak, as he frequently does in his own diocese, like a missionary providing a mission service." The Primus said that without an explanation from the Archbishop any expression of opinion should await another time.

Rev J Brodie Innes: Having been asked why he had drawn a distinction between the two prelates in his speech, Mr Brodie Innes stated: "The distinction … is this – that the Bishop of Winchester, according to his own statement, conducted mission services, with the addition of an extempore prayer, in the absence of the minister. On the other side, it is said that the Archbishop of York conducted an entirely Presbyterian service, in the presence of the parish minister."

Very Rev Provost Powell: "In a letter I had from the Bishop of Winchester, he says, 'I consider myself in no way mixed up with the Presbyterian service, except to borrow the kirk for a service of my own'."

Rev W West: "Mr West said the Bishop of Winchester's letter was evasive. He spoke of a Bishop's service; but that service he did not deny was exactly as described by an eye witness from beginning to end. Many of the members of Synod feel thankful to Mr Brodie Innes for having brought forward the subject. This is a melancholy instance of the spirit of the time overcoming one who had been a firm supporter of the truth, and a staunch friend to their Church. Still this should not prevent them from expressing their great regret that his lordship should have so acted."

Rev J Macdonald, Synod Clerk: "It occurs to me that the Bishops intended the service as a missionary service entirely, and that they wished to educate these people up to the mark of the Liturgy."

Very Rev Provost Powell: "Whatever colour may be given to [the Bishop of Winchester's] acts by other people, he certainly does not consider that he was mixed up with the Presbyterian service. It seems to me that we are bound to accept [his] disclaimer. … As regards the Archbishop of York we do not know what account he may give. We may charitably suppose that he will give as complete a disclaimer."

Rev E Owen: "Mr Owen thought it was unfortunate that the service at Glengarry was such that both the Episcopalian body and the Presbyterian body could claim it for themselves. While they could not adopt the original resolution of Mr Innes, and ignore the explanations they had heard, might it not be well to place on record an expression of regret that the service was so indefinite, and so leave the matter open?"

The Primus: "The Primus signified that if they wished to express in general terms their regret that the service of the Church was not actually performed, he could not oppose it – at the same time guarding the right of bishops to sanction abbreviated services."

Rev J Ferguson: "Mr Ferguson asked if it would not make the matter worse and intensify the feeling on the subject by taking notice of it by a resolution."

The Primus: "The Primus said that there was a good deal in that view; still the clergy of the diocese might be anxious to express some opinion, and provided that opinion was properly guarded he would not be disposed to say that they ought not to do so."

The Resolution: The Inverness Courier continued that following further consultation the resolution was agreed to in the following form:-

"The Synod regrets that his Grace the Archbishop of York and the Bishop of Winchester, in conducting public service at Glengarry, did not use the entire service as prescribed by the Prayer Book, as by so doing they would have prevented reports which are injurious to the peace and well doing of the Churches. This Synod having read the letter addressed by the Bishop of Winchester to Dr Mackarness [*see comment at 18 September, above*], and having received explanations from the Primus and the Provost that the service intended as a mission service was in so sense a Presbyterian one, desires to express its satisfaction with this disclaimer. And his lordship, the Primus, having intimated that he had communicated with his Grace the Archbishop of York, defers the expression of any opinion on the statements which have been publicly made respecting the manner in which his Grace conducted the service at Glengarry.""'

28 September: Comments from Christian journals
[Contained within the Inverness Courier, 28 September]

"The *Church Herald* has three leaders on the subject, and says 'there is evidently arising, alike among the laity and the clergy of the Church of England, very strong feelings of indignation and disgust at such latitudinarian and lawless conduct on the part of the two right rev. prelates.'

The *Independent*, which is the organ of the English non-conformists, thinks that one reason which may have swayed the prelates in what they did was to strengthen the remaining Church Establishment. On this point it observes – 'These wide-awake leaders of the English Church see to how great a danger the Establishment here is exposed by the isolation in which it stands. If the Establishment of the three kingdoms are to be attacked in detail, and brought down like that in Ireland, the English Church will be left so weak that it will be impossible to maintain it. When the Scotch have lost their Establishment they will not improbably help to destroy the privileges of a neighbouring clergy of which they will then be naturally impatient and jealous. Moreover, it is felt to be impossible to maintain an Episcopal Establishment on the old high grounds of Divine commission while a Presbyterian Establishment is kept up just over the Border. The only hope for Establishment now is in making common cause, and offering a united front to the foe. Broaden the Church, so far, at least, as to comprehend in it all vested interests – that is to be the cry and that the policy of the future.'"

28 September: Comment on the Primus' Letter
["Our London Correspondent", Inverness Courier, 28 September]

"The High Church papers and High Church men are much exercised here with the subject of the English Bisshops preaching in a Highland parish church a few Sundays ago. Their concern is mainly with Dr Wilberforce, the Bishop of Winchester, who is the light and soul of the High Church party. Any fall on his part from the pure and sound primitive form would be a fall indeed. As to Dr. Thomson, the Archbishop of York, he is such a notorious Low Churchman that the Anglican party have given up all concern with him – all interest in him; and they would – oh, how gladly – make a present of him, if they could, to any Presbyterian or Dissenters. But the Bishop of Winchester's defection would, indeed, be as when a standard-bearer fainteth. There is, therefore, great comfort in the assurance of the Primus of the Scotch Episcopal Church that no harm was meant or done; that the forms of the Church were all, or nearly all, preserved; and that only one departure of consequence from the Episcopal form was sanctioned in the extempore prayer at the close – just as an acknowledgement to the place, a sort of quit rent paid to the Presbyterians for the use of the church."

28 September: York to Moray, about the service of 10 September
[Letter from Archbishop of York to Bishop Eden, published in The Times, 2 October]

"In answer to your letter, I write to say that the service which I conducted at Glengarry on the 10th September was precisely the same as that which the Bishop of Winchester held the previous

Sunday. A selection from the Liturgy was used as a prayer, the lessons for the day were read, an extempore sermon preached, an extempore prayer offered, and the benediction pronounced. Several psalms were sung from the Scotch version, the only one which was available. The service was exclusively conducted by myself, and no restriction at all was imposed on me as to the manner of conducting it. I cannot accept the view that it was wholly intended for the Episcopalians in the Glen. It was a mission service conducted by a Bishop, in a building placed unconditionally at his disposal for a mixed congregation, consisting of all those who chose to attend. The population of the Glen is very small; it consists of Episcopalians, Presbyterians, and Roman Catholics, the first being perhaps the least, and the last the most numerous. Such services have been lawful in the Church from the beginning. It is needless for me to say to you that nothing could have been farther from my thoughts than to injure or weaken the Church over which you preside. Had there been an Episcopal Church anywhere within reach on that Sunday, I should have been there to worship or to serve, with the same brotherly readiness which caused me to alter my route and forego other engagements a few days before in order to hold a confirmation for one of your bishops."

[The Archbishop had conducted a Confirmation at Fort William for the Bishop of Argyll before arriving at Glengarry]

29 September: A simple, conclusive test

[Letter from Colin Mackenzie of Edinburgh, published in The Scotsman, 30 September]

"SIR, - I have read the correspondence in your columns, your leading article, and the speeches at the Synod of Moray and Ross on this subject with much interest. I think the disputants have omitted to apply one simple, and yet very conclusive test, to ascertain whether the service was Episcopal or Presbyterian. Were the Psalms sung during it the Scotch metrical version or the English version of Tate and Brady? If the former, the service, according to the facts admitted on both sides, squares substantially with the forms of the Establishment; if the latter, it may fairly be styled an Episcopalian Mission service."

29 September: "... this is what actually took place"
[A second letter from "Veritas", published in The Scotsman, 2 October, reiterated his account of 20 September and countered claims made at the Synod]

" ... on the overwhelming testimony of the minister ... elders, and the whole congregation of Glengarry, to whom appeal can be made, this is what actually took place, and therefore what, in the absence of fuller official explanation, we must accept as an example of the service in question – viz., the Bishop obtained the use of the Glengarry pulpit to officiate, in the Presbyterian form, for the benefit of the *whole congregation* of Glengarry, and did so officiate – without vestments, be it known to Bishop Eden, since he seems to consider acceptable Christian worship cannot be celebrated without vestments."

30 September: A cat, or a dog?
[Amongst an Editorial dissecting the meeting of the Synod of Moray, The Scotsman, 30 September, offered the following observation. Unfortunately much of the archived item is indecipherable]

"The whole affair, it must be admitted, has a strongly Presbyterian look. Nevertheless, it is the view of the Synod, "in no sense Presbyterian." The animal has the head, the body, the legs, and especially the tail of a cat, but, for all that, it is a dog."

30 September: In defence of Mr Ellice

[Letter to the *Record*; the Inverness Courier (printed on 5 October) believed its author to be Dr Cumming, of London]

"Sir, - I have had some opportunity of analysing the somewhat complicated and partially conflicting evidence on this subject – 1. Mr Ellice, M.P., a member of the Church of England, regularly attends the Scotch parish church where he statedly resides. 2. Had he desired to have the English Liturgy read he could have easily persuaded either of his guests, the prelates in question, to perform this service in his drawing-room. 3. The two prelates preferred to officiate in the Scotch parish church, and elected to do so. 4. The Rev. Mr Cameron, minister of the parish, allowed and invited them to occupy his pulpit, but on distinct and definite conditions – viz., that the service should be that used in the Established Church of Scotland – and that there might be no misunderstanding, he placed in their hands the rubrical laws by which it is governed. 5. The prelates engaged to officiate in praise and prayer according to these rubrics, and they did so. 6. Mr Ellice did not, in the parish church, hear read the Liturgy of the Church of England. He did not expect there and then to hear it read. 7. Bishop Eden's statement is totally inapplicable. The service did not meet, nor attempt to meet, the wishes of the Episcopalians. The Bishop and Archbishop did not try to do so. Every Highland peasant in the church joined in the regular forms of his own Church, and recognised no act or utterance at variance with it on the part of either prelate. 8. May not this be the inauguration of an united attempt on the part of our two Established Churches to defend that great principle relinquished in Scotland by certain bodies outside the National Church, and vehemently opposed by Dissenters in England – the principle of national responsibility and national religion as embodied in the Articles and Confessions of the two Established Churches?"

30 September: Bishop Wilberforce to the Dean of Chichester
[Part of letter reproduced in "Life of the Rt. Rev. Samuel Wilberforce," A R Ashwell and R G Wilberforce, New York, 1883, 520,521]

"I *must* ask you to *show* me where I am wrong. I am quite ready to say that I am sorry to have done anything to pain one true-hearted friend like you, and would never have done what I did had I foreseen it. But I *cannot* say that I think, in what I did, there was any ground for the offence. I think there was abundant ground in what W. Ebor did. He identified himself with the unapostolic intrusive Presbyterian ministry. I did nothing of the sort. As to using the kirk, I no more encouraged Presbyterianism in that than, if I had preached the Gospel in a cow-house, I should have encouraged vaccination. But you say I ought to have said our whole Office. Why? I did say it privately in my own room. I did not consider the Morning Service one fit for it. if you went into a heathen land to preach the Gospel to half-taught Christians, would you feel bound to read the whole Office first? I do not feel bound in England, if I take a Mission Service in a school, to do so. On the contrary, I have too much veneration for our Service to have done so. I showed my colours: began with our Confession, got no response, saw it was maltreating our Service; so I read openly out of the Prayer Book, to show that I was so reading it, the prayers I could, collects, etc. Now do explain to me why you object to this. *The* thing I thought it my duty to avoid, was to give any sanction to the Presbyterian asserted ministerial Commission, and this I did. But except as a public service of our Church, I have never felt any obligation to perform her Service. The truth is that, if I was in fault, it was rather in thinking myself in Heathendom in a Kirk, than anything else. I *could* not have read out our Communion Office in it. Now, do you really think that the Apostolic Office has lost the power of free Mission-teaching and praying, under such circumstances?

If you have seen the *resolution* of the Synod of Moray; it was in yesterday's *Daily Telegraph* – when the Synod after discussion voted a resolution of satisfaction with the explanations rendered by me – but required them of W. Ebor."

2 October: The true location of Glengarry!

[Reproduction of part of a letter from Bishop Ewing (Argyll) to the Archbishop of York, dated 2 October; Inverness Courier, 23 November]

"My Dear Lord Archbishop, - I do not know that any letter from me can be of use at this moment; but as I believe that Glengarry lies in this diocese, and not, as has by mistake been supposed, in Moray and Ross, it may be that I am called upon to say a word on the subject. At the same time, as I claim no territorial jurisdiction in the district save over those congregations which submit themselves to my Episcopate, it may seem superfluous to express any opinion as to what takes place in other churches. But as to some people this may not appear to be the case, and as I am called on for an expression of opinion, I cannot but say that your Grace's officiating in the Parish Church of Glengarry gave me well-founded pleasure; for I looked upon it as a step towards that great goal to which I hope all Churches alike are tending, where the distinctions of their various ministries shall be lost and swallowed up in the common objects for which they exist."

1 November: Meeting of the Presbytery of Abertarff

[Inverness Courier, 9 November. The Presbytery minute of this meeting is very much briefer than the newspaper's account which reported Mr Clerk's address at length]

"The Presbytery of Abertarff met at Invergarry on the 1st instant, and this being the first meeting since the month of August last, Mr

Cameron, minister of Invergarry, reported that on the 30th (*sic*) September the Right Rev. Bishop of Winchester had preached in the parish church of Invergarry, and that on the 10th of the same month the Right Rev. the Archbishop of York had preached there; that on both occasions the services were conducted in accordance with the forms of the Church of Scotland.

Having in view the discussions that had already taken place on this subject throughout the country, Mr Clerk, minister of Kilmallie, proposed a deliverance by the Presbytery to the following effect:- "The Presbytery find that Mr Cameron was fully authorised ... to avail himself of the services of the Right Rev. the Archbishop of York and the Right Rev. the Bishop of Winchester, inasmuch as they are both ordained ministers of the Church of England – the other Established Church of this Empire – and conducted the said services according to the usual forms of worship observed in the Church of Scotland. The Presbytery further express their earnest wish that the time may soon come when there shall be a free and brotherly interchange of ministerial services among all the Churches which agree in the essential doctrines of our common Christian faith."

Mr Clerk, in moving this finding, said that with the matter to which Mr Cameron's report referred, as it first stood, they, as a Presbytery of the Church of Scotland, had every reason to be satisfied. When they considered the sacred duty of promoting unity and brotherhood among all the followers of Christ, how necessary, according to the solemn words of our Saviour, the manifestations of this unity to the world was to the universal triumph of His blessed cause; or on the other hand, what distressing results had flowed, and did still flow, from division and strife among professed Christians, they must rejoice in seeing ministers of a Church differing from theirs in forms and observances, but agreeing in the infinitely more important matter of doctrine, cast off the trammels of these forms, and on the ground of their common faith and common hope occupy their pulpits as Christian brethren. He would willingly avoid saying more, but he felt himself in duty bound to protest openly and strongly against the treatment their Church had received in many of the extra-ordinary letters which had appeared on the subject of the now famed Glengarry preachings. In doing so he did not wish to disparage or vilify other Churches, but merely to defend the position and the privileges of their own. If the distinguished prelates who conducted their latest of missionary enterprises among the benighter (*sic*) heathens of Glengarry had seen proper, in their letters published in reference to it, manfully to vindicate the step of Christian liberty which they had taken, they might have inaugurated a brighter day for all the Churches in our land, a day of greater freedom and love. But after having done a truly worthy act they laboured hard to destroy its value, and to throw contempt upon those in whose behalf it was due. They would not acknowledge that they preached in a Presbyterian church – it was merely a building. They did not preach to fellow-Christians, but merely conducted a mission service, as if among the heathen – as the Apostle Paul did at Philippi, where there were no Christians till he made converts by his preaching. This ignoring of the previous existence of Christianity in Glengarry was all the more absurd from the fact that the programme of the usual service in the parish church was faithfully followed out, leaving it uncertain which the converts really were. The tone of their letters became still further unintelligible, when it was remembered that they were both distinguished members of the legislature by which the Church of Scotland, as well as the Church of England, was upheld, and could not be ignorant that the leading doctrine of both Churches was the same. One would fain hope that it had become unnecessary to assert that holding the truth as it is in Jesus, and not a prelatic form of Church government or ceremonial observances, constitutes a church. The Church of Scotland might claim to have received the truth at the Reformation, to say the least of it, as fully as the Church of England, and to have maintained it as strenuously under circumstances the most trying ever since; nor could it be said that their Church in the northern part of the island had been less successful in introducing the people in the truths of religion than the more wealthy and powerful Church of the South. In these letters they figured, as the *Kirk*, not the Church of Scotland – a mode of attempted disparagement which he would characterise as spiteful, small, and exceedingly vulgar. In treating of the subject which was then before the Presbytery, the Episcopal Synod of Moray and Ross had exhibited a spirit more in keeping with the 9th than with the 19th century. Bishop Eden not only regretted that the Bishops had preached in Glengarry, but seemed by some mysterious process to conjure up dread visions of Atheism and Communism in connection with following out such a practice. Could he for a moment believe that the Gospel could not be acceptably preached without certain robes and without reading prayers from a book it would certainly lead him to Atheism. And as to Communism – the chief danger to their country in the future arose from the antagonism of class to class, which Bishop Eden and his Scottish Episcopal brethren help to aggregate, by striving to gain over certain classes to a form of worship which had always been disliked by the great body of the people. Scotland had long resisted the ritualism which many would thrust upon them, and he had no doubt would continue to do so; preserving the simple forms of her own worship and the free constitution of her Church, whose pulpits was open to clergymen of all kindred denominations. He hoped that in this other Churches would follow their example, that they might all co-operate in overthrowing the kingdoms of darkness and sin, and in advancing the Redeemer's kingdom of light, and righteousness, and peace.

The finding was supported by Mr Macintyre of Boleskine, and Mr Cameron of Kilmonivaig, and approved of. Mr Cameron of Urquhart dissented for reasons to be given in. *[In fact, his dissent was never presented.]*

A similar case, in which a clergyman of the Church of England had preached in the parish church of Kilmonivaig, was reported by the minister, Mr Cameron, and the Presbytery pronounced the same deliverance on it as in the Invergarry case."

The Presbytery minute records that "Mr Cameron Minister of Glengarry was fully authorised ... to employ the services of the Archbishop of York and the Bishop of Winchester in the Parish Church in as much as they are both ordained ministers of the Church of England, the other Established Church of this Empire, which holds the same doctrines with those set forth in the Confession of Faith and that the said Archbishop and Bishop conducted the said services according to the usual forms of worship conducted in the Church of Scotland."

14 November: Bishops "... a source of annoyance"
[From The Scotsman Editorial, 14 November]

"BISHOPS have always been a source of annoyance in Scotland, but never in history have they annoyed it more than when a detachment of them recently thought it good to invade it by the Glengarry route. It seems we are never to hear the last of that celebrated Episcopal foray. We had fondly hoped that it had been dead and buried ...

16 November: Comments on the Presbytery Report
[Report from the Church Herald reproduced in the Inverness Courier, 16 November]

"The resolution (of the Presbytery) states that the services were 'according to the usual form of worship observed' in the Kirk. This virtually contradicts the pleas which both the primates have set up in excuse for what they did. There can now be no doubt that they did actually conform to the Presbyterian form, and thus all the more closely identified themselves with that Scotch Presbyterianism which has usurped the place of the true Church of Scotland, and is still her determined and bitter opponent. No wonder our sister Church should feel it keenly. But this is not all. The acts of the two prelates were gross breaches of discipline and of duty. With what reason, or with what justice, therefore, can they call to account any of their clergy for breaches of discipline and of duty!"

16 November: A View from St Andrews

[The Inverness Courier carried a report of a recent address by Principal Tulloch, St Mary's College, St Andrews, which touched on the Glengarry case]

"The marvellous ignorance with which many people, otherwise in as to the relations of Churches and their doctrines to one another, is astonishing, and helps to keep floating in the newspapers and society a mass of prejudices and absurdities of the most aggravating character. The recent discussions as to the English Bishops preaching in a parish church in the Highlands was an illustration of this, especially on the part of the English newspapers and the English clergy. A more lamentable display could hardly have been given of bigotry and ignorance, of that blind adherence to a petty circle of ideas which characterised many of the Anglican clergy – in some respects as to their own profession the least educated clergy in the world. The slightest knowledge as to the historical relations of the two national Churches to one another, and as to the two types of Protestantism which they represent, would have saved us from all that nonsense."

20 November: The Archbishop to Mr Cameron, Glengarry
[Letter from the Archbishop of York to the minister of Glengarry, published in the Inverness Courier, 23 November]

"My Dear Sir, - I learn from several Scotch papers that I have been represented as having called the service which I held at Glengarry 'a mission service to the benighted heathen' of that place. I never said – never thought or dreamed of saying – anything so absurd. A 'mission service' is not necessarily addressed to the heathen. We have just held a week of 'mission services' in York. No one has taken offence at the title, nor has the fear of being considered 'heathens' deterred the numerous worshippers.

A mission service is a service of a special kind or with a special object, as distinguished from the ordinary services of the Church. I used the word, in speaking of Glengarry, to explain that as there was no regular Episcopalian service in the place, I was acting lawfully in holding a service applicable in my judgement to the unusual circumstances."

22 November: Comment on the Archbishop's letter
[The Scotsman (22 November) carried a long editorial on the Glengarry case, ending with an amusing comment of the Archbishop's letter to Mr Cameron]

"The only condition apparently required of a 'mission service' is that it be 'distinguished from the ordinary services of the Church.' It may be of any 'special kind,' and for any 'special object.' At this rate, there is no possibility of saying what an Episcopal 'mission service' may be like, or for what object it may not be employed. It appears to be Protean in its form and universal in its aim; one thing at York, and another at Glengarry. That this is no exaggeration we are compelled to conclude from the Archbishop's own self-defence. At Glengarry he 'acted lawfully in holding a service applicable, in his judgement, to the unusual circumstances of the case.'   These circumstances were, how to conduct the worship of a Presbyterian congregation by means of Episcopalian rites – circumstances which many people would think not only unusual, but impossible.   A 'mission service,' however, is equal to any emergency, for it can be of any 'special kind' and for any 'special object,' and the 'special kind' which the Archbishop selected in the present instance was the Presbyterian kind; the 'special object' we do not know, except that it was not to convert 'benighted heathens.'   There is evidently not the slightest reason why the Archbishop should not hold Episcopal 'mission services' at Rome, Mecca, Benares, or Pekin.   All that he would need to do would be to use what was 'applicable in his judgement to the unusual circumstances.'"

23 November: A view from the sidelines
[Letter from "Tullochgorum" to The Scotsman, 25 November]

"Are the two contending parties the only ones who arrogate to themselves the title of "the Church of Scotland?"   I have a lively recollection of the "Disruption" period, when the ministers of the newly-formed body called it "the Church of our Fathers," and I also remember a worthy clergyman, now a Professor in the Free Church College, telling his audience that the Erastian Establishment [*implying the Church of Scotland*] was not a church at all."

23 November: Letter from Mr Clerk, Kilmallie
[The Scotsman, 25 November, commenting on the Archbishop's letter]

"As I was the proposer of the judgement to which the Presbytery came to this case, I feel called upon again to assert the truth of what is therein stated as to the services having been ... conducted according to the usual forms of worship observed in the Church of

Scotland. His Grace was furnished with a full programme of these forms, and he followed it to the minutest detail. From the very first Psalm to the benediction he conformed in every respect to the mode of worship observed in the Presbyterian Church of Scotland. This may be called a 'mission service,' or designated by any other name; but the facts which I have here stated are beyond contradiction."

28 November: Presbytery responds to Bishop Ewing
[At a meeting of Abertarff Presbytery, Mr Clerk, Minister of Kilmallie, presented a copy of Bishop Ewing's letter to the Archbishop of York, dated 2 October, which was earlier published in the Inverness Courier, and which the Bishop wished to be communicated to the Presbytery]

"The Presbytery in considering this letter resolve to record their thanks … to the Rev Bp Ewing for communicating it to them. They are glad to find that he entertains the same views with the Church of Scotland on the subject of a true exchange of ministerial services among all churches, which are sound in the faith. They entirely agree … that the manifestation of brotherly love among the followers of Christ is the only effectual guard against the crying evils which the present troublous times threaten to destroy, weaken or impair Civil Society, and they earnestly pray for the hastening of the day when this brotherly love shall be manifested by all true believers."

28 December: Dean Ramsay's comments
[On the above date the Inverness Courier reproduced part of a new preface to the recently published 20th edition of Dean Ramsay's "Reminiscences of Scottish Life and Character." An extract is copied below]

"The act of two English prelates officiating in one of the Established Churches has called forth a storm of indignation as loud and vehement as if in a heathen land they had fallen down before the image of a heathen deity, and worshipped in a heathen temple. Then the explanation which has been given by apologists for these services is not the least remarkable feature of the transaction. These ministrations have been called 'mission services,' and, in so far as I enter into the meaning of the phrase, I would solemnly and seriously protest against it being made use of in such a case. '*Mission service*' can only be applied to the case of a missionary raising his voice '*in partibus infidelitum*,' or, to say the least of it, in a land where no Christian church was already planted. When I think of the piety, the Christian worth, and high character of so many friends in the Established and other Presbyterian Churches in Scotland, I would again repeat my solemn protestation against such religious intolerance, and again declare my conviction that Englishmen and Scotchmen, so far from looking out for points of difference and grounds for separation on account of the principles on which their Churches are established, should endeavour to make the bonds of religious union as *close* as possible."

Postscript: 1883
[The Glengarry Affair erupted again in 1883 following the publication of Volume 3 of "Life of the Rt. Rev. Samuel Wilberforce." The authors prefaced their reproduction of two letters to The Times as follows (taken from the New York one-volume edition, 1883, 520,521)]

"The service in the little Glengarry church, which the Bishop gave at Mr. Ellice's request, was thus reported by the *Scotsman*: 'The Bishop of Winchester officiated at Glengarry, strictly following throughout the service of the Presbyterian order of the worship of the Church of Scotland.' On the following Sunday, September 10, the Archbishop of York, who was at the time Mr. Ellice's guest, performed a service in the same church, in ordinary walking-dress, and used a mixture of the Scotch and English Services. A rumour was thus spread that these two Prelates had performed service conforming to the Presbyterian service. The Bishop's conduct was approved of by the Episcopalian Synod of Moray, and he received the full approval of the Primus of Scotland."

17 January 1883: Rev. Dr. Clerk on the "Glengarry Raid"
[The Times, 23 January, 1883. Dr Clerk, Minister of Kilmallie, had contributed to the Presbytery of Abertarff meeting on 1 November, 1871: see above]

"Sir, - I am not desirous of prolonging the controversies which have been raised by the third volume of the late Bishop Wilberforce's biography: but I consider it due to the cause of truth that I should state some facts regarding his preaching at Glengarry in 1871 – facts with which the words in the biography do not tally, but of which I am full cognizant and which I am ready to prove.

I begin by mentioning that all which the Bishop did in this now notorious case was entirely of his own free will. No one asked him to visit Glengarry, far less to preach in its parish church. He came to the Glen unsolicited by any one there, and offered to preach in the church on Sunday, September 3. The offer was gladly accepted, but the parish minister – Rev. A. Cameron, now in Sleat, Isle of Skye – was from home; so it became necessary to consult a layman as to the usual order of service. Bishop Wilberforce expressly asked for a written programme. Mr. Malcolm, banker and factor at Invergarry, furnished him with this, and he, with many others present on the occasion, declares that the Bishop openly referred to the programme at every various stage of the service, following it faithfully and minutely.

The wonderful interest in the "mission" at Glengarry which had led to the Bishop to undertake such a toilsome journey speedily took possession of the breast of the Archbishop of York as well, and he volunteered his services for the following Sunday, September 10. The parish minister had by this time returned home, and at his Grace's request wrote out a directory for him, which was followed as fully as that of the preceding Sunday had been. Both programmes are still preserved, and there are many witnesses to testify that both the prelates conformed to them at every point.

There were some circumstances of a rather ludicrous nature connected with this Glengarry raid, one of which may be mentioned. Bishop Eden, of the Scottish Episcopal Church at Inverness, according to the report of the papers at the time, complained loudly of the invasion of his diocese by the English Church dignitaries without his episcopal permission being even asked for, and he conjured up dread visions of "communism," even of "atheism," as likely to result from the desecration implied in Apostolically-descended Bishops preaching within a Presbyterian building. On inquiry it turned out that the now famous Glen was entirely beyond his jurisdiction – that it was within the so-called Diocese of Argyll and the Isles, consequently under the charge of the truly pious and large-minded Bishop Ewing, who earnestly desired free and unfettered intercourse between Christian Churches, more especially between the two Established Churches of the kingdom.

I will not dwell on the politico-ecclesiastical object freely spoken of at the time as having moved both the prelates in question to make the extraordinary raid on Glengarry; but I assert that both of their own accord asked leave to preach in the parish church there well knowing it to be a parish church; that both asked for, and complied with a directory for the usual form of service in that church; that both set at naught the Scottish Episcopal Church, and honoured the Scottish Presbyterian Church – as far as their conducting her worship according to her wonted forms was an honour. Nor will the pitiful word – twisting and the spiteful nicknaming of that Church which are so painfully resorted to in their letters of attempted exculpation tend in the least degree to alter the facts of the case, which are undeniable."

26 January 1883: An Episcopalian Response
[The Times on 30 January; letter from Rev J Brodie Innes, who had moved the resolution at the Synod of Moray on 27 September 1871, attempting to counteract Dr Clerk's letter]

The letter began by quoting Dr Clerk's fourth paragraph and comments:
    "This passage is full of misrepresentations. The Primus of Scotland (Bishop Eden, as Dr Clerk terms him) did not initiate any action in the matter, nor make any 'loud complaint of the invasion of his diocese.' No such words as those quoted by him were used by him, or any one who took part in the Synodical discussion. It was of no importance to the question whether Glengarry is in the diocese of Moray or any other in Scotland.
    The Bishop of Oxford [*sic: this was his appointment prior to moving to Winchester*] (Wilberforce) and the Archbishop of York (Thomson) each on one Sunday preached in the Established Kirk at Glengarry. The fact was largely published, and commented on in Presbyterian papers as evidence of the relations between the Church of England and the Presbyterian Establishment in Scotland. Clearly it would also have relation to the Episcopal Church in Scotland. Acting entirely on my own responsibility, and without any previous conference with the Primus, I brought the matter before the Synod of the diocese held at Inverness, and after conference it was decided to address the two Prelates on the subject, not in the language said to be quoted by Dr. Clerk nor in the least degree resembling it. Dr. Clerk uses the words, 'according to the report of the papers of the time.' I saw many of the reports at the time, but none of them with

anything similar to Dr. Clerk's version. As he says he is 'ready to prove,' I call on him to produce his authority."

Mr Brodie Innes then refers to Dr Clerk's third paragraph and states:

"I have no means of estimating the energies of the Archbishop of York, but from long knowledge of the Bishop of Oxford [*sic*] I should say there must have been some very deep political end in view to induce him to take 'such a toilsome journey' for the purpose of preaching at Glengarry.

As the portion of Dr. Clerk's letter with which I am concerned appears, until proof is afforded, so extremely inaccurate, it may be concluded that in other portions he may have been misled by erroneous information or trusted to imperfect memory.

I have not yet seen the third volume of the Bishop's life."

There, it would appear, the "Glengarry Affair" came to an end.

ANNEX 4:

FORT AUGUSTUS COMMUNION ROLL: 1880-81

Findlay MacDonald	m	Auchterawe	
Mary Fraser	s	Bridgend	
Colin Campbell	m	Rose Cottage	
Mrs Hector Munro	m	Bridgend House	
Eliza MacBean	s	Isle	
Jane Park	s	Isle	
J MacLean	m	Isle	Shepherd
John Aitchison	m		Baker
Mrs Aitchison	m		
James Aitchison	s		Baker
Thomas Aitchison			Baker
Maggie Munro	s	Bridgend House	
Mrs Grant	m	The Isle	Farmer
Alexander Munro	m		Carter
Mrs Munro	m		
James Munro	s		Student
Miss Macrae	s	Ardachie	
Charles MacLean	m		Surgeon
Mrs MacLean	m		
Widow Macrae	m	Fort Augustus	
Donald Campbell	m	Fort Augustus	
Mrs D Campbell	m	Fort Augustus	
Andrew Brown	m	Cullachie	
Mrs Brown	m	Cullachie	
Miss Brown	s	Cullachie	
Miss E Brown	s	Cullachie	
Miss Campbell	s	Rose Cottage	
Mr Gray	m		Carpenter
James Fraser			Minister

Taken from Kirk Session minutes: CH2/792/3.

APPENDIX: ROLL OF PARISH MINISTRY

Details derived from FASTI volumes of the Church of Scotland, Free Church and United Free Church; Abertarff Presbytery Minutes and other sources as credited.

Dates in bold type denote the year(s) a minister or missionary served in the charges/parishes in each section.

Abbreviations:

adm	admitted
app	appointed
ass	assistant
b	Born
CF	Chaplain to the Forces
CU	Congregational Union
dr	daughter
d	Deceased
dem	demitted
ed	educated
EPC	English Presbyterian Church
FC	Free Church
ind	inducted
lic	licensed
min	minister
missy	missionary
ord	ordained
OSC	Original Secession Church
P	Presbytery
PM	Presbytery Minute
res	resigned
s	son
tr	translated
U	University/universities
UFC	United Free Church
URC	United Reformed Church

1: CHURCH OF SCOTLAND

A. ABERTARFF/FORT AUGUSTUS

Appointments with reference to Abertarff:

"Gillibride": prior to 1216

"Persona de Abirtarff" mentioned by Bricius, Bishop of Moray. *E C Batten, "The Charters of the Priory of Beauly", The Grampian Club, 1877, 34*

James Duff: 1567 *[other references in 1563,1574,1580,1582?]*

"Exhorter and Reader" for Dores, Boleskine and Abertarff. *"Register of ministers, exhorters and readers", Maitland Club, 1830*

Patrick Dunbar: 1579

Presented to Abertarff, December 1579 upon the death of ? Brown

Andrew Macphail: 1607–1608

min of Farnua (Kirkhill) in 1575; tr Kingussie 1581; tr Abertarff, Boleskine, Moy, Daviot and Dunlichity 1590; d 1608

Andrew Dow Fraser: 1607–1646(?)

Minister of Abertarff 1607; Dalarossie, Moy, Boleskine and Abertarff c1616; Boleskine and Abertarff c1625. *Murdered c1645 "because he had obtained an order for a legal glebe." "Parson and vicar of Abertarff" – so described in 1635. Walter MacFarlane, "Geographical Collections", Vol 1, p218*

Thomas Houston: 1648?–1704

From 1676–1688 Abertarff was removed from Boleskine and associated with Glenmoriston: in 1688 Abertarff was again joined to Boleskine

Robert Munro: 1676–1688(?)

b Kiltearn; ord Abertarff and Glenmoriston at Kilchuimen 12 March, 1676; d post-1697

Ministers of Boleskine and Abertarff:
John Morrison: 1706–1711
b Lewis; lic P Argyll 1698; ord Glenelg 1699, tr Boleskine 1706, tr Gairloch 1711; tr Urray and Tarradale 1717, d1747
Thomas Fraser: 1713–1766
lic P Lorn 1712; ord 1713, d 1766
Patrick Grant: 1770–1800
b 1773; U Edinburgh, Aberdeen; lic P Aberdeen 1760, ord Daviot and Dunlichity 1761; tr Boleskine 1770; tr Inverness 1st Charge 1800; tr Kiltarlity 1800; d 1807
William Fraser: 1800–1840 *See below*
lic P Inveraray 1788; ord missy Fort Augustus 1790; dem 1793; app CF (79th Foot); adm Boleskine 1800; d 1840
Donald Chisholm: 1840–1857
b 1797; U Aberdeen; ord 1829 to ?; adm Boleskine 1840; d 1857
Malcolm MacIntyre: 1859–1893
b Balquidder 1832; U Glasgow; ass Lismore 1852; ord Tobermory 1855; adm Boleskine 1859; d 1893

Specific appointments to Abertarff/Fort Augustus:
Thomas Montfod: 1726
missy Glenmoriston and Kilmonivaig in 1725; app Catechist Abertarff and Glenmoriston 1726; lic P Abertarff 1728; app missy-min to P Abertarff 1730; adm Kilmallie 1732; d 1750
George Anderson 1728–1729
CF Scot's Greys, serving in Netherlands until 1717; app Royal Bounty Cttee 1728; ord missy Maryburgh [Fort William] and Kilchuiman 1728-9 and Maryburgh 1733 on; later Master of George Watson's Hospital, Edinburgh 1741-52
Patrick Grant: 1739–1740, 1741
ord 1739 to Fort Augustus and Glenmoriston; to Fort William 1740, returned 1741; to Kilmonivaig Mission 1741; adm Logie Easter 1744; d 1778
Alexander Dallas: 1741–1750
Catechist at Fort Augustus and Schoolmaster 1741-50 [SSPCK Schoolmasters 1709–1872; A S Cowper, SRS, Edinburgh 1997]

William Grant: 1743–1750
b.1712; lic. P Abernethy 1741; ord 1743; tr Kilmonivaig 1750; d 1775
John Grant: 1751–1753
b 1725; lic P Abertarff 1750; ord 1751; *described in 1752 as Minister and Catechist at the Garrison of Fort Augustus and officiating at Glenmoriston*; tr Dores 1753; d 1784
Ludovic Grant: 1755
ord 1755 *[Described as Preacher and Catechist at the Garrison of Fort Augustus and officiating at Glenmoriston. Mentioned in "Reports on the Annexed Estates" (Scottish Record Office, 1973, p45) as an itinerant preacher "in both languages", and located at Fort Augustus, with a salary of £30]*
Andrew Gallie: 1756–1758
b Tarbat 1730; lic P Tain 1753; ord missy 1756; adm Laggan 1758; tr Kincardine (P Tain) 1774; d 1803
Alexander Falconer: 1758–1763
b Inverness 1730; ord missy 1758; adm Edrachillis 1763; d 1802
Colin M'Farquhar: 1759–1761
b Killearnan c1733; lic P Chanonry 1756; ord 1759; adm Applecross 1.4.1761 *[dem 1775 to emigrate with members of his congregation to Pennsylvania; no record of death: Directory of Settlers in North America 1625–1825, Vol V]*
George Watson: 1762–1770
b c1737, ord c1762; adm Kiltearn 1770; tr Inverness (3rd Charge) 1775, adm 2nd Charge 1778, d 1798. *May have overlapped with …*
James Grant: 1769–1775
app missy, Fort Augustus 1769; tr Laggan 1775; CF Perthshire Volunteers (90th Foot) 1794; d 1801 *["A man of cultivated tastes and amiable in manner, and greatly revered and loved". Married Anne MacVicar, only child of Capt. Duncan MacVicar, Barrack Master of Fort Augustus and Fort George, on 1779]*
John M'Kilican: 1776–1785
b Croy 1744; lic P Inverness 1768; missy Boleskine; ord 1776 serving Glengarry and Glenmoriston; adm Dores 1785; d 1819
John MacDonell: 1786–1788
Appointed to Boleskine, Urquhart and Kilmonivaig
William Fraser: 1790–1793 *See above*
lic P Inveraray 1788; ord missy Fort Augustus 1790; dem 1793; app CF (79th Foot); adm Boleskine 1800; d 1840

James Fowler: 1791–1799
lic P Dingwall 1787; ord missy (with Glenmoriston) 1791; tr Urquhart and Glenmoriston 1799; d 1814
Hugh Ross: 1799–1800
b Tarbat 1760; ord missy 1799; adm to Gaelic Chapel, Cromarty 1800; tr Fearn 1809; d 1844
George Ross Monro: 1800
b 1770 s of min Cromarty; lic P Chanonry 1793; app missy Fort Augustus 1800; ord ass Bellie 1800; adm Huntly 1801; d 1822
William Macrae: 1801–1813
b Black Isle 1776; lic P Lochcarron 1801; ord missy 1801; also Glenmoriston, and Glengarry to 1806; tr Barvas 1813; d 1856
Colin Fraser: 1813–1823
b Ross-shire 1781; lic P Dingwall 1809; ord missy Brae-Badenoch & Brae-Lochaber 1810; app 1813 to Fort Augustus, Glenmoriston and Glengarry; tr Kiltarlity 1823; d 1853
John M'Intyre: 1824–1828
b Camusnaherie 1794, s of Duncan, min Kilmallie; Tutor to Aeneas, s of Col Alexander MacDonnel of Glengarry; lic P Abertarff 1820; ord 1824; married 1826 Eliza, eldest dr of Thomas Clark, Auchterawe, Elder at Abertarff; tr Kilmonivaig 1828; d 1870. *One son became minister of Shieldaig, another (John Walker MacIntyre) minister of Kilmonivaig (1901–24)*
James Stewart: 1829–1835
No information; recorded present in 1829–1835
William Sutherland: 1843–1844 *See also Glengarry*
b Dornoch 1822; app 1843 (also to Glenmoriston and Glengarry); ord Harris 1844; tr Laggan 1846; tr Dingwall 1850; d 1867
1846–1847: *Royal Bounty Committee Return for 1.11.1846 states Fort Augustus as "Vacant" (Abertarff Presbytery – CH2/7/13/46)*
Edward Baynes Rodgers: 1849–1852
ord 1849; adm Tweedmouth 1852; emigrated to Canada 1870; adm Leith and Johnson (Ontario) 1870; tr Meaford 1879; then missy in Brice Peninsula and Maintoulin Island; d 1906
John William Tolmie: 1853–1854
b Uiginish, Skye 1831; app 1853; ord Strontian 1854; tr Bracadale 1856; tr Contin 1863; d 1886

William MacDonald: 1854–1856

b Urray; Scripture Reader and Catechist 1850-54; app Glengarry 1852 [see Bardgett, 299]; lic P Abertarff 1853; app Fort Augustus and Glengarry 1854; ord 1855; adm Urray 1856; d 1860

Alexander Maclean: 1856–1858

app 1856, ord 1857 *(see APM: away by 3.8.1858)*

James Skinner Mackenzie: 1858–1860

b 1834 Fox Harbour, Nova Scotia; missy at Strathglass *(APM 3.11.58)*; app Abertarff 1858; ord 1859; tr Carnoch [Contin] 1860; tr Little Dunkeld 1866; d 1918.

Peter Calder: 1860–1862

b 1829; schoolmaster in Grantown; ord 1860; tr Kinlochbervie 1862; tr Clyne 1864; d 1870. *At Fort Augustus "he laboured with exemplary diligence and great acceptance (APM 5.5.1862)*

Donald Macleod: 1862–1863

b 1839, Laggan, Strathspey [*a history of Nether Lochaber Church gives birthplace as Onich Manse, where his father was minister before translation to Laggan*]; ord 1862; tr Dornoch 1863; tr Greyfriars, Dumfries 1866; tr Montrose 1867; tr St Marks Dundee 1870; tr Jedburgh 1877; tr London Crown Court 1881; tr London St Columba's 1884 *(upon the creation of the new congregation which was originated by Dr Macleod in 1883)*; dem 1901; d 1911

John Macdougall: 1864–1866

b Argyll, ord 1864; tr Carnoch [Contin] 1866; dem 1897; d 1912

Robert Cumming Macdougall: 1867–1868

b Moy 1839; ord missy at Tayvallich 1866; adm 1867; ass Kilmonivaig 1868-70; adm Resolis 1871; d 1911

James Macdonald: 1868–1869

b Perthshire 1825; ord Knock 1861; dem 1864; worked abroad; Gaelic Church, Saltcoats; app Fort Augustus 1868; app Oban 1869; tr Glenelg 1876; d 1890

John Menzies: 1870–1875

b Weem 1845; ed U St Andrews; lic P Weem; app 1870; ord 1872; tr Fordoun 1875; d 1902

James Fraser: 1876–1881
b Abernethy 1834; schoolmaster at Elchies; lic P Aberlour 1862; ass Cromdale; ord 1876; tr Erchless 1881 and adm first min of the parish 1884; dem 1914; d Dornoch 1924

Simon Macgregor: 1881–1882
b Nova Scotia 1831; ord min at East River of Pictou, NS 1860; tr 1870 St Andrew's Church, Victoria BC; adm 1881; tr Glencoe 1882; tr Appin 1884; d 1906

John Alexander Campbell: 1882
Served in Glenmoriston and Fort Augustus – see Glenmoriston

James Munro: 1882–1883
b Fort Augustus; ed Edin 1880; app Fort Augustus 1882; ord 1882; missy Glenmoriston from June 1882; refused a call to Fort Augustus in 1885; tr Logie Easter 1886; d 1915. *"Held in high esteem and respect by all in the district, as an excellent man and as an able preacher." [Northern Chronicle, 21.1.1885]*

James Robertson: 1882–1884
[First Minister of Fort Augustus: 1883]
b Kirkmichael, Perthshire 1858; ass Langholm 1880-1; ord 1882; adm first minister of the parish 1883; tr Garturk 1884; tr Fetteresso 1890; tr Anderston Glasgow 1904; d 1911

William Craig Flint: 1885–1921
b 1850 Morpeth; ord 1878; min of EPC, Pendleton, Manchester; adm CofS 1885; ind 1885; res 1921; dec 1933

Neil Louis Arthur Campbell: 1922–1925
b Dalmellington 1892, s of FC min; lic P Glasgow 1920; ass Bluevale, Glasgow; ord 1922; tr Chapel of Garioch South 1925, united charge of Chapel of Garioch 1941; d 1962

August John Kesting: 1925–1939
b Inverness 1874; lic P Inverness 1897; ord 1898; missy in Nyasaland; res 1901; locums at Midcalder, Leslie; in charge St John's Mission Kirkcaldy 1903-088; adm St Fitticks Aberdeen 1908; res 1910; min Scots Kirk Paris 1911-18; adm Mossgreen, Fife 1918; ind 1925; dem 1939; d 1947

Hugh Malcolm Gillies: 1939–1980
b Strontian 1913; student ass Partick Old 1938-39; lic P Glasgow 1939; ord and ind 1939; ret 1980, d 2000
Gilbert Stuart Cameron: 1980–1986
b 1919, ord CF 1942; ind Campbeltown Highland 1947; tr Broughty Ferry St Stephen's and West 1963; app Nassau St Andrews 1974; ind Fort Augustus 1980; ret 1986; d 1992

B. GLENGARRY

John M'Kilican: 1776
See Fort Augustus; app also to Fort Augustus and Glenmoriston
Thomas Campbell: 1786
John MacDonell: 1788–1790
app to Boleskine, Urquhart and Kilmonivaig.

Locharkaig and Glengarry Catechist District: 1800–1811
Alexander McIntosh: 1806–1811
Later app Glengarry and Knoydart, 1811–1813

Glengarry and Knoydart Mission District: 1811–1824
John Ross: 1814
Alexander MacIver: 1821
app Arnisdale and Knoydart 1824

Glengarry Mission District: 1811–1867
Colin Fraser: 1813 *See Fort Augustus*
Donald MacDonald: 1816–1824
b Rannoch 1783; ord 1816; emigrated to Cape Breton as missy 1824; to Prince Edward Island in 1826 where his ministry was marked by outstanding revivals in 1829 and 1860; d 1867
Farquhar McIver: 1827–1828
tr Glenmoriston 1828; tr Glensheil 1840

James MacIntyre: 1829–1839
Described in 1839 as missy at Laggan, Loch Lochy
William Lauder: 1840–1843
b Ballachulish 1807; ord missy Glengarry 1840; into FC 1843; min
Glengarry FC 1843-4; Strachur FC 1844-85; d 1885
Peter Grant: 1843–1844
William Sutherland: 1843–1844 *See Fort Augustus*
James MacNaughton: 1846–1847
b Glenlyon 1822; ed U Edinburgh; app missy Glengarry; ord Dores 1848;
dem 1888; d 1890
James Keith: 1851–1852
b Keith 1825; lic P Aberlour 1849; app Glengarry 1851; ord missy at
Grantown 1852; tr Forres 1853; d 1905
William MacDonald: 1852–1855 *See Fort Augustus*
Donald Fraser: 1855–1857
b 1822; app missy Glengarry and Glenquoich 1855; ord 1855; adm to
Fearn 1857; d 1869
Patrick MacGregor: 1857–1859
b 1830; lic P St Andrews; app 1857, ord 1857; adm Logiealmond 1859; d
1899. *In 1858 deemed to be "deficient in Gaelic"*
John Cameron: 1859–1864
b Abernethy 1832; lic P Abernethy; app 1859; ord 1859; tr Urquhart and
Glenmoriston 1864; d 1879
Donald Cameron: 1864–1871
[First Minister of Glengarry: 1867]
b Blarachaorain, Fort William 1827; ord Rothesay Gaelic Chapel 1862; tr
Glengarry 1864; adm min of Glengarry 1867; tr Kilmonivaig 1871; d
Blarour, Spean Bridge 1897
Alexander Cameron: 1871–1881
b 1845, s min of Lochbroom; missy in Strathglass; ord 1871; tr Sleat 1881;
dem 1914; d Perth 1923
Thomas Sinton: 1882–1890
b Aberarder 1855; lic P. Abernethy 1881; ass Blair Atholl; ord 1882; tr
Dores 1889; d 1923. *A noted writer and Gaelic scholar*

Farquhar MacRae: 1889–1895
b Kirkmichael, Banffshire 1856; lic P. Dingwall 1888; missy at Kyleakin and Dunvegan; ord Truimisgarry 1888; tr Glengarry 1889; tr Glenorchy 1894; dem 1930; d 1943

John McGilchrist: 1894–1896
b Bowmore 1866; missy at Ford (Lochawe); ord Glengarry 1894; tr Fodderty 1896; tr Skelmorlie 1899; tr West St Giles, Edinburgh 1911; tr Govan 1913; tr Old Machar, Aberdeen 1923; d 1928. *"Known as one of the most influential preachers in the Church" – Times Obituary, 24.8.1928*

Norman MacLean: 1897–1903
b Braes, Portree 1869; ord Halin in Waternish 1892; tr Glengarry 1897; tr Colinton 1903; tr The Park, Glasgow 1910; tr St Cuthbert's Edinburgh 1915; **Moderator of the General Assembly 1927–8**; dem 1937; d 1952 *"One of the foremost ministers of the Church of Scotland" – Times Obituary, 17.1.1952*

Donald MacKinnon: 1903–1909
ord Stornoway 1897; tr 1903; tr Kilninian and Kilmore 1909; tr Milton, Glasgow 1914; tr Assynt 1919; tr Cumlodden 1927; d 1939

Kenneth Olaus MacLeod: 1909–1911
b 1878; ord 1909; tr Caputh 1911; dem 1948

Alexander MacDonald: 1911–1914
b N Uist 1885; ord Glengarry 1911; tr Glassary 1914; tr Stevenston 1921; tr Alloa 1927, tr St Columba's Glasgow 1929; **Moderator of the General Assembly 1948–1949**; dem 1954; d 1960.

James Robert Lee: 1914–1917
b North Berwick 1885; lic P. Glasgow 1909; ass Govan; ord Glengarry 1914; tr Cellardyke 1917; d 1951

Robertson McCallum Millar: 1917–1921
b Lesmahagow 1888; lic P Lanark 1915; ass Alloa, Tullibody; ord Glengarry 1917; tr Ladyburn Greenock 1921; tr Stronsay (Orkney) 1929; dem 1931; went to Canada

James Hill: 1921–1940
b Girvan 1888; lic P Ayr 1919; ass Kilmorack (Beauly); ord Glengarry 1921; tr Teviothead 1940; ret 1.1963; d 1973

Donald MacLean: 1940–1943
ord Glengarry 1940; tr Corby 1943; tr Alves 1947 (1948?); d 1950

Daniel Murray Stewart: 1943–1947
b Muthil 1899; ord Kingarth 1926; dem 1931; ind Innerleithen Craigside
1940; tr Glengarry 1943; tr Benholme & Johnshaven 1947; ind Lonmay
1949 with Rathen from 1958; ret 1967; d 1987
Ian Fife Montgomery: 1948–1955
b 1904, South Africa; lic 1928; ass John Knox Mounthooly Aberdeen; ord
Kinlochluichart 1930; tr Aberdeen Middlefield 1940; tr Glengarry 1948; tr
Inverness Queen Street 1955; ret. 1970; d 1987
Robert Black Notman: 1955–1957
b 1909, lic P Annandale 1933; ass Edinburgh St Stephens 1933–5; ord ass
1934; ind Restalrig 1935; tr Glengarry 1955; d 1957
Robert Milne Tuton: 1957–1964
b Castle Douglas 1929; ord Glengarry 1957; tr Glasgow Colston Wellpark
1964; tr Shettleston Old 1973; ret 1995
John Dale: 1964–1967
ord 2.9.1964; dem 8.9.1967

Glengarry & Kilmallie: "Area of Re-adjustment" 1968–1974

Arthur Law – Associate: 1968–1970
ord Associate Glengarry 1968; ind Redding & Westquarter 1970; tr
Glassary & Kilmartin 1975; tr Kincardine in Menteith with Norrieston
1981; ret 1988

William M M Campbell – Associate: 1970–1973
b 1942; ord Associate. Kilmallie and Glengarry 1970; ind Braes of
Rannoch with Kinloch Rannoch 1973 (linkage with Foss and Rannoch
1977); tr Lundie and Muirhead of Liff 1978; app Chaplain Royal Cornhill
& Woodlands Hosps, Aberdeen 1986

Glengarry linked with Kilmonivaig: 1974–1987
Grahame McLaren Henderson: 1974–87
b Aberdeen 1943; U Aberdeen; ord 1974; tr Dingwall Castle Street 1987;
thereafter at Dunoon

Student Missionaries recorded at Lochourn/Glenquoich
1875: Duncan MacLennan; 1876: Dugald McPhee; 1877: Dugald
Carmichael; 1878: Alexander Stewart; 1879: John C Mackinnon; 1880:
Angus MacDonald; 1883: W Tolmie; 1884: Mr MacLean; 1886: Charles
Bentick; 1887: Peter Macgregor; 1888: A Mactaggart

C. FORT AUGUSTUS AND GLENGARRY

Linked from 26 March 1987

George W Charlton: 1987–1992
b 1926 Mauchline, Ayrshire; HM Forces 1944-7; ord ass Govan Old 1952;
ind Islay Kilmeny 1953; tr Tullibody St Serfs 1961; tr Musselburgh St
Ninians 1968; tr Fort Augustus 1987; ret 1992; d 2010
Alan Lamb: Associate 1992–1994
b Croydon 1931; min CU and URC; app Ass Fort Augustus and Glengarry
1992; later Associate at Arisaig; d 2020
Moses Donaldson: 1993–1999
b Kirkmuirhill 1935; ord Associate. Kilninian and Kilmore with
Tobermory etc. 1972; ind Duneaton 1978; tr Fort Augustus and Glengarry
1993; ret 1999; d 2005
Adrian Varwell: 2001–2011
b London 1946; U Durham, Aberdeen, Edinburgh; ass Dunblane
Cathedral; ord Benbecula 1983; app Director, St Ninian's Centre, Crieff,
1997; adm Fort Augustus and Glengarry 2001; ret 2011
Tabea Baader – Exchange 2012–2016
Minister of the Evangelical Lutheran Church of Bavaria
Anthony Jones: 2017–

D. GLENMORISTON

Donald Maculloch: 1647–
tr from Inverness 2nd Charge
Robert Munro: 1676–1688(?)
ord Abertarff and Glenmoriston at Kilchiumen 12 March, 1676. See
Annex 1
Alexander Macbean: 1725
SSPCK missionary
Thomas Montfod: 1726 *See Abertarff*
Patrick Grant: 1739 *See Abertarff*
William Grant: 1743–1750 *See Abertarff*
John Grant: 1751–1753 *See Abertarff*
Ludovik Grant: 1755 *See Abertarff*
William MacLeod: 1768
Named as Catechist
John MacDonell: 1786–1788
Named as Missionary-minister serving Boleskine, Urquhart and Kilmonivaig
William MacLeod: 1788
Named as Catechist
James Fowler: 1791–1799 *See Fort Augustus*
Simon Fraser: 1799–1815
b Ross-shire 1773; lic P Chanonry 1799; app missy Glenmoriston 1799; tr
Stornoway 1815; drowned at sea 1824

Glenmoriston Mission District: 1811–41
Colin Fraser: 1813–1823 *See Fort Augustus*
app 1813 to Fort Augustus, Glenmoriston and Glengarry
John MacKenzie: 1818–1823
b Gairloch 1792, U Aberdeen; lic P Lochcarron 1817; ord missy
Glenmoriston 1818; tr Rogart 1823; tr Resolis 1843; d 1870
Alexander M'iver: 1824–1826
b 1801, s of min of Glenelg; U Aberdeen; schoolmaster Glenelg 1816; lic
P Lochcarron 1820; ord missy Arnisdale & Knoydart 1821; missy 1824-6;
adm Sleat 1826; tr Dornoch 1843; d 1852

Farquhar MacIver: 1828–1840 *From Glengarry*
tr Glensheil 1840
William Sutherland: 1843–1844 *See entries above*
ord to Glengarry, Fort Augustus and Glenmoriston
Alexander Gair: 1853–1874(?)
ord 1857 P Abertarff; d 1874; Acted as physician and pastor! *[Alexander MacDonald, "Story and Song from Loch Ness-side", Inverness, 1914 (reprinted edition 1982), 66,152]*
Malcolm MacCallum: 1876
b Craignish, Mull, 1852; lic Pres Inveraray 1873; ass Inveraray; served Glenmoriston prior to ord Knoydart 1876; tr Strontian 1882; tr Muckairn 1886; res 1921
George Johnston Birrell: 1878–1881
app 15.6.1878; removed 1881 due to "lack of Gaelic"; served subsequently at Cairndow and Ollaberry, Shetland
Alexander Duff: 1880
b Salen, Mull 1855; lic P Islay 1880; served in Glenmoriston prior to ord Kilmeny, Islay, 1882; tr Oban 1891; res 1922
John Alexander Campbell: 1881–1882
b Dervaig, Mull, 1847; U Glasgow; lic P Kintyre 1876; ass Kildalton; missy; ord Portnahaven, Islay, 1882; res 1916; d 1916
James Munro: 1883–1886
b Fort Augustus; U Edin 1880; app to Fort Augustus 1882; ord missy Glenmoriston 4.9.1883; refused a call to Fort Augustus in 1885; tr Logie Easter 19.4.1886; d 9.9.1915. *"an excellent man and ... an able preacher."* [Northern Chronicle, 21.1.1885]
William Birrell: 1885
Robert Cumming: 1886
b Duthil 1858; U Aberdeen, Glasgow, app 1886; received medical qualifications 1903
Archibald M'Neill: 1891–1929
[First Minister of Glenmoriston: 1891]
b Tongue 1859; lic Pres Tongue 1887, ass Urquhart; ord 1891; dem 1929; d 1929

Walter James Gordon: 1929
b Coatbridge 1909; missy at Dalchriechart for 4 months 1929; ord & ind St Monance 1934; tr Larbert & Dunipace Old 1944; tr Aberdeen East & Belmont 1962; ret 1974; d 1998

Evan Mackenzie: 1930–1934
b Daviot 1868; FC missy India & Nepal 1897-1930; adm to CofS; adm 1930; d 1934

Neil MacInnes: 1933
b Breakish, Skye 1892; war service 1917-19; student missy including Glenmoriston 1933 and Arnisdale 1933-4; ord & ind Hylipol, Tiree 1938; CF 1942-6; tr Glenshiel 1945; ret 1967; d 1973

Donald Cameron: 1934
b 1909; student missy, including Glenmoriston 1934 [*Bardgett, p338*]; ord Kildalton 1938; tr Blair Atholl 1947; ret 1979; d 1990

Archibald McCall: 1934–1939
b Luib, Skye 1867; lic P Glasgow (FC); ord & ind Shapinsay (UFC) 1903; tr Kirkbean & Southwick 1910; tr Ardeonaig 1919; tr Portpatrick 1926; tr Helmsdale 1929; ind Glenmoriston (CofS) 1934; dem 1939, d 1939

Duncan McMillan Turner: 1940–1949
b Glasgow 1907; ord Thornhill Cong Church 1934-7; tr Aberfeldy Cong Church 1937-8; adm CofS, Rothienorman 1938-40; ind 1940; served in Civil Defence; MBE 1944; dem 1948; Chaplain and Welfare Officer 1949; ind Montrose St George's and Trinity 1952; tr Alford 1958; tr Innerwick and Spott 1964; ret 1997; d 2001

Peter Fraser: 1949–1980
b 1914, Beauly; lic P Inverness 1939; ass Edinburgh St Matthew's; CofS Huts and Canteens 1940-41; ord 1941; Scottish Secretary SCM 1941-43; Chaplain Achitoma College, Gold Coast 1943-49; ind 1949; ret 1980; d 1993

E. URQUHART AND GLENMORISTON

Linked 30.4.1980; United 27.8.1992

Frary Barton Buell: 1980–1995
min of united charge from 1992; ret 1995
Hugh Finlay Watt: 1996–

2: FREE CHURCH OF SCOTLAND

For further details see Ian Allan's "West the Glen", "Annals of the Free Church 1900–1986" and www.ecclegen.com

A. FORT AUGUSTUS & GLENMORISTON: 1843–78

William Lauder: 1843–1844 *See also Appendix 1.B*
missy at Glengarry; adhered to the FC 1843 and played a pivotal role in establishing the congregation in Fort Augustus
Francis McBean: 1844–1869
b Corpach c1794; missy-min with OSC; went to FC 1843; app to assist in Glenurquhart then Fort Augustus; ind 1844; d 1869
Alexander McColl: 1870–1877
b Lochcarron 1815; ord Duirinish, Skye, 1852; ind 1870; tr Lochalsh; d 1889

B. FORT AUGUSTUS: 1878 – 1908

Donald Alexander MacDonald: 1878–1888
b Iona 1847; ord 1878; ind Kilmuir, Skye 1888; went into the 1900 and 1929 unions, becoming minister of the united charge of Kilmuir 1926; dem 1934, d 1934
John Stuart MacKay: 1889–1900
b Farr, Sutherland, 1838; ord Altnahara 1871; ind 1889; went into UFC – *Appendix 3*

C. GLENMORISTON: 1879 – 1900

Donald MacInnes: 1879–1889
b Glendale, Skye, 1838; teacher in Uist; ord Glenmoriston 1879; d unmarried 1889
William MacKinnon: 1891–1894
b Strath, Skye, 1843; ord North Ballachulish 1878; tr North Uist 1884; ind 1891; tr Gairloch 1894; **Moderator of the General Assembly, 1908–1909**; d 1925
Donald A MacInnes: 1895–1900
b Portree, Skye, 1862; ord Glenmoriston 1895; went into the 1900 Union, *see Appendix 3*; left Glenmoriston in 1907; ind Kinlochspelvie (CofS) 1910; d 1916

D. FORT AUGUSTUS & GLENMORISTON: 1908–83

Kenneth MacRae: 1909–1915
ord Glenshiel 1898; ind 1909; tr Lochalsh 1915; d 1928
Duncan MacDougall: 1918–1921
b Islay; ord Ness, Lewis 1909; ind 1918; app missy Vancouver, BC 1921; ind Dunoon 1938; ret 1947; d 1954

Murdo MacKay: 1921–1929
ord Kincardine and Croick 1910; Kilmuir Easter 1915; served in Canada,
then Burghead; provided pastoral care 1921–29
Murdoch Campbell: 1930–1935
b Lewis 1900; ind 1930; tr Partick Highland 1934; tr Resolis 1951;
Moderator of General Assembly 1956-1957; ret 1968; d 1974
Donald G Ferguson: 1937–1947
b St Kilda 1880; ord Minard 1924; tr Ayr 1928; tr Scalpay 1933; ind 1937;
tr Kilbrandon 1948; d 1967
William J MacLeod: 1948–1958
b Knock, Lewis 1897; ord Tobermory; tr Fort William, Ontario 1936; ind
1948; d 1958
John Fraser: 1965–1983
b Strathnairn 1914; ord Wick 1955; ind 1965; ret 1983

E. GLENURQUHART & FORT AUGUSTUS: 1983 –

Ian M Allan: 1984–1999
b Inverness 1948; FC missy Glenelg 1973-76; ord & ind 1984; tr
Bishopbriggs 1999; tr Carbost 2005; tr Rogart 2010; ret 2014
John MacKay: 2001–2011
John Ross: 2012–2017
Sean Ankers: 2020–

3: UNITED FREE CHURCH

A. FORT AUGUSTUS: 1900 – 1929

John Stuart Mackay: 1889–1907
[from Free Church, see Appendix 2] Fort Augustus UFC from 1900; ret 1907;
d 1908

Donald John MacInnes: 1909–1913
b Scarp, Harris, 1869; ord Kilchoman, Islay, 1900; tr 1909; tr Knockbain 1913; war service with YMCA in France; tr Stornoway 1924; tr Lochbroom 1927; min united congregation 1929-34; tr Helmsdale 1935; d 1935

Thomas William Armour: 1913–1917
ord into Baptist ministry; ind 1913; tr Inverness Ness Bank 1917; res 1924; ind Christchurch NZ; d 1947

William Doig Dunbar: 1918–1922
b Dundee 1884, lic P Edinburgh 1914; ass Dundee St Johns 1914-15; ord & ind Cleland 1915; tr Fort Augustus 1918; tr Dunnet 1922; tr Gateshead 1927

Frederick Smith: 1922–1925
b Bangor, Co Down 1888; ord P Toronto 1914; war service with YMCA in France; CF 1917-19; ind 1922; tr Glencraig 1925; tr Canonbie 1927; tr Alloa 1929; tr Montreal 1929; tr Blythbridge 1934; tr Kirkurd 1935; ret 1959; d 1979

Angus MacIntyre: 1926–1933
b Glencoe 1863; lay then ord missy Assynt, then Strathglass 1912-23; ind Strathglass 1923; tr Fort Augustus 1926; went into 1929 Union as Minister of Inveroich CofS; dem 1933; d 1938

B. GLENMORISTON: 1900 – 1907

Donald A MacInnes: 1900–1907
[from Free Church, see Appendix 2] Glenmoriston UFC 1900 - ?; joined CofS, adm Kinlochspelvie, Mull, 1910; tr Tiree 1914; d 1916

REFERENCES

Foreword

[1] Walter MacFarlane, "Geographical Collections", SHS, Edinburgh, 1906, Vol 2, 169
[2] Edward C Ellice, "Place Names of Glengarry and Glenquoich, London 1898, facsimile edition, Glengarry Visitor Centre, 1999, 49,51
[3] Edmund Burt, "Letters", XXVI, p320–343, passim
[4] OSA, Vol XX, 31
[5] Matthew 5:13-16; 28:19,20
[6] William Mackay, "Urquhart and Glenmoriston", Inverness, 1893
[7] Ian M Allan, "West the Glen", Inverness, 1997
[8] Fr Andrew Joseph MacDonald, "Glen Albyn: Tales and Truths of the Central Highlands", Abbey Press, Fort Augustus 1909 and 1953; Peter Anson, "The Catholic Church in Modern Scotland, Burns, Oates and Westbourne, 1937 and his "Underground Catholicism in Scotland", Standard Press, Montrose, 1970; Dom Odo Blundell, "The Catholic Highands of Scotland, 2 vols, Sands & Co., Edinburgh, 1909 & 1917
[9] Alan B Lawson, "A Country Called Stratherrick", South Loch Ness Heritage Group, 2006

Chapter 1

[1] John 1:1
[2] Quoted in John Finney, "Recovering the Past: Celtic and Roman Mission", Darton, Longman & Todd, 1996, 7
[3] The late Alistair Grant, an Elder at Glengarry Church, wrote a novel in which he envisaged a Roman soldier sharing his faith as he travelled through the Highlands! Alistair Grant, "Mist in the Corries", Pentland Books, 2001, 82
[4] J D Mackie, "A History of Scotland", Penguin, 1964, 3
[5] "St Ninian's Church, Glenurquhart", leaflet, n.d.
[6] J D Mackie, op cit, 35

[7] F F Bruce, "The Spreading Flame", Paternoster Press, 1982, 354

[8] Ian Finlay, "Columba", Edinburgh 1992, pp14,15,103

[9] ibid, 104-107

[10] Ian Bradley, "Argyll, The Making of a Spiritual Landscape", St Andrew Press, Edinburgh, 2015, 50

[11] Duncan MacDonald, "Reflections on Glenurquhart and Beyond", 2019, 169,170

[12] Ian Finlay, op cit, 122

[13] Bruce Ritchie, "Columba: The Faith of an Island Soldier", Christian Focus, Fearn, 2019, 384

[14] George F Campbell, "The First and Lost Iona: A Secret History of Fort Augustus", Candlemass Hill Publishing, Glasgow, 2006, 64,113

[15] Ian Bradley, op cit, 57,58

[16] Bruce Ritchie, op cit, 129

[17] George F Campbell, op cit, 65

[18] Bruce Ritchie, op cit, 352

[19] George F Campbell, op cit, 68,69,86,89

[20] William Mackay, op cit, 333

[21] ibid, 337

[22] Katherine Stewart, "The Story of Loch Ness", Luath Press, 2005, 25

[23] John Finney, op cit, 126,127

[24] Acts 18:3

[25] Ian Finlay, op cit, 132–135

[26] Tim Clarkson, "The Picts", Birlinn, Edinburgh, 2016, 139

[27] William MacKay, op cit, 336

[28] ibid, 225

[29] Bruce Ritchie, op cit, 401

[30] Thomas Williams, "Viking Britain", William Collins, London, 2017, 52,53

[31] James Hunter, "The Last of the Free, A Millennial History of the Highlands and Islands of Scotland," Mainstream Publishing, Edinburgh, 1999, 82

[32] William MacKay, op cit, 9,10; Katherine Stewart, op cit, 33

[33] Else Roesdahl, "The Vikings", Penguin, 2016, 167

[34] George F Campbell, op cit, 43

[35] Alexander MacDonald, "Story and Song from Loch Ness-side", Inverness, 1914, 75,76

[36] George F Campbell, op cit, 46; Jonathan Clements, "A Brief History of the Vikings", Constable and Robinson, London, 2005, 174,231

[37] J D Mackie, op cit, 42

[38] David Turnock, "Patterns of Highland Development", MacMillan, London, 1970, 2,3

[39] Catriona Fforde, "The Great Glen", Neil Wilson Publishing, 2011, 59

[40] Chris Tabraham (ed), "Urquhart Castle", Historic Scotland, 2002, 19

[41] Edward C Ellice, op cit, 3

[42] Iain R Thomson, "The Long Horizon", Birlinn, Edinburgh, 2008, 199

[43] George F Campbell, op cit, 24–27

[44] Ian Bradley, op cit, 114

[45] W Douglas Simpson, "Beauly Priory", HMSO Guide, 1974, 1,2

[46] Iain R Thomson, op cit, 26,27

[47] Ian Donnachie, "Economy and Society in the 17th Century in the Highlands" in "The Seventeenth Century in the Highlands", IFC, 1986, 56,57

[48] "Historical Guide to Glengarry", Glengarry Visitor Centre, 1999, 9. A pig of iron cast at Invergarry in 1732 is displayed at the Bonawe Iron Furnace in Argyll.

[49] William Mackay, op cit, 54

[50] Leonella Longmore, "Land of Churches", Inverness, 2000, 44

[51] James Kirk, "The Jacobean Church 1567–1625" in "The Seventeenth Century in the Highlands, IFC, 1986, 26

[52] ibid, 42

[53] James Hunter, op cit, 174

[54] See, for instance "The Reformation", The New International Dictionary of the Christian Church, Ed J D Douglas, The Paternoster Press, Exeter, 1974, 830,831

[55] "Register of ministers, exhorters and readers, and of their stipends, after the period of the Reformation", Maitland Club, Edinburgh, 1830, 58,59

[56] ibid, 60–62

[57] William Mackay, op cit, 518

[58] James Kirk, op cit, 27

[59] ibid, 32

[60] William Mackay, op cit, 115

[61] Peter Anson, 1970, op cit, 6,7

[62] James Kirk, op cit, 45,48

[63] A M Renwick, "The Story of the Church", IVP, London, 1962, 158

[64] Peter Anson, 1970, op cit, 18,40,59,69-72,82

[65] Alan Lawson, op cit, 77

[66] Katharine Stewart, "Women of the Highlands", Luath Press, Edinburgh, 2006: Ch.11, 64–77 is devoted to Anne Grant

[67] Duncan MacDonald, op cit, 43

[68] James Kirk, op cit, 37

[69] George F Campbell, op cit, 115 – 117

[70] Catriona Fforde, op cit, 86,115,119 et seq

[71] Rory Fitzpatrick, "God's Frontiersmen: The Scots-Irish Epic", Weidenfeld and Nicolson, London, 1989, 45

[72] Peter Anson, 1970, op cit, 100

[73] Douglas Ansdell, "The People of the Great Faith: The Highland Church 1690–1900", Acair, 1998, 27

[74] Peter Anson, 1970, op cit, 101

[75] A S Cowper, "SSPCK Schoolmasters, 1709–1872", SRS, Edinburgh, 1997

[76] OSA, Vol XX, Urquhart and Glenmoriston, 315

[77] J MacInnes, "The Evangelical Movement in the Highlands, 1688-1800", Aberdeen, 237

[78] Edward C Ellice, op cit, 29

[79] Peter Anson, 1970, op cit, 123,124

[80] ibid, 117,118

[81] Bruce Lenman, "The Jacobite Clans of the Great Glen: 1650-1784", Methuen, London, 1984, 21

[82] Map 20: see Bibliography

[83] Douglas Ansdell, op cit, 31

[84] Norman Macleod, "Reminiscences of a Highland Parish", S W Partridge, London, n.d., 86

[85] John Knox, "A Tour through the Highlands of Scotland and the Hebride Isles", London, 1786, clxii

[86] A Drummond and J Bulloch, "The Church in Late Victorian Scotland 1874–1900", St Andrew Press, 1978, 83

[87] Fitzroy Maclean, "Bonnie Prince Charlie", Canongate, Edinburgh, 1989, 296

[88] ibid, 283

[89] Peter Anson, 1970, op cit, 146

[90] ibid, 150

[91] ibid, 162

[92] ibid, 162, footnote

[93] ibid, 152

[94] ibid, 153

[95] Chris Tabraham & Doreen Grove: "Fortress Scotland and the Jacobites", Historic Scotland, Batsford, 1995

[96] Peter Anson, op cit, 232

[97] Mrs Grant, "Letters from the Mountains – being the real correspondence of a lady, 1773–1807", 1809, 187

[98] APM, 1.4.1818

[99] Archibald Clerk, "Notes of Everything", Kilmallie Parish Church, 1987, 2

[100] Ian M Allan, passim: Gairlochy Church had been ruinous for many years and has now been demolished.

[101] Rev A Russell, "A History of Mission in Lochaber from the Reformation", Lochaber Presbytery, 1992, 33

[102] Archibald Clerk, op cit, 31

[103] John Gifford, "The Buildings of Scotland: Highlands and Islands", Yale University Press, London, 2003, 59,60

[104] Rev A Russell, op cit, 43

[105] Alexander MacDonald, op cit, 350,351

[106] C A McAllister, "Fort Augustus and Glen Urquhart", MA Thesis, St Andrews University, 1963, 41–43

[107] John Prebble, "The Highland Clearances", Penguin, Harmondsworth, 1969, 189

[108] bid, 137–145

[109] Quoted in T M Devine, "Clearance and Improvement: Land, Power and People in Scotland 1700–1900", John Donald, Edinburgh, 2006, 202

110 Duncan MacDonald, op cit, 36

111 ibid, 51–58, where a detailed account of this estate may be found.

112 Edward C Ellice, op cit, 114,115

113 James Miller, "The Foresters", Birlinn, Edinburgh, 2009, 50,98

114 ibid, 98

115 Brian Osborne, "The Last of the Chiefs", Argyll Publishing, Glendaruel, 2001, 172–6

116 Ian Keillar, Electricity in the North, Moray Field Club, March 1981

117 James Miller, "The Dam Builders: Power from the Glens", Birlinn, Edinburgh, 2002

118 SSE: "Glendoe: Hydro is back", Scottish and Southern Energy plc, Perth, 2009; "Divine help for tunnellers", Light of the North, 4, Winter 2006/7, 8

119 SSE Renewables Ltd, "Generating Benefits in the Great Glen", Perth, 2020, Appendix 1

Chapter 2

1 Thomas Pennant: "A Tour of Scotland 1769", Birlinn, Edinburgh, 2000, p133 footnote; OSA, Vol XX, 20; Archibald Clerk, op cit, 33

2 Map 6.

3 Fr Andrew Joseph MacDonald, op cit, 93; E C Batten, "The Charters of the Priory of Beauly", The Grampian Club, 1877, 320

4 George F Campbell, op cit, 22,68,69

5 William Mackay, op cit, 337

6 Alan Lawson, op cit, 4,5

7 E C Batten, op cit, 34; George F Campbell, passim

8 E C Batten, ibid; Pont's map of c1583–96; Map 1

9 www.canmmore.org.uk/site/12197/abertarff

10 E C Batten, op cit, 39,240,241; J Cameron Lees, "History of the County of Inverness", William Blackwood, Edinburgh, 1897, 23

11 Alan Lawson, op cit, 21

12 Some details in the preceding three paragraphs are based on a talk by Dr Richard Oram of Stirling University to the Fort Augustus Heritage Group, 4 April 2016

[13] Alan Lawson, op cit, 22

[14] ibid, 25

[15] Iain R Thomson, op cit, 199

[16] Alan Lawson, op cit, 6

[17] Walter MacFarlane, op cit, Vol 1, 221

[18] ibid, Vol 2, 170-172

[19] Map 1

[20] George F Campbell, op cit, 21,22

[21] IPM, 28

[22] ibid, 65,66

[23] IPM, 66–69

[24] ibid, 70

[25] ibid, 67,68,69. "Infeftment" implies the investing of the rights of possession to a new owner.

[26] ibid, 81–84

[27] Walter MacFarlane, op cit, Vol 1, 221

[28] IPM, 84

[29] William Mackay, op cit, 363,364

[30] Map 1

[31] George F Campbell, op cit, 24

[32] Map 5

[33] Map 7

[34] Map 11

[35] Map 12

[36] Map 15

[37] Map 17

[38] www.canmore.org.uk/site/12204/cille-chuimein. The ancient Celtic tradition of burying the dead alongside running water perhaps underlines the fact that churches were not always alongside graveyards.

[39] NSA, Vol XIV, 61

[40] IPM, 82

[41] C A McAllister, op cit, 37,58,59

[42] Boleskine, Register of Baptisms & Marriages, CH2/792/7

[43] Lachlan Shaw, "History of the Province of Moray", revised by J F S Gordon, Vol iii, Glasgow, 1882, 443,444

[44] Jamie Kelly, "The Mission at Home: The Origins and Development of the SSPCK, 1709 – 1767", Glasgow University, 2016; "Record of SSPCK Schools, 1733", www.janeology.co.uk

[45] APM, 6.10.1725

[46] Duncan MacDonald, op cit, 75

[47] Walter MacFarlane, op cit, Vol 1, p221. Some details of boats working on Loch Ness are recorded in Duncan MacDonald, op cit, 134–136

[48] Map 13

[49] Chris Tabraham (ed), "Fort George", Historic Scotland, 2001, 17

[50] Alexander Dow, "Ministers to the Soldiers of Scotland", Oliver and Boyd, Edinburgh, 1962, 241

[51] Alexander Dow, ibid; FASTI, Vol IV, 130; ODNB Vol II, George Anderson 1676/7–1756, 31f

[52] APM, 14.5.17829, 9.8.1732, 11.10.1732

[53] FASTI, Vol IV, p131; Vol VII, 63

[54] John Gifford, op cit, 56

[55] William Mackay, op cit, Appendix II, 495–498

[56] Alexander Dow, op cit, 212

[57] Caledonian Mercury, 15 August 1745

[58] Charles Fraser-Mackintosh, "Antiquarian Notes, Historical, Genealogical and Social (Inverness)", A & W Mackenzie, Inverness, 1897, ChVI; A S Cowper, op cit

[59] www.ambaile.org.uk/asset/7455/1/

[60] Alexander Dow, ibid, 218

[61] Rev Dr John Ross, "The Jacobite Chaplains at Culloden", Glenurquhart Bulletin, Drumnadrochit, 2016, 32f

[62] The Duke of Cumberland's description of Fort Augustus quoted in John Prebble, "Culloden", Penguin, 1967, 177: the whole of Prebble's Chapter 4, 177–205, gives a graphic description of events at Fort Augustus.

[63] Caledonian Mercury, 19.6.1746

[64] John Prebble, 1967, op cit, 177

[65] Caledonian Mercury, 19.6.1746

[66] ibid, 23.6.1746; John Prebble, 1967, op cit, 184,185

[67] John Prebble, ibid, 188,189

[68] Caledonian Mercury, 23.6.1746

[69] Caledonian Mercury, 30.6.1746, quoted in ibid, 194

[70] APM, 11.6.1746

[71] Cumberland was awarded £25,000 per annum by Parliament "for his late signal service in extinguishing the Rebellion in Scotland: Caledonian Mercury, 19.5.1746

[72] Catriona Fforde, op cit, 170

[73] John Prebble, 1967, op cit, 311,312

[74] Alexander Dow, 224

[75] APM, 28.11.1752

[76] NSA, Vol XIV, 56

[77] Boleskine, Register of Baptisms & Marriages, CH2/792/7

[78] Charles Fraser-Mackintosh, op cit, passim

[79] See Appendix 1.A

[80] FASTI, Vol IV, 131,132; SRO, "Reports on the Annexed Estates", Edinburgh, 1973, 45

[81] Alexander Dow, op cit, 241,242

[82] Rev T M Murchison, "The Synod of Glenelg: 1725–1821", TGSI, vol 38, 85

[83] Cill Chuimein Heritage papers; T M Murchison, op cit, 91

[84] Charles Fraser-Mackintosh, op cit, passim

[85] APM, 7.9.1758

[86] SHS, Forfeited Estate Papers, Vol 57, 112,113,129

[87] APM, 23.11.1774

[88] SHS, Forfeited Eastate Papers, op cit, 68

[89] APM, 10.8.1773

[90] APM, 23.11.1773

[91] APM, 5.4.1774

[92] Iain R Thomson, op cit, 77,78

[93] APM, 23.11.1774

[94] APM, 11.4.1775

[95] APM, 18.6.1776

[96] APM, 7.12.1784

[97] APM, 2.6.1785, 29.11.1786

[98] Mrs Grant, op cit, Vol I, 186

[99] ibid, 118

[100] ibid, 187

[101] Map 19

[102] NSA, Vol XIV, 61,62

[103] SHS, Scottish Forfeited Estate Papers, Vol 57, 1909, 68. The galleries were not mentioned in earlier accounts of the church: they were perhaps added at a later date and may have contributed to the building's later problems.

[104] Mrs Grant, op cit, Vol I, 108–210 and Vol II, 36–41, passim

[105] ibid.

[106] Duncan MacDonald, op cit, 64

[107] APM, 2.6.1785

[108] APM, 29.3.1808

[109] APM, 12.5.1808

[110] APM, 29.11.1808

[111] APM, 12.5.1808, 24.5.1808

[112] Joseph Mitchell, "Reminiscences of my life in the Highlands", Vol I, 37,38

[113] Robert Southey, "Journal of a Tour in Scotland in 1819", ed. C H Herford, John Murray, 1929, 182

[114] A D Cameron, "The Caledonian Canal", Birlinn, Edinburgh, 2005, 89

[115] Joseph Mitchell, op cit, 27,82

[116] Boleskine Register of Baptisms and Marriages, CH2/792/7: the baptism of two of Joseph Mitchell's siblings are recorded in 1808 and 1809 whilst his father was resident at Bunoich. Joseph's son, James, entered the ministry of the Church of Scotland and served as Moderator in 1907.

[117] Marjory Harper, "Adventurers and Exiles: The Great Scottish Exodus", Profile Books, London, 2003, 46,47; Charles Fraser-Mackintosh, "Antiquarian Notes, Historical, Genealogical and Social (Inverness)", A & W Mackenzie, Inverness, 1897, op cit

[118] A D Cameron, op cit, 111 et seq

[119] Boleskine & Abertarff Kirk Session, 23.9.1824, CH2/792/1

[120] NSA, Vol XIV, 51,57

[121] Rev T Brown, "Annals of the Disruption", MacNiven and Wallace, Edinburgh, 1892, 217

[122] Inverness Courier, 1.1.1845

[123] Boleskine & Abertarff Kirk Session, 22.1.1845, CH2/792/1

[124] APM, 24.9.1846

[125] Inverness Courier, 1.2.1855

[126] Inverness Courier, 13.8.1857

[127] The annual fair is described by Alexander MacDonald, op cit, 199

[128] Fort Augustus School Minutes, 1811–35, 10.8.1811, 3.4.1812, 4.2.1828, CH2/1433/4

[129] Norman Macleod, op cit, 204,205

[130] Fort Augustus School Minutes, 8.10.1819, CH2/1433/4; A Drummond and A Bulloch, "The Scottish Church, 1688–1843", St Andrew Press, Edinburgh, 1973, 153

[131] FASTI, Vol VII, 176

[132] Inverness Courier, 7.11.1894

[133] Quoted in Frank D Bardgett, "Devoted Service Rendered", St Andrew Press, Edinburgh, 2002, 302

[134] APM, 1.10.1840

[135] APM, 8.5.1844

[136] APM, 2.7.1844

[137] APM, 25.9.1845

[138] APM, 7.5.1845, 17.6.1845, 24.9.1845

[139] APM, 24.12.1845

[140] Inverness Courier, 8.6.1847

[141] APM, 3.5.1848, 22.8.1848, 28.11.1848

[142] https://leithchurch.ca/history

[143] APM, 3.8.1858

[144] APM, 14.9.1858, 15.9.1858, 22.9.1858

[145] Archibald Clerk, op cit, p8

[146] This and the following two sections draw upon the minutes of the Congregational Committee 1860–1867 held at Fort William Archive Centre; CH2/1433/2

[147] Fort Augustus School Minutes, CH2/1433/4; APM, 3.11.1858

[148] APM, 4.8.1863

[149] Duncan MacDonald, opcit, 172,173

[150] APM, 9.5.1865

[151] https://queenscollegestourbridge.weebly.com/prescot-house---a-potted-history.html

[152] Inverness Courier, 28.9.1871

153 The Commissioners of Woods, Forests and Land Revenues was established in 1810 by the merger of two offices managing Crown lands; they were responsible for managing the lands around the Garrison.

154 APM, 13.6.1865, 27.3.1866

155 John Gifford, op cit, 247

156 APM, 27.3.1866

157 APM, 25.4.1866

158 John Gifford, op cit, 243,262,264

159 Inverness Courier, 28.6. 1866, 5.7.1866

160 FASTI, vol IV, 132

161 Andrew J. Macdonald, op cit, 76–78; Alexander MacDonald, op cit, 137,138. Sincere thanks are due to Jane Patten, Fort Augustus, who has researched the history of this colourful man and has supplied other relevant information.

162 The purchase of these materials for "the erection of a new church" was noted by the Inverness Courier, 30.8.1866

163 Inverness Courier, 11.7.1867

164 APM, 6.11.1866

165 Daily Telegraph, 8.9.1871

166 APM, 3.7.1867, 6.8.1867, 10.9.1867

167 APM, 5.11.1867, 26.11.1867

168 APM, 22.9.1868

169 APM, 2.11.1869

170 APM, 26.6.1878, 26.11.1878

171 APM, 24.11.1880, 2.8.1881

172 APM, 29.11.1882

173 Malcolm sent copies of a circular with a letter to the Secretary of the SSPCK, 19.12.1882; held at the Glengarry Heritage Centre.

174 APM, 18.9.1882 – 25.4.1883

175 Presbytery Archive, CH2/7/12/99, 16.2.1884

176 Presbytery Archive, CH2/7/12/104, 5.8.1884

177 APM, 28.11.1888, 15.6.1892

178 APM, 24.11.1897

179 APM, 5.7.1898

[180] J C & S J Leslie, "The Hospitals of Lochaber", Old Manse Books, Avoch, 2013, 57–65

[181] Extract from verses by Dom R Alexander, op cit, 11

[182] Ian M Allan, op cit, 113–122; a detailed account of Francis MacBean is to be found in John MacLeod's "By-Paths of Highland Church History", Knox Press, Edinburgh, 1965, 22 et seq

[183] ibid, 126–129

[184] ibid, 129

[185] James Carron, "Tin Tabernacles and other corrugated iron buildings in Scotland", 2017

[186] Map 18

[187] Dom Odo Blundell, op cit, Vol 2, 183

[188] Peter Anson, 1970, op cit, 324 footnote

[189] Dom Aelred Grugan OSB, "Red Coats and Black Habits, private paper, Fort Augustus Abbey, 1998; The Scotsman, 14.9.1876

[190] Sir David Hunter Blair, "An Abbey School in the Making"

[191] The Scotsman, 14.9.1876

[192] Alasdair Roberts and Ann Dean, "Northern Catholic History Notes", Aberdeen, 2019, 58

[193] J C & S J Leslie, op cit, 67,70,71

Chapter 3

[1] The words of Alasdair Grant in a poem, reproduced later in the chapter, are surely a reference to "Creagan an Fhithich", the Raven's Rock, the traditional war-cry of the Macdonell's and the site of Invergarry Castle.

[2] Map 3

[3] Edward C Ellice, op cit, 43

[4] A Drummond and J Bulloch, op cit, 83

[5] W Kilgour, "Lochaber in Peace and War", Paisley, 1908, 159

[6] Edward C Ellice, 71,77

[7] IPM, 82 (referring to Aeneas Macdonell, Lord Macdonell and Aros), 100

[8] Peter Anson, op cit, 162

[9] Catriona Fforde, op cit, 166

[10] Quoted in Dom Odo Blundell, op cit, Vol 2, 188

[11] Peter Anson, 1970, op cit, 261

[12] Inverness Courier, 4.1.1948

[13] Dom O Blundell, op cit, 189

[14] John Gifford, op cit, 248

[15] Bruce Lenman, op cit, 19

[16] T M Murchison, op cit, 74, 75

[17] Rev A Russell, op cit, 11,12

[18] APM, 7.12.1784

[19] Boleskine Register of Baptisms and Marriages, CH2/792/7. It is recorded that Margaret Macdonell was baptised in 1775, but she was not born until 1782: the entry must refer to Elizabeth who was born in 1775.

[20] APM, 18.6.1776

[21] APM, 7.12.1784

[22] APM, 5.5.1785

[23] C Fraser-Mackintosh, "Antiquarian Notes, Historical, Genealogical and Social (Inverness)", A & W Mackenzie, Inverness, 1897, 128

[24] John Prebble, 19699, op cit, 137–145; for details of the evictions see Fraser-Macintosh, op cit, 120–128

[25] More information on Gillespie is contained within James Hunter, op cit, 242-244

[26] APM, 29.11.1786

[27] APM, 6.5.1789; CH2/792/7

[28] APM, 6.10.1806

[29] APM, 31.3.1812

[30] APM, 24.11.1812

[31] APM, 26.7.1814

[32] KKS, 26.11.1836, 9.4.1837

[33] APM, 3.1.1844

[34] APM, 9.11.1848

[35] APM, 3.7.1867; NSA, Vol XVI, 425

[36] KKS, 13.5.1838, 21.10.1861

[37] David Turnock, op cit, p5

[38] Edward C Ellice, op cit, p5

[39] John Prebble, 1969, op cit, p75,179

[40] David Paton, "The Clergy and the Clearances", Birlinn, Edinburgh, 2006, p94

[41] Dictionary of Canadian Biography, Vol 9, "Edward Ellice": he also received £35,000 in compensation following the liberation of over 300 slaves on sugar estates he co-owned in the West Indies – "Legacies of British Slave-ownership, Rt Hon Edward Ellice" (www.ucl.ac.uk/lbs/person/view/27776)

[42] John Prebble, 1969, op cit, p82,283

[43] Inverness Courier, 1.11.1860

[44] David Turnock, op cit, 30

[45] J C & S J Leslie, op cit, 46,47

[46] J Cameron Lees, op cit, 340

[47] David Turnock, op cit, passim

[48] Alexander MacDonald, op cit, 299,405

[49] Ian M Allan, op cit, 143

[50] Inverness Courier, 21.12.1847

[51] Inverness Courier, 28.12.1847

[52] John Prebble, 1969, op cit, 274

[53] Inverness Courier, 28.12.1847: the new missionary was William Sutherland, appointed to serve Glengarry and Fort Augustus and Glenmoriston too!

[54] Inverness Courier, 4.1.1848

[55] Ian M Allan, op cit, pp144,145

[56] See map of the "Ladies' Schools" -in- Rev T. Brown, op cit

[57] The text of the English sermon at Glengarry Church, 27.8.1867

[58] Rev A Russell, op cit, 25

[59] APM, 28.11.1854

[60] APM, 29.8.1854, 1.11.1854

[61] APM, 9.5.1865: a parish "quoad omnia" is one that exercises pastoral and civil functions.

[62] APM, 3.7.1867

[63] Inverness Courier, 5.9.1867: Mr Cameron, minister of Urquhart, had been the missionary at Glengarry from 1859–1864.

[64] APM, 27.8.1867

[65] Inverness Courier, 22.9.1896

[66] The Scotsman, 14.9.1871

[67] Peter Anson, 1970, op cit, p32,333. Anson here emphasises the minority position of the Episcopal Church which numbered only 55,000 members in the early 1870s, compared to 300,000 Catholics and 3 million Presbyterians.

[68] Inverness Courier, 13.9.1866; see also correspondence published there 25.10.1866 and 8.11.1866

[69] ODNB, Robert Eden: 1804–1886

[70] Peter Anson, ibid, 333

[71] ODNB, Samuel Wilberforce: 1805–1873

[72] ODNB, William Thomson: 1819–1890

[73] A Drummond and J Bulloch, "The Church in Victorian Scotland: 1843–1874, St Andrew Press, Edinburgh, 1975, 327,328

[74] The Scotsman, 19.9.1871

[75] Inverness Courier: 28.9.1871

[76] The Scotsman, 22.9.1871

[77] The Scotsman, 30.9.1871

[78] Marion Lochhead, "Episcopal Scotland in the Nineteenth Century", John Murray, Edinburgh, 1966, 141

[79] Inverness Courier, 23.11.1871

[80] Marion Lochhead, op cit, 178

[81] A R Ashwell and R G Wilberforce, "Life of the Rt. Rev. Samuel Wilberforce", New York (where published as a one-volume edition), 1883, 519–521

[82] The Times, 23.1.1883, 30.1.1883

[83] APM, 24.11.1880

[84] APM, 26.3.1895

[85] cf 1 Peter 2:4,5; Inverness Courier, 22.9.1896

[86] TSA, Vol XVI, 425

[87] Sir David Hunter-Blair, "A New Medley of Memories", London, Edward Arnold, 1922, 204.

[88] Glengarry History Society, "Wartime in Glengarry", Glengarry, 2005?, 6,7

[89] Poem reproduced by kind permission of the Grant family. The "dreaming woman" is a reference to Eliza Ellice who was responsible for the extension of the Parish Church in 1896 and the subsequent installation of an organ.

[90] James Miller, 2002, passim

[91] Information provided by Mrs Helen Allan, Glengarry Lodge.

[92] Correspondence quoted in Brian D Osborne, op cit, 172

[93] Ian M Allan, op cit, 147

[94] Brian D Osborne, op cit, 50

[95] Ian Allan, op cit, 151

[96] Brian D Osborne, op cit, 154

[97] ibid, 155

[98] NSA, Vol XIV, 511

[99] A Drummond and J Bulloch, 1978, op cit, 83

[100] KKS, CH2/433/1, CH2/433/2

[101] A Drummond and J Bulloch, 1973, op cit, 254

[102] Ian M Allan, op cit, 145

[103] More information on Laggan Church is related within ibid, 146–154

[104] Quoted in Edward C Ellice, op cit, 86

[105] APM, 26.3.1811

[106] Rev A Russell, op cit, 24

[107] A Drummond and J Bulloch, 1978, op cit, 83,84

[108] Edward C Ellice, op cit, p88; Joseph Mitchell, "Reminiscences of my life in the Highlands", Vol 2, David and Charles, Newton Abbot, 1971, 123–125

[109] ODNB: Edward Ellice, 1783–1863; Edward Ellice 1810–1880

[110] Edward C Ellice, op cit, 93,94

[111] Iain Thornber, "James Henderson – a Highland deer stalker", Oban Times, 25.6.2017

[112] George Malcolm to Mr Bass, 13.4.1882: letter held by Glengarry Heritage Centre.

[113] ibid, 17.4.1882

[114] ibid, 23 May, 2 August, 19.12.1882

[115] Mary Miers, "Western Seaboard: An Illustrated Architectural Guide", Rutland Press, 2008

[116] Letter from George Malcolm, 25.4.1883

[117] ibid, 19.12.1882

[118] Peter R English, "Arnisdale and Loch Hourn", Arnisdale and Loch Hourn Community Association, 2000, 410,411,438

[119] APM, 24.11.1897, Presbytery Archive, CH2/7/12/83

[120] APM, 29.3.1904

[121] Frank D Bardgett, op cit, 100

[122] Abertarff Presbytery papers, CH2/7/12/229

[123] David Kellas, "Cill Chuimein, A History of the Parish Church of Glenelg", Glenelg, 2009, 23

[124] Peter R English, op cit, 301. The FASTI entry for Glenelg (Vol VII, 149) refers to a "mission chapel" at Lochhournhead: this may refer to the schoolroom.

Chapter 4

[1] William Mackay, op cit, 322–325

[2] Alexander MacDonald, op cit, 14. It is suggested that "Erchard ... should be placed in the ranks of the early heroes of the early Pictish church in Alba, alongside the better known Ternan and Drostan." www.cushnieent.com/saints/sterchard.html

[3] "There is no trace or any local knowledge of a church" at the graveyard: https://canmore.org.uk/site/12157/st-merechards-church; Kenneth MacDonald, "A Modern Raid in Glengarry and Glenmoriston" in TGSI, Vol XV, 1888–1889, 11–35

[4] William Mackay, op cit, 460 footnote

[5] Walter MacFarlane, op cit, Vol 2, 171; the appellation perhaps indicates a dedication to Merchard?

[6] William Mackay, op cit, 333,334,337

[7] ibid, 117 footnote, 342,460,518

[8] ibid, 383

[9] FASTI, Vol VI, 453

[10] William Mackay, op cit, 348–350

[11] Walter MacFarlane, op cit, Vol 2, 171

[12] William Mackay, op cit, 352,353

[13] ibid, 361,362

[14] IPM, pp81–83

[15] William Mackay, op cit, 363

[16] IPM, 123

[17] Note provided by Duncan MacDonald, Drumnadrochit.

[18] William Mackay, op cit, 372–374

[19] ibid, 375,397,398

[20] A S Cowper (ed), op cit. The appellation "St Richard's" is recorded in 1783 in the Abertarff Marriage Register as the residence of a bride; CH2/792/7

[21] Alexander MacDonald, op cit, 69

[22] APM, 8.5.1776

[23] OSA, Vol XX, 316,317

[24] John Prebble, "Mutiny", Penguin, Harmondsworth, 1977, 289 et seq

[25] William Mackay, op cit, 376,384

[26] A S Cowper, op cit

[27] J MacInnes, op cit, 238

[28] William Mackay, op cit, 294

[29] Alexander MacDonald, op cit, 26,27

[30] ibid, 302–310; John Prebble, 1967, op cit, 302–304

[31] William Mackay, op cit, 296,297

[32] William MacKay, op cit, 299

[33] ibid, Appendix II, 495–498. William Grant also served in Abertarff.

[34] Thomas Pennant, op cit, 131

[35] William Mackay, op cit, 554,555

[36] Annette Smith, "The Work of the Forfeited Estates Board Around Loch Ness" – in – IFC, 1991, 63,65. Alexander MacDonald (op cit, 37) suggests the linen works were in use until 1791: today the building is known as Invermoriston Home Farm.

[37] Rev A Russell, op cit, 14; CH2 /792/7; Fr A J Macdonald, "Glen Albyn: Tales and Truths of the Central Highlands", 1953, 92,93

[38] OSA, Vol XX, 313,314

[39] APM, 7.12.1784; 31.3.1801

[40] Duncan MacDonald, "The Stipend", Glenurquhart Bulletin, 2020, 27

[41] William Mackay, op cit, 384

[42] APM, 31.3.1812

[43] Glenmoriston Kirk Session, 1827–87, CH2/434/6

44 APM, 30.11.1813
45 Glenurquhart Heritage Group, "Glimpses of Glenurquhart: Tales from a Highland Glen", 2018, 187
46 NSA, Vol XIV, 49
47 APM, 11.9.1827
48 APM, 1.12.1841
49 APM, 13.7.1843
50 APM, 28.11.1848
51 APM, 26.6.1878
52 Rev A Russell, op cit, 25
53 APM, 25.11.1896; 30.11.1898
54 Census summaries in www.glenmoriston.org.uk, and Ian M Allan, op cit, 99
55 Ian M Allan, op cit, 85–87
56 It is interesting to note that the footprints are also attributed to a Jesuit, Alexander MacRae! Rt Rev Mark Dilworth, writing in "Scalan News", 23, November 2001, 17
57 NSA, Vol XIV, 47
58 Glenmoriston Minutes, CH2/434/6, 61–72. Those proposing the new parish may have been encouraged by the creation of the Parish of Erchless in Strathglasss in 1884, IPM, 1.4.1884
59 See Appendix 1.D for the missionaries and ministers serving in Glenmoriston.
60 Letter within Kirk Session minutes of 1910. In her Will (reproduced at www.glenmoriston.org.uk) Mrs Morrison left £20,000 to various Christian causes.
61 Session Minute, 1.4.1913; 6.4.1915
62 Session Minute, 17.5.1929. Mr Gordon's sojourn could not have been long for his name does not appear in the Register of Lay Missionaries, 1930–1988, within Frank D Bardgett, "Devoted Service Rendered", St Andrew Press, Edinburgh, 2002, 335-360. The FASTI entry for Glenmoriston (Vol VI, 453, published in 1926) states that "there is now a mission chapel … at Dalchreichart": this cannot be confirmed and may refer to the school.
63 Session Minute, 6.3.1932

[64] Session Minute, 12.7.1953

[65] Ian M Allan, op cit, 88,109

[66] Report reproduced courtesy of Rev Duncan Turner's son, Hamish Turner.

[67] James Miller, "The Dam Builders", 2002, 22-26, 88

[68] Session Minute, 13.7.1952, 7.12.1952

[69] Session Minute, 5.4.1953

[70] Session Minute, 3.12.1955

[71] Session Minute, 10.7.1955

[72] E Wood, "The Hydro Boys", Luath Press, Edinburgh, 2010, 99

[73] Congregational Board Minute, 11.12.1980, 18.8.1981

[74] Session Minute, 8.3.1986

[75] Congregational Board Minute, 13.3.1986

[76] Session Minute, 2.3.1987

[77] Congregational Board Minute, 10.3.1988, 17.4.1990; Session Minute, 31.8.1989

[78] Congregational Board Minute, 17.4.1990

[79] Congregational Board Minute, 30.5.1991

[80] Rt Rev Mark Dilworth, writing in Scalan News, No. 23, November 2001, 15

[81] OSA, Vol XX, p315; NSA, Vol XIV, 49,50

[82] John Gifford, 181

[83] Alasdair Roberts and Ann Dean, op cit, 60

[84] Moriston Matters, No.1, 4: at www.glenmoriston.org.uk

[85] Ian M Allan, op cit, 88,89

[86] ibid, 100–103

[87] See the Reminiscences of Pat MacDonald at www.glenmoriston.org.uk

[88] Kenneth A Macrae, "Highland Handshake, Northern Chronicle, Inverness, 1954

[89] Ian M Allan, op cit, passim

[90] Moriston Matters, No.45, 7

[91] Broadcast on 1.9.1968, from a recording kindly loaned by Mrs Helen Macleod, daughter of Rev Peter Fraser.

[92] TSA, Vol XVI, 243

Chapter 5

[1] Alex Motyer, "Isaiah", Tyndale Old Testament Commentaries, Inter-Varsity Press, 1999, 271

[2] NSA, Vol XIV, 58

[3] Katharine Stewart, "A School in the Hills" – in – "A Life in the Hills", Birlinn, Edinburgh, 2018, 393

[4] Ian M Allan, op cit, passim

[5] John Benton, "Whatever happened to the local church?", Evangelicals Now, February 2021, 7,9

[6] Paul Williams, "The Revelation of the Lockdown", The Bible in Transmission, Summer 2020, 24,25, The Bible Society, Swindon

[7] This is but one strand of various new approaches to worship and witness: www.freshexpressions.org.uk

[8] Alan J Roxburgh, "The Missionary Congregation, Leadership and Liminality", Trinity Press International, Harrisburg, Pennsylvania, 1997, 57

[9] ibid, 59,61,64

[10] John Inge, "A Christian Theology of Place", Routledge, 2003, 111–115

[11] "The Bible for Today", Oxford University Press, 1941, editorial comment, 1100

[12] ibid, 515

[13] Paul Williams, op cit

[14] Steve Aisthorpe, "The Invisible Church", St Andrew Press, Edinburgh, 2016, 194–196

[15] Steve Aisthorpe, "Rewilding the Church", St Andrew Press, Edinburgh, 2020, 26,27,38,48

[16] Church of Scotland Theological Forum, "Five Marks of Mission", Finalised Report, 20.8.2020

[17] John Inge, op cit, 36

[18] Steve Aisthorpe, 2020, op cit, 22

[19] "The Bible for Today", op cit, editorial preface to the Gospels, 950

[20] Matthew 1:23, cf Isaiah 7:14; John 1:14, The Message

[21] Dr Anne Richards, "Rights of Common", Country Way, Issue 84, Summer 2020, 22, The Arthur Rank Centre

[22] John Inge, op cit, 58

[23] Dr Anne Richards, op cit, 23

[24] John Inge, op cit, 103

[25] Steve Aisthorpe, 2016, op cit, 189

[26] Aisthorpe 2020, op cit, 59

[27] Luke 10:30–37; John 4:5–42

[28] Very Rev A Bogle, "Crossing the divides", Life and Work, October 2019, 16

[29] Hebrews 13:12; Acts 8:26–39; 9:1–19; 10:28–48; 16:13–15

[30] Revelation 3:20

[31] Philip Sheldrake, "Living Between Worlds: Place and Journey in Celtic Spirituality", London, Darton, Longman and Todd, 1995, 7

[32] Al Barrett and Ruth Harley, "Being Interrupted: Reimagining the Church's Mission from the Outside In", London, SCM Press, 2020, 165

[33] Paul Williams, op cit, 25

[34] D Bonhoeffer, "Christology", Collins, 1978, 60

[35] Paul Williams, op cit, 26, quoting Matthew 6:10

[36] Alan J Roxburgh, op cit, 54

[37] Map 1; ODNB, Robert Pont, Timothy Pont

[38] Acts 17:26,27

[39] Steve Aisthorpe 2020, op cit, 41

[40] John 17:14–18

[41] Paul Williams, op cit, 26

[42] Hebrews 13:15,16

[43] Alan J Roxburgh, op cit, 1

[44] Charlotte Runcie, "Salt on your tongue", Canongate, Edinburgh, 2020, 179

[45] Quoted in James Hunter, op cit, 381; emphasis added

[46] Steve Aisthorpe 2020, op cit, 2

[47] ibid, 158

[48] Alan J Roxburgh, op cit, 29,45,46

[49] Steve Aisthorpe, 2016, op cit, 204; quoting "The Special Committee anent Review and Reform, 2001, A church without walls", Edinburgh, The General Assembly of the Church of Scotland, 8

[50] John Benton, "Why small churches are closing", Evangelicals Now, December 2019, 16

[51] John Finney, op cit, 6

[52] 'Columba's Herding' –in– Alexander Carmichael, "Carmina Gadelica", 1997 edn, Floris Books, Edinburgh, 338,339; emphasis added.

BIBLIOGRAPHY

National Archives of Scotland

Boleskine & Abertarff Kirk Session, 1801-57; CH2/792/1
Boleskine, Register of Baptisms & Marriages; CH2/792/7
Fort Augustus Church Committee, 1860-67; CH2/1433/2
Fort Augustus School Minutes, 1811-3; CH2/1433/4
Glenmoriston Kirk Session, 1827-87; CH2/434/6
Kilmonivaig Kirk Session; CH2/433/1,2
Kilmonivaig, Register of Baptisms & Marriages; CH2/433/3
Presbytery of Abertarff; CH2/7/1-9
Presbytery of Abertarff, miscellaneous papers;
    CH2/7/12/83,99,104,229,230

Newspapers and Journals

Caledonian Mercury*
Daily Telegraph*
Glasgow Herald*
Glenurquhart Bulletin
Inverness Courier*
John Bull*
Light of the North
Moriston Matters
Scalan News
Scots Magazine*
The Scotsman*
The Times*

* Accessed at: www.britishnewspaperarchive.co.uk

Printed Sources

Aisthorpe, S., "The Invisible Church", St Andrew Press, Edinburgh, 2016

Aisthorpe, S., "Rewilding the Church," St Andrew Press, Edinburgh, 2020

Alexander, Dom R., "The Great Venture – or – Fort Augustus in View", Inverness, c1928

Allan, I. M., "West the Glen", Inverness, 1977

Ansdell, D., "The People of the Great Faith: The Highland Church 1690-1900", Acair, 1998

Anson, P.F., "The Catholic Church in Modern Scotland, Burns, Oates and Westbourne, 1937

Anson, P.F., "Underground Catholicism in Scotland", Standard Press, Montrose, 1970

Ashwell A. R. & Wilberforce R. G., "Life of the Rt. Rev. Samuel Wilberforce", New York, 1883

Bardgett, F. D., "Devoted Service Rendered", St Andrew Press, Edinburgh, 2002

Barrett A. & Harley R., "Being Interrupted: Reimagining the Church's Mission from the Outside In", SCM Press, London, 2020

Batten, E. C., "The Charters of the Priory of Beauly", The Grampian Club, 1877

Benton J., "Why small churches are closing", Evangelicals Now, December 2019

Benton J., "Whatever happened to the local church?", Evangelicals Now, February 2001

Blundell, Dom O., "The Catholic Highands of Scotland", 2 vols, Sands & Co., Edinburgh, 1909 & 1917

Blundell, Dom O., "Kilcumein and Fort Augustus", The Abbey Press, Fort Augustus, 1915(?)

Bogle, Very Rev A., "Crossing the divides", Life and Work, October 2019

Bonhoeffer, D., "Christology", Collins, 1978

Bradley, I., "Argyll, The Making of a Spiritual Landscape", St Andrew Press, Edinburgh, 2015

Brown, Rev T., "Annals of the Disruption", MacNiven and Wallace, Edinburgh, 1892

Bruce, F. F., "The Spreading Flame", Paternoster Press, Carlisle, 1982

Burt, E., "Letters", vol XXVI, c1725

Cameron, A.D., "The Caledonian Canal", Birlinn, Edinburgh, 2005

Campbell, G.F., "The First and Lost Iona: A Secret History of Fort Augustus", Glasgow, Candlemas Hill Publishing, 2006

Carmichael, A., "Carmina Gadelica", Floris Books, Edinburgh, 1997

Carron, J., "Tin Tabernacles and other corrugated iron buildings in Scotland", Createspace, 2017

Charlton, Rev G., Note on Glengarry Church, 1989

Clarkson, T., "The Picts", Birlinn, Edinburgh, 2016

Clements, J., "A Brief History of the Vikings", Constable and Robinson, London, 2005

Clerk, Rev Dr A., "Notes of Everything", Kilmallie Parish Church,1987 (with West Highland Museum, Fort William)

Cowper, A.S. (ed), "SSPCK Schoolmasters, 1709–1872", Scottish Record Society, Edinburgh, 1997

Denoon, B., "Do you say 'Sir' to your father? Tales and memories of the Great Glen", Ardvreck Publishing, Inverness, 2009

Devine, T.M., "Clearance and Improvement: Land, Power and People in Scotland 1700–1900", John Donald, Edinburgh, 2006

Donnachie, I., "Economy and Society in the 17th Century in the Highlands", in IFC, 1986

Douglas, J.D. (ed), The New International Dictionary of the Christian Church, The Paternoster Press, Exeter, 1974

Dow, A., "Ministers to the Soldiers of Scotland", Oliver and Boyd, Edinburgh, 1962

Drummond, A. & Bulloch, J., "The Scottish Church, 1688–1843", St Andrew Press, Edinburgh, 1973

Drummond, A. & Bulloch, J., "The Church in Victorian Scotland: 1843–1874", St Andrew Press, Edinburgh, 1975

Drummond, A. & Bulloch, J., "The Church in Late Victorian Scotland: 1874–1900", St Andrew Press, Edinburgh, 1978

Ellice, E.C., "Place Names of Glengarry and Glenquoich", London, 1898, facsimile edition, Glengarry Visitor Centre, 1999

English, P.R., "Arnisdale and Loch Hourn", Arnisdale and Loch Hourn Community Association, 2000

Fforde, C., "The Great Glen", Neil Wilson Publishing, 2011

Finlay, I., "Columba", Chambers, Edinburgh, 1992

Finney, J., "Recovering the Past: Celtic and Roman Mission", Darton, Longman and Todd, 1996

Fitzpatrick, R., "God's Frontiersmen: the Scots-Irish Epic", Weidenfeld and Nicolson, London, 1989

Forestry Commission, "The forest is a beautiful place to be: The Story of Forestry in the Great Glen in the 20th Century", Forestry Commission, Edinburgh, 2008

Fraser-Mackintosh, C., "Antiquarian Notes, Historical, Genealogical and Social (Inverness)", A & W Mackenzie, Inverness, 1897

Gifford, J., "The Buildings of Scotland: Highlands and Islands", Yale University Press, London, 2003

Glengarry History Society, "Wartime in Glengarry", Glengarry, 2005?

Glengarry Visitor Centre, "A Short History of the Ellice Family", n.d.

Glengarry Visitor Centre, "Historical Guide to Glengarry", 1999

Glenmoriston Congregational Board Minutes, kindly loaned

Glenmoriston Kirk Session Minutes, kindly loaned

Glenurquhart Heritage Group, "Glimpses of Glenurquhart: Tales from a Highland Glen", Drumnadrochit, 2018

Grant, A., "Mist in the Corries", Pentland Books, 2001

Grant, Mrs [Anne], "Letters from the Mountains – being the real correspondence of a lady, 1773–1801"

Grugen, Dom A., OSB, "Red Coats and Black Habits", Fort Augustus Abbey, 1998

Harper, M., "Adventurers and Exiles: The Great Scottish Exodus", Profile Books, London, 2003

Hunter, J., "Last of the Free: A Millennial History of the Highlands and Islands of Scotland", Mainstream Publishing, Edinburgh, 1999

Hunter-Blair, Sir D., "A New Medley of Memories," London, Edward Arnold, 1922

Hunter-Blair, Sir D., "An Abbey School in the Making," www.corbie.com, 2000, o.o.p.

IFC, "The Seventeenth Century in the Highlands", Inverness, 1986

IFC, "The Hub of the Highlands", The Mercat Press, Edinburgh, 1990

IFC, "Loch Ness and Thereabouts", Inverness, 1991

Inge, J., "A Christian Theology of Place", Routledge, 2003

IPM, "Records of the Presbyteries of Inverness and Dingwall, 1643–88", SHS, Vol 24, 1896

Keillar, I., "Electricity in the North", Moray Field Club, Elgin, 1981

Kellas, D., "Cill Chuimen, A History of the Parish Church of Glenelg", Glenelg, 2009

Kelly, J., "The Mission at Home: The Origins and Development of the SSPCK, 1709–1767", 2016 gla.ac.uk/media/Media_461957_smxx.pdf

Kilgour, W.T., "Lochaber in War and Peace", Alexander Gardner, Paisley, 1908

Kirk, J., "The Jacobean Church in the Highlands, 1567–1625" –in– IFC, 1986, above, 24–51

Kirk, J. (ed), "The Church in the Highlands", Scottish Church History Society, Edinburgh, 1998

Knox, J., "A Tour through the Highlands of Scotland and the Hebride Isles", London, 1786

Lawson, A.B., "A Country Called Stratherrick", South Loch Ness Heritage Group, 2006

Lees, J.C., "History of the County of Inverness", William Blackwood, Edinburgh, 1897

Lenman, B., "The Jacobite Clans of the Great Glen: 1650–1784", Methuen, London, 1984

Leslie, J.C. & S.J., "The Hospitals of Lochaber", Old Manse Books, Avoch, 2013

"Light of the North", Aberdeen RC Diocese Magazine

Lochhead, M., "Episcopal Scotland in the Nineteenth Century", John Murray, Edinburgh, 1966

Longmore, L., "Land of Churches", Inverness, 2000

McAllister, C.A., "Fort Augustus and Glen Urquhart", MA Thesis, St Andrews University, 1963

Macdonald, A., "Story and Song from Loch Ness-side", Inverness, 1914 (reprinted edition 1982)

Macdonald, Fr. A.J., "Glen Albyn: Tales and Truths of the Central Highlands", The Abbey Press, Fort Augustus, 1909 and 1953

Macdonald, D., "Reflections on Glenurquhart and Beyond", Compilations from the Glenurquhart Bulletin, Inverness, 2019

Macdonald, D., "The Stipend", Glenurquhart Bulletin, 2020

Macdonald, K., "A Modern Raid in Glengarry and Glenmoriston" -in- TGSI, Vol XV, 1888–89, pp11–35, 26

Macfarlane, W., "Geographical Collections", Vols 1 & 2, SHS, Edinburgh

Macinnes, J., "The Evangelical Movement in the Highlands, 1688–1800", Aberdeen University Press

Mackay, W., "Urquhart and Glenmoriston", Inverness, 1893

Mackie, J.D., "A History of Scotland", Penguin, Harmondsworth, 1964

Maclean, F., "Bonnie Prince Charlie", Canongate, Edinburgh, 1989

Macleod, J., "By-paths of Highland Church History", Knox Press, Edinburgh, 1965

Macleod, N., "Reminiscences of a Highland Parish", S W Partridge, London, n.d.

Macrae, K.A., "Highland Handshake", Northern Chronicle, Inverness, 1954

Maitland Club, "Register of ministers, exhorters and readers, and of their stipends, after the period of the Reformation", Edinburgh, 1830; NLS

Miers, M., "Western Seaboard: An Illustrated Architectural Guide", Rutland Press, 2008

Miller, J., "The Dam Builders: Power from the Glens", Birlinn, Edinburgh, 2002

Miller, J., "The Foresters", Birlinn, Edinburgh, 2009

Mitchell, J., "Reminiscences of my life in the Highlands", 2 vols, David and Charles, Newton Abbot, 1971

"Moriston Matters", archived at www.glenmoriston.org.uk

Motyer, A., "Isaiah", Tyndale Old Testament Commentries, Inter-Varsity Press, Leicester, 1999

Murchison, Rev T.M., "The Synod of Glenelg: 1725–1821" –in– TGSI, Vol 38, 63ff

NSA, "The New Statistical Account of Scotland", Vol XIV

ODNB, Oxford Dictionary of National Biography

OSA, "A Statistical Account of Scotland" (the Old Statistical Account), Vols XVII, XX, XXI

Osborne, B., "The Last of the Chiefs", Argyll Publishing, Glendaruel, 2001

Paton, D., "The Clergy and the Clearances", Birlinn, Edinburgh, 2006

Pennant, T., "A Tour of Scotland, 1769", Birlinn, Edinburgh, 2000

Prebble, J., "Culloden", Penguin, Harmondsworth, 1967

Prebble, J., "The Highland Clearances", Penguin, Harmondsworth, 1969

Prebble, J., "Mutiny", Penguin, Harmondsworth, 1977

Renwick, A.M., "The Story of the Church", Inter-Varsity Press, London, 1962

Richards, A., "Rights of Common", Country Way, Issue 84, Summer 2020, The Arthur Rank Centre

Ritchie, B., "Columba: The Faith of an Island Soldier", Christian Focus, Fearn, 2019

Roberts, A., "Roman Catholicism in the Highlands" –in– Kirk, J. 1998, above, 63–88

Roberts, A., "Chapels of the Rough Bounds", Mallaig Heritage Centre, 2015

Roberts, A. & Dean, A., "Northern Catholic History Notes", Aberdeen, 2019

Roesdahl, E., "The Vikings", Penguin, Harmondsworth, 2016

Ross, Rev. Dr. J., "The Jacobite Chaplains at Culloden", Glenurquhart Bulletin, Drumnadrochit, 2016

Roxburgh, A. J., "The Missionary Congregation, Leadership and Liminality", Trinity Press International, Harrisburg, PA, 1997

Runcie, C., "Salt on your tongue", Canongate, Edinburgh, 2020

Russell, Rev. A., "A History of Mission in Lochaber from the Reformation", Lochaber Presbytery, 1992

Russell, Rev. A., "Abertarff/Lochaber Presbytery: A History", Lochaber Presbytery, 1995

"Scalan News", Newsletter of The Scalan Association

Shaw, L., "History of the Province of Moray", revised by J F S Gordon, 3 vols, Glasgow, 1882

Sheldrake, P., "Living Between Worlds: Place and Journey in Celtic Spirituality", Darton, Longman and Todd, London, 1995

SHS, "Forfeited Estate Papers", SHS Publications, Vol 57, 1909

SHS, "Records of the Presbyteries of Inverness and Dingwall, 1643–88", SHS Publications, Vol 24, 1896

Simpson, W. D., "Beauly Priory", HMSO Guide, 1974

Smith, A., "The Work of the Forfeited Estates Board around Loch Ness" –in– IFC, 1991, above, 56–73

Southey, R., "Journal of a Tour in Scotland in 1819", ed. C H Herford, John Murray, 1929

SRO, "Reports on the Annexed Estates", Edinburgh, 1973

Scottish and Southern Energy plc, "Glendoe: Hydro is back", Perth, 2009

SSE Renewables Ltd., "Generating Benefits in the Great Glen", Perth, 2020

St Ninian's Church, Glenurquhart, descriptive leaflet, n.d.

Stewart, K., "The Story of Loch Ness", Luath Press, Edinburgh, 2005

Stewart, K., "Women of the Highlands", Edinburgh 2006

Stewart, K., "A School in the Hills" -in- "A Life in the Hills", Birlinn, Edinburgh, 2018

Stiubhart, D.U., "The genesis and operation of the Royal Bounty Scheme, 1725–30", SHS, 2003, 63–141

Tabraham, C. (ed), "Fort George", Historic Scotland, 2001

Tabraham, C. (ed), "Urquhart Castle", Historic Scotland, 2002

Tabraham, C. & Grove, D., "Fortress Scotland and the Jacobites", Historic Scotland, Batsford, 1995

TGSI, Transactions of the Gaelic Society of Inverness

"The Bible for Today", Oxford University Press, London, 1941

Thomson, I.R., "The Long Horizon", Birlinn, Edinburgh, 2008

Thornber, I., "James Henderson–a Highland Deer Stalker", Oban Times, 25.6.2017

TSA, "The Third Statistical Account of Scotland", Vol XVI, Inverness, Scottish Academic Press, 1985

Turnock, D.,"Patterns of Highland Development", Macmillan, London, 1970

Williams, P., "The Revelation of the Lockdown", "The Bible in Transmission", Summer 2020, The Bible Society, Swindon

Williams, T., "Viking Britain", William Collins, London, 2017

Wood, E., "The Hydro Boys", Luath Press, Edinburgh, 2010

Wynne, T., "The Forgotten Cameron of the '45: The Life and Times of Alexander Cameron S.J.", Fort William, n.d.

Maps Consulted

1. c1583-96: Timothy Pont, "The Great Glen and Glen Garry" https://maps.nls.uk/view/00002291
2. 1636-52: Robert and James Gordon, "Aberdeen, Banf, Murrey & c." https://maps.nls.uk/view/00000356
3. 1636-52: Robert and James Gordon, "A detailed map including Glenmore" https://maps.nls.uk/view/00000190
4. 1636-52: Robert and James Gordon, "Lochabyr" https://maps.nls.uk/view/00000557
5. 1654: Blaeu Atlas of Scotland, https://maps.nls.uk/view/00000456
6. 1689: "A New Map of Scotland", https://collections.leventhalmap.org/search/commonwealth:cj82kz36p
7. 1718: Dumaresq & Bastide, "A Plan of the Barrack at Kiliwhiman" https://maps.nls.uk/view/00002988
8. 1718: Herman Moll, "A pocket companion of ye roads" https://maps.nls.uk/view/00001267
9. 1722: Andrew Johnston, "New map of the north part of Scotland" https://maps.nls.uk/view/102190054
10. 1724-5: R Debize, "A plan of the Barracks ..." https://maps.nls.uk/view/00001154
11. c1724-45: R Debize, "A Plan of Killwhymen" https://maps.nls.uk/view/00001153
12. c1727: Joseph Avery, "Plan containing Lochness ..." https://maps.nls.uk/view/00003052
13. 1729?: John Romer, "A Plan of the intended Fortress" https://maps.nls.uk/view/00001156
14. 1746: Thomas Willdey, "A map of the King's Roads" https://maps.nls.uk/view/74400311
15. 1747-55: Roy's Military Survey, https://maps.nls.uk/roy/
16. 1750: Daubant, "A Plan of Fort Augustus" https://maps.nls.uk/view/00002927
17. Post-1775: Wade, "Plan of Fort Augustus" https://maps.nls.uk/view/00003223

18. 1796: George Brown, "Plan of intended road ..."
    https://www.scotlandsplaces.gov.uk/record/nrs/RHP1160
19. c1800: Plan of Crown Lands at Fort Augustus, British Waterways
    Collection, Inverness Archive, BW1 5/14/3/3
20. 1825: Aaron Arrowsmith, "Ecclesiastical Map of Scotland"
    https://maps.nls.uk/view/74400708
21. 1840: G Campbell Smith, "Map of the Lands of Glengarry"
    https://maps.nls.uk/view/216443669
22. 1876: Lovat Estate, "Fort Augustus Estate Map"
    https://maps.nls.uk/view/190781209

Selected Websites

www.ambaile.org.uk (Highland history resource)
www.archive.org (for Fasti Ecclesiae Scoticanae)
www.britishnewspaperarchive.co.uk (British Newspapers)
www.canmore.org.uk (for archaeological information)
www.cushnieent.com (The Early Church in Northern Scotland)
www.ecclegen.com (Free Church Ministers 1843–1900)
www.glenmoriston.org.uk (Glenmoriston Archive)
www.stataccscot.edina.ac.uk (for the Statistical Accounts)

Printed in Great Britain
by Amazon

86912315R00235